PowerBook®
and iBook®
Digital
Field Guide

Todd Stauffer with Dennis R. Cohen

WILEY

Wiley Publishing, Inc.

PowerBook® and iBook® Digital Field Guide

Published by
Wiley Publishing, Inc.
111 River Street
Hoboken, N.J. 07030
www.wiley.com

ISBN-13: 978-0-7645-9680-3

ISBN-10: 0-7645-9680-2

Manufactured in the United States of America

10 9 8 7 6 5 4 3 2 1

1K/RY/RQ/QV/IN

For general information on our other products and services or to obtain technical support, please contact our Customer Care Department within the U.S. at (800) 762-2974, outside the U.S. at (317) 572-3993 or fax (317) 572-4002.

Wiley also publishes its books in a variety of electronic formats. Some content that appears in print may not be available in electronic books.

Library of Congress Control Number: 2005926046

WILEY

About the Authors

Todd Stauffer is the author or coauthor of more than three dozen books on computing, technology, and the Internet, including *iMovie 2 For Dummies*, *Macworld Mac Upgrade and Repair Bible*, and *Upgrading and Repairing Macs and iMacs For Dummies*. Todd is also a magazine writer, a documentary filmmaker/editor, and the publisher of the *Jackson Free Press*, a newsweekly and city guide in Jackson, Mississippi. He's used a PowerBook as his main Mac since well before the turn of the century.

Dennis R. Cohen started programming with toggle switches, paper tape, punch cards, and teletype terminals about the time Voyager started its journey to Jupiter and beyond (he was working at the Jet Propulsion Laboratory's Deep Space Network at the time). He got started with Apple products with the Apple III and, after a short stint with the Lisa, moved to the Macintosh when it was released — his dual G5 is his 12th Mac (four of them are still in use). He's authored or coauthored more than a dozen books, has contributed to almost 20 others, and been the technical editor on almost 200 titles. Dennis lives in Sunnyvale, California, with his Boston Terrier, Spenser (who knows which key to hit to make the CD tray open).

Credits

Acquisitions Editor
Michael Roney

Project Editor
Cricket Krengel

Technical Editor
John C. Welch

Copy Editor
Kim Heusel

Editorial Manager
Robyn Siesky

Vice President & Group Executive Publisher
Richard Swadley

Vice President & Publisher
Barry Pruett

Project Coordinator
Maridee Ennis

Graphics and Production Specialists
Denny Hager
Jennifer Heleine
Clint Lahnen
Lynsey Osborn
Brent Savage

Quality Control Technician
Laura Albert

Cover Design
Michael Trent

Proofreading and Indexing
Vicki Broyles
Infodex Indexing Services, Inc.

*I dedicate this book to my nephew, Owen,
in part because it's probably the first one of mine
he'll be able to pick up. — T.S.*

Acknowledgments

I'd like to thank Mike Roney for accepting my proposal to write this book and I'd like to thank whoever thought of the Digital Field Guide series only a few months before I thought I had invented it! (There's always someone out there smarter than you are.) Thanks also go to Cricket Krengel for taking what I presented and developing it into a much better framework, while keeping me on task and helping me all along the way.

Thanks also to Laura Lewin, who sent this book proposal to many different editors and helped me get it done with the wonderful folks at Wiley; thanks also to the entire cast of characters at the Studio B literary agency for the excellent services they provide.

On a similar note, I'd like to thank Dennis Cohen for the help he gave me in meeting some key deadlines and filling in gaps with his enormous wealth of Mac knowledge. And John Welch did an excellent job as technical editor, making sure this book is quite a bit more accurate and useful than it would have been if you were just relying on me and the stuff that comes off the top of my head.

Thanks to the staff of the *Jackson Free Press* for taking up the slack as I hid away in my office or at home trying to write this book, which happened to be a title that was important to me to write well.

And thanks, as always to Donna Ladd and all her cats for keeping me sane or, if they're not doing that, then at least keeping me entertained as I slowly go crazy.

Preface

Well, it goes without saying that notebook computers are getting more powerful all the time, and they're increasingly giving us a certain freedom of mobility, even if that freedom means that we're constantly connected to the Internet, our work, our play, and our e-mail.

Maybe it's a mixed blessing.

There's no question that both of Apple's portable lines — the consumer-oriented iBook and professional-series PowerBook — prove the point every day. These are fast little workhorse computers that are easy to carry with you pretty much anywhere. They're so light, in fact, that these days I'm slinging my backpack over one arm like I did back in my college days.

And there's certainly something to being able to take your work with you so that you're no longer tethered to the desk and a little more able to make your own schedule. And there's absolutely nothing like the freedom of not having to worry about having some incredibly important computer file with you on your big trip because—well—you've got *all* your computer files with you.

I use my PowerBook as a "desktop replacement" — meaning it can do anything that I would do with a desktop computer, *plus* it's portable. In fact, the current PowerBook I have actually replaced an older PowerBook that, itself, was the real desktop replacement. My PowerBook offers plenty of computing horsepower for me in the office — where I hook it up to a nice monitor, mouse, and keyboard. Then, when I disconnect it and head home — or to a meeting, a coffee shop, an airport, or on a road trip — I've still got everything I need with me, all squirreled away on the internal drive, including my e-mail, notes, calendar, address book, and key applications.

And don't tell that PowerBook of mine, but I've been eying an even smaller (but more powerful) iBook that might just become a PowerBook replacement in its own right.

Given the increases in power and options in portables, the explosion in wireless Internet offerings, and the persistent travel that is the hallmark of many of our lives, I think there's room for an important little book. How about a book specifically about the iBook and PowerBook that is *also* extremely portable and dense with handy information and ideas?

And lets make it colorful and fun to open up, just like the iBooks and PowerBooks themselves (not to mention this somewhat painful metaphor).

In the *PowerBook and iBook Digital Field Guide*, you find that if there's anything we make a point of doing, it's cutting to the chase. This isn't just another primer on using a Mac or using the Macintosh operating system — instead, we focus exclusively on portable computing issues, from synchronizing data to securing that data to configuring wired and wireless Internet connections to troubleshooting tips to my recommendations on the topic of what else should be in your bag whenever you travel with your Mac.

You'll also find the book easy to jump into and out of as well as attractively designed and, hopefully, at least a bit of fun in the process. I had fun writing it, and I hope it's worth many, many times its weight in tips, techniques, and lifesavers on the road with your portable Mac.

If you need to reach me with questions or suggestions, please visit my Web site at www.macblog.com/ or send an e-mail with a meaningful subject line (for example, "I have a question about page 123") to fieldguide@macblog.com.

Todd Stauffer

Contents at a Glance

Contents

Chapter 2: Setting Up Your Portable Mac 49

Chapter 3: Security Basics for Your Portable Mac 75

Part II: Getting the Most from Your Portable Mac   103

Chapter 4: Online on the Road   105

Chapter 5: Networking Your Portable Mac   131

Chapter 6: Tips and Techniques for a Better Portable Mac Experience 163

Chapter 7: Troubleshooting and Maintaining Your Portable Mac 233

Appendix A: Upgrading Your Portable Mac 253

Quick Tour

I f you haven't spent much time with a PowerBook or iBook — even if you've worked with other Macintosh models in the past — you'll find something a little different about the portable experience. Obviously, the main difference is the fact that you can get up and go with your portable Mac, but that mere fact can result in some other, more subtle differences as well. For example, portable Macs can take a slightly different path to expansion, offering a few different ports and slots than desktop Macs. And they behave a little differently, too, with a battery and battery-management issues thrown into the mix.

At the same time, though, Apple's iBook and PowerBook models are 100 percent Macintosh. That means you can use nearly any of your Macintosh applications, including Apple's famous iLife applications (iMovie, iLife, GarageBand, even iDVD if you have a SuperDrive built in), as well as favorites like Adobe Photoshop, Apple Final Cut Pro, Microsoft Office, and many others.

And, what would any computer be like without Internet access? Your Mac portable offers a variety of options and approaches for getting you on the Internet, which are discussed in this chapter.

A Bit about Setting Up

If you're lucky enough to just be pulling your Mac out of the box, then you'll have some steps to take before you get it up and running. First of all, you'll probably need to plug the PowerBook or iBook in, as its battery may not have a full charge. Your manual can walk you through the basics of getting plugged in and charging, but I do want to quickly hit on some highlights.

First, you should know that it's OK to run with the computer on AC power when you first get it — you don't have to wait a number of hours for the battery to charge before starting to work with it. Unlike some electronic devices, the batteries in modern PowerBooks and iBooks don't have battery memory problems or whatnot, so you can use them without a full charge.

That said, the *first time* you use your portable Mac (or anytime that you begin working with a new battery), it's a good idea to calibrate the battery, according to Apple. Here's how:

1. **Plug one end of the adapter into your Mac and the other end into an electrical wall socket.** Allow the Mac to fully charge, until the adapter indicates that it's done (or the battery indicators on your toolbar shows it's fully charged, in case you have an older adapter that doesn't show different colors).

2. **Unplug the adapter from your Mac and work with the Mac until the battery is completely depleted.** Go past the warnings that appear when the battery gets very low.

3. **Work until the PowerBook or iBook puts itself into Sleep mode.** At that point, you've almost fully drained the battery.

4. **Now, plug in the adapter and fully charge the Mac again.** Don't take it off power until the adapter indicates that it's full. When you plug your newer iBook or PowerBook in, you may need to deal with Apple's 45-watt or 65-watt "brick" Apple Power Adapter. This square device is pretty ingenious, in that it is a bit more flexible than many other power adapters (see figure QT.1).

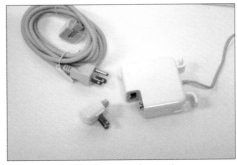

QT.1 The Apple Power Adapter is adjustable, enabling you to connect it directly to an outlet or to a longer cable.

Your PowerBook or iBook comes with both an AC plug adapter and a longer AC cord for the Apple Power Adapter; you can slide one or the other of these onto the Apple Power Adapter, depending on your needs. Note also the small feet that pop out of the back of the adapter to allow you to wrap the thin power cable around it.

The other side of the Apple Power Adapter is the thin power cable and its small DC connector that plugs into the power port on the side or back of your PowerBook. The uniqueness of this adapter is the colors that appear on the adapter's ring — the adapter glows amber when your Mac is charging and green when the adapter feels that the battery is fully charged (see figure QT.2). Once the adapter goes to green, it means it is being used only to meet whatever power needs the Mac has, whether you're using it or the Powerbook/iBook is in Sleep mode.

QT.2 The DC connector glows green when the PowerBook or iBook is charged.

Startup and setup

Once your Mac is plugged in — or if it has a full battery charge and is ready to be used without its AC adapter — you can open it and press the Power button on its case to start it up. (You should press it once for less than a second.) If the Mac is totally shut down, you should hear the startup tone if the Mac's volume is set to an audible level, which indicates that it's beginning the startup process. Then, after a moment, the screen will flicker to life. (If the Mac wasn't totally shut down, then it should start up from Sleep mode the moment you open the clamshell.)

During the startup process, the Mac goes through a self-diagnostic that checks internal memory and some other key hardware systems, and then it locates the Mac OS version that has been selected as the current default. Normally, it is the Mac OS version that's installed on the internal hard drive. Once found, the Mac begins the process of launching the operating system, which means certain items are read from the hard drive into system memory and those items are then acted upon — files are written, ports are opened, and services, like those that write to the display and those that deal with network connections, start.

Finally, if this is the first time you've launched your Mac, you are greeted by the Setup Assistant, which walks you through the process of getting a user account on your Mac, setting up your Internet connection, and sending registration information to Apple. That process is generally self-explanatory, so I won't cover it in depth, but I have a little advice for how to approach a few of the items that the Startup Assistant covers:

✦ When your Mac asks you to choose a username and password, that's because it's creating the first administrative account on this Mac as well as the keychain that goes with that account. You may want to consult the password discussion (and keychain discussion) in Chapter 3 before getting too deep into the Assistant, although you can always change your password later.

✦ Because you are asked for information about your Internet connection by the Assistant, you might want that information at your fingertips from your ISP, if appropriate. Or, if you have a DSL modem, AirPort base station, or any sort of device that needs to be on and functional, it's advisable to plug all that in and get it started before you launch into the Setup Assistant. Likewise, connect any Ethernet or phone cables that are necessary for your Internet connection.

Tip *By default, you are logged on to your Mac account automatically whenever you start your Mac. Read Chapter 3 to learn more about setting up your Mac so that you have to log on using your username and password, which is a more secure approach, particularly for mobile computing.*

Carrying it around

Whenever possible, it's best to shut your Mac's screen before carrying it; this puts the Mac into Sleep mode while making it easier to grip and carry. If you ever do need to move it while open, grasp it on the side of the base of the Mac, not by the display; the display's hinges are considerably more fragile than the main body and are not designed to support the weight of your PowerBook or iBook.

 Note *iBooks are a bit more sturdy than the PowerBooks, but handling an iBook by its display is still not a good idea.*

Probably the biggest issue to remember when you get up to move with your PowerBook or iBook is the fact that one or more cables may be plugged in. Look around carefully to make sure you aren't pulling your Mac away from something to which it's connected.

When you put your PowerBook or iBook in a bag, consider whether or not there are loose items in the bag that could slide down between the keyboard and display, get caught in a port, or otherwise do damage to the outside of the portable. Seek out a protective laptop sleeve for your Mac if you plan to use a bag that's not specifically designed for carrying a laptop.

 Cross-Reference *See Chapter 2 for some examples of protective sleeves and carrying cases for Mac portables.*

Apple notes in its documentation that its portables can get warm on the bottom — you may have noticed this too if you've tried to use your laptop, well, on your lap. Your portable is really designed to sit on a desk or flat table; the small feet on the bottom lift it to allow a little air to circulate. Usually you're okay with any sort of computer stand or desktop attachment as well. More important than that, though, is to avoid something that you might not have thought about — using a Mac portable on a pillow, blanket, or something else that doesn't allow air to circulate well underneath the machine. As much as you may love to sit in bed and compute, it's better if you use either a special pad for the bottom of your Mac or something like a lap desk (available in department stores and office stores) that has a hard top for a workspace and a softer bottom.

And if you really do want to compute in your lap, you can try a special cooling accessory, like the iLap from Rain Design (www.raindesigninc.com/ilap_features.html), shown in figure QT.3 or the Lap Protector by J.R. Hill and Company (www.jrhillandcompany.com).

Courtesy of Rain Design

QT.3 The iLap is a fun device designed to help keep both your portable Mac and your lap cooler.

Managing Your Power: Sleep, Restart, Shutdown

When you're ready to stop working with your Mac, you've got two choices — sleep or shutdown. You can put your Mac into Sleep mode by simply closing the clamshell — when it latches, your Mac should go automatically into Sleep mode, which is a low-power mode that uses only a trickle of power from your battery in order to maintain the contents of system memory. What Sleep mode enables you to do is pick up with your work where you left off — assuming nothing goes wrong with your battery or you don't wait too long before powering back up (too long meaning many days or weeks), you can wake your Mac from Sleep almost instantly and begin working again where you left off.

Shutting the clamshell isn't the only way to put your portable to sleep; you can also choose Apple ⇨ Sleep, or you can press the Power button on your Mac and then click the Sleep button that appears in the dialog box on your screen. To wake your Mac up, simply press the space bar. (Actually, any key will work, but the keystroke may register, so the space bar is often the best choice.)

If you won't be working on your Mac for quite some time, you can shut it down instead of putting it to sleep. To do that, choose Apple ⇨ Shut Down and in the dialog box that appears, choose Shut Down. You can also press the Power button and then choose Shut Down from the dialog box that appears.

 Note *Most modern Mac portables have a sleep indicator of some kind that can tell you when a Mac is in Sleep mode as opposed to shut down. Look for the light on the Mac that pulses (I think of it as snoring) or a similar glowing indicator. Also, if your Mac's Apple logo lights up when it's working, it should dim when your Mac is in Sleep mode; if it doesn't dim after an interval of 30 seconds or so, you might need to check and make sure the Mac has gone to sleep. A closed, running Mac portable can overheat.*

As part of the Shut Down procedure, you may be asked to save changes in any open applications that have documents or settings that haven't been saved. And, occasionally, you'll find that an application is busy and stops the shutdown procedure, in which case you may have to stop the application yourself and initiate Shut Down again. Once your Mac gets past those hurdles, you'll see applications and the Finder disappear and, eventually, your personal user account will be logged out and the Mac powers down. To start up again, press the Power button.

You'll find occasionally that it make sense to restart your Mac, whether you've just installed important updates or if you feel you need to restart for diagnostic reasons or to enter Target Disk Mode or startup from another disk. To restart, choose Apple ⇨ Restart or press the Power button, and then click Restart. From there, the process is the same as Shut Down, except that your Mac immediately starts up again after shutting down.

Your Mac's Ports and Connections

Either on the side or back of your Mac (and often both) are the ports that are used to connect your Mac to peripherals, to phone lines, and to other Macs, depending on what you're trying to accomplish. Most modern PowerBook and iBook models offer a similar array of ports, with just a few differences among them. PowerBook G3 and earlier PowerBook G4 models put many of their ports behind a small door that folds down in the back; figure QT.4 shows the ports for a PowerBook G4/500. Figure QT.5 shows the ports on a much newer iBook G4 model, which, like the latest PowerBook G4 models, has its ports out in the open.

Here's a quick look at the ports that you'll encounter and a little about them:

✦ **FireWire.** The FireWire port offers a high-speed connection to external hard drives, iPods, digital video camcorders, and similar devices that move a lot of data from an external device to and from your Mac. FireWire devices can be *daisy-chained* together, which means you can plug one device into your Mac and then other devices into that first device if it offers a second FireWire port. (If it doesn't you might want to opt for a FireWire hub if you need multiple devices.) All portable Macs that support FireWire support the FireWire 400 (400 megabits per second) technology; a few top-end PowerBooks (at the time of this writing) support FireWire 800, which has a different-shaped port. FireWire technology is Apple's trademark for the type of port called "IEEE-1394" or "i.Link" on other computing platforms, such as Microsoft Windows-compatible PCs.

✦ **USB.** The Universal Serial Bus is a common port connection for all sorts of peripherals that range from keyboards and mice to printers, scanners, business card readers, adapters, and even cable and DSL modems. USB comes in two versions — USB 1.1 and USB 2.0. All Macs that offer USB ports support USB 1.1, which tops out at 12 megabits per second; later PowerBooks and iBook G4 models support USB 2.0, which works at up to 480 megabits per second. USB 2.0 is better suited to external hard drives and other devices that need fast data transfer speeds (and Apple offers some iPod models that support USB 2.0).

✦ **Ethernet.** The Ethernet port is used for connecting an Ethernet cable, which looks a lot like a typical telephone cable, only slightly thicker, with a wider connector. Ethernet is generally used to connect to a cable or DSL modem, to a network printer, or to an Ethernet network. You can also connect your Mac to another Mac (or PC) using Ethernet.

 Consult Chapter 4 for details about Ethernet and other cables.

✦ **Modem.** The modem port accepts a standard RJ-11 connecter on the end of a telephone wire, with the other end destined for a wall phone socket. This connects your Mac's modem to the outside world so that it can be used to connect to the Internet or send and receive faxes.

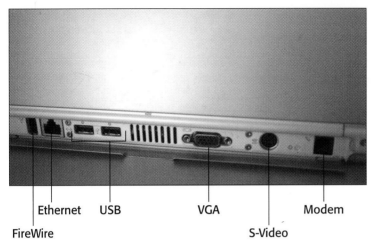

Ethernet   USB   VGA   Modem
FireWire   S-Video

QT.4 The ports on the back of a PowerBook G4/500.

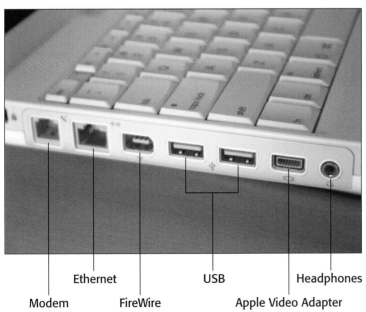

　　　Ethernet　　　　　　USB　　　　Headphones
Modem　　　FireWire　　　　Apple Video Adapter

QT.5 The ports on the side of a 2005-model iBook G4.

Caution

Your Mac's modem should only be connected to an analog phone jack. Never connect it to a digital phone jack (part of a PBX system or any other digital system). In hotel rooms, for example, you'll want to use the special data port for modem connections if one is provided.

✦ **VGA/DVI.** PowerBooks tend to have either a DVI or VGA (for older PowerBooks) port on the back, which can be used to connect the PowerBook to an external display. VGA is the standard for analog CRT (cathode-ray tube) monitors and analog LCD (liquid crystal) flat-panel displays. DVI is the digital interface for digital CRTs and LCDs, which tend to offer better results, but may be pricier. Apple's latest aluminum-edged LCD displays are DVI. (On PowerBook 12-inch models, Apple offers a mini-VGA or mini-DVI connector, which requires an external adapter before it works with a display.

✦ **Apple Video Adapter.** iBooks offer a special port that can accept an adapter that enables you to connect an external VGA monitor *or* a different adapter that lets you connect to a TV or video component.

✦ **Audio.** All PowerBooks and iBooks have a headphone jack so you can listen to your Mac without bothering others. On some PowerBook G4 17-inch models, the headphone jack is also an optical audio-out port. Some PowerBook models also include a mini-jack audio-in port; a few 17-inch models include an optical audio-in port.

When it comes to ports, probably the most important thing you can do is keep them clean and avoid forcing plugs into the wrong ports. All of the ports on your Mac are designed so that there's one right way to plug into them, and all but the Ethernet and modem ports are very different in size and configuration. Ethernet and modem cables are similar, although the RJ-45 connector on an Ethernet cable is visibly larger.

USB and FireWire enable you to plug in devices while your Mac is up and running. Most of the time, that device is recognized automatically and made available to you or to an application with which it's compatible. (For example, when you plug in a digital camera, iPhoto might launch.) If your Mac doesn't recognize the device, a dialog box should appear that asks if you need to install driver software or something similar.

When you're done working with a FireWire or USB peripheral, depending on the device, you may need to "eject" it in the Finder or in its associated application before unplugging it. This is particularly true of external hard disks (or even iPods) that are connected to your Mac and then mounted on your Desktop or in the Finder. You need to eject these disks before unplugging them to avoid damage to your documents. To eject a disk, you have a few choices:

✦ You can locate the disk's icon on the Desktop and then drag the icon to the Trash icon in the Dock. You will see the Trash icon change to a special eject icon to show that you're ejecting the disk (and not throwing it away!).

✦ If you see the icon in the Sidebar of a Finder window, you can click the small eject icon that appears next to the disk (see figure QT.6).

✦ If the external device is an iPod, you can eject it via the iTunes application.

QT.6 Click the small eject icon next to your external disk's entry in the Finder window to eject that disk so that it can be safely unplugged from your Mac.

Getting Started in Mac OS X

Once you start up your Mac and are done with the Setup Assistant, you should see the Finder. At the top of the screen is the menu bar, at the bottom is the Dock, and in the background is the Desktop. These, along with the menu commands in the menu bar and the Finder window that appears, are the tools you use to manage files, launch applications, and set options on your Mac (see figure QT.7).

The Finder, Desktop, and Dock

The Finder is where you do most of your file management including copying and deleting files, renaming them, and burning them to CDs or DVDs (if your Mac has an optical drive that allows you to create data discs). In particular, Finder windows include the Sidebar, which, by default, houses some of the key folders that are accessible to your Mac user account, as well as your Mac's internal hard drive and any other computers that your Mac is connected to through a local network.

To view a particular folder, you can select it from the Sidebar, or select the main hard drive icon, and then open folders and subfolders until you find the items you're looking for. The Finder offers a special Columns view, which is a quick way to move through the hierarchy of folders. If you find you don't like the Columns approach, you can choose View ➪ as Icons or View ➪ as List to change that view, as well as the buttons found in the Finder toolbar that correspond to Icon and List view (see figure QT.8).

You can create new folders for organizing other folders and files, if desired, by selecting a location in the Finder (or on the Desktop by clicking it once) and choosing File ➪ New Folder. In the folder that is created, begin typing to give it a name. Now you can drag-and-drop items into it.

Tip *Mac OS X version 10.4 and later can create other types of folders for different reasons. A Smart Folder automatically gathers file icons based on search criteria that you specify when you create the folder by choosing File ➪ New Smart Folder. A Burn Folder can be used to copy data to CD-R or DVD-R. See Chapter 6 for more on Burn Folders.*

Apple menu   Menu bar   Finder window

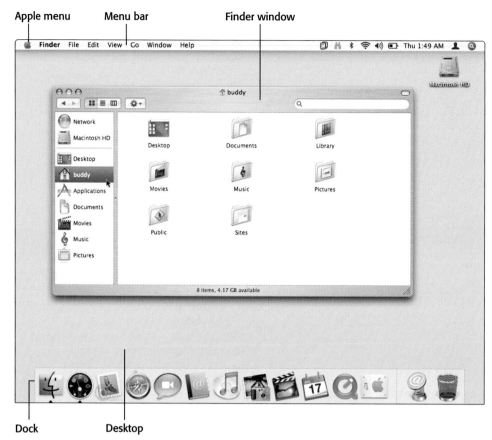

Dock   Desktop

QT.7 The Finder and other Mac OS X interface elements.

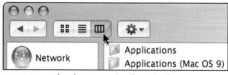

QT.8 Use the buttons in the Finder to change views.

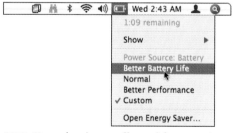

QT.9 Menu bar icons offer quick access to settings.

At the top of the screen, the menu bar holds menu commands for the active application, including the Finder. On the right side of the menu bar, however, are *menu bar icons*, which are generally small menus that give you access to quick options and settings, including things such as volume control and information about battery life and energy savings, as shown in figure QT.9.

At the bottom of the screen is the Dock, which is used to launch and switch applications. It is also for dealing with the minimized application window and for holding the Trash icon, which is where you click and drag files that you want to delete from the Finder. The Trash can be emptied by Control-clicking the icon and choosing Empty Trash or by choosing Finder⇨Empty Trash from the menu bar. (Note that when you empty the Trash this way, you won't see a dialog box asking if you're sure you want to empty the Trash; if you choose Finder⇨Empty Trash, you will see the warning by default.)

 Cross-Reference *I discuss the Dock in more detail in Chapter 1.*

One of the key elements of the Mac interface is one you've already seen — the Apple menu. It's in the Apple menu that you access frequent commands such as Sleep, Shut Down, and Log Out. You can also access the About This Mac command from the Apple menu, where you see about your Mac, including the processor speed and how much RAM is installed. Click More Info to launch the System Profiler, which tells you in-depth information about your Mac (see figure QT.10).

○ ○ ○   About This Mac

Mac OS X
Version 10.4

(Software Update...)

Processor 1.2 GHz PowerPC G4

Memory 512 MB DDR SDRAM

Startup Disk ToddsiBook HD

(More Info...)

TM & © 1983–2005 Apple Computer, Inc.
All Rights Reserved.

QT.10 The About This Mac window offers some handy info.

How your hard drive is organized

I mentioned the Sidebar in the previous section, which is part of the Finder; another interesting thing about the Sidebar is that it gives you a glimpse of the way Mac OS X files are organized on your hard drive when it's installed. Mac OS X is pretty logical and dogmatic about this, separating things into basic folders that you can see if you click your hard drive's icon in the Sidebar (see figure QT.11).

Here's a look at the main-level folders:

✦ **Applications.** On the main level of your hard drive is the Applications folder where most applications are installed by default. You can choose another folder for an application, but this is the folder that's used to make an application publicly available to users on your system. To launch an application, all you have to do is open this folder, locate an application, and then double-click its icon.

✦ **Library.** The Library folder is where your Mac keeps files that should be accessible to third-party applications, or are common to all users on a specific Mac. This is where fonts, color profiles, and even HTML Web documents and scripts are stored for use by various applications and system components. Again, items in here are accessible to all users (and the applications they launch) on your Mac.

QT.11 The main level of folders gives a sense of how Mac OS X likes to parcel a hard drive into special folders.

✦ **System.** The System folder is where the Mac OS puts system components that you and third-party applications are not supposed to access or alter as much. Almost everything in the System folder is put there by Apple; few third-party items are put in this folder. As a general rule, you don't want to move or change anything inside it.

✦ **Users.** The Users folder is where individual users' home folders are stored on the Mac. It's within those home folders that users on your Mac (even if there's only one – you) keeps their documents, pictures, movies, mail, personal preference files, and many other items. In this folder is a subfolder called Shared that can be used by multiple users on your Mac if desired.

✦ **Applications (Mac OS 9) and System Folder.** When launched, the Classic environment uses these two folders to run older Classic Mac programs, meaning those designed to run in Mac OS 9 prior to the arrival of Mac OS X.

So, now you know that your home folder is stored in the Users folder; you can open up the Users folder and select your home folder to see many of the same folders that appear on the lower part of the Sidebar in a Finder window for quick access. Select your home folder and you'll see its subfolders in the Finder (see QT.12).

Each of these subfolders has a purpose, and, although you don't have to use them for their intended purposes, you may find it handy:

✦ **Desktop.** The Desktop folder represents the contents of your Desktop – you can open this folder to access those same files in another way. Likewise, items placed in this folder appear on the Desktop.

✦ **Documents.** The Documents folder is where it's suggested that you store the bulk of your stuff. In here you can create subfolders for different types of files, different applications, different projects, different topics, or whatnot – or just dump them all in there and use Spotlight (if you have Mac OS X 10.4 or higher installed) or the Finder window's search box to sort them out.

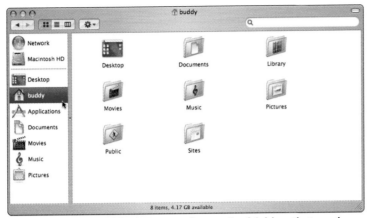

QT.12 Your home folder has a certain set of subfolders that can be used to organize your documents and files.

✦ **Library.** The Library folder in your home folder is similar to the main Library folder on your hard drive, except that the settings and application support files stored here are specifically for your account's use. Fonts, browser bookmarks, settings, and options that you make in your applications are stored here and used when your account is active.

✦ **Movies.** The Movies folder is where iMovie will place movie files by default; and for any movie downloads or editing projects, it's a handy place to put your clips and project files.

✦ **Music.** By default, iTunes stores music files in the Music folder and organizes them within a hierarchy of subfolders. You're free to do the same with any music files that you work with outside of iTunes.

✦ **Pictures.** The Pictures folder is used by iPhoto to store and organize images, although, again, you can use it yourself for image files if desired.

✦ **Public.** The Public folder is a special folder that enables you to make your files available to others. By *others*, I mean both other users who have an account on your Mac and guest users who connect to your Mac via a network connection. And the "sharing" can go two ways — inside the Public folder is a Drop Box subfolder that other users can use to send you files. You should be careful with what you put in the Public folder because files may be accessible to more users than you realize; likewise, watch out for items placed in your Drop Box and only work with them if you're sure they came from a trusted source.

✦ **Sites.** The Sites folder is used to store personal Web pages; when you turn on Web Sharing on your Mac, others can access not only your Mac's main Web server, but also your personal pages, which are made available for others to see if they're stored in this folder.

Nothing about the hierarchy of folders is set in stone, particularly if you have administrative capabilities. (The first user on a new Mac always has admin privileges, so more than likely you're working in such an account.) You can copy items from anywhere to anywhere, for the most part, and you're free to store files and folders on your desktop or in the Shared folder or even on the main level of your Macintosh hard drive. I don't recommend that you do that, but in most cases you can.

There are a few things that are nice about using this hierarchy. First, if all your documents are in the Documents folder, it makes them a lot easier to back up, because they're all in one place. Also, as you see in Chapter 3, Mac OS X has a feature that allows you to encrypt your home folder, which secures the files from being accessed by anyone who doesn't have your password. In order for you to pull that off, your files need to be in your home folder. And, finally, if you place files outside of your home folder, you make them available to other user accounts on your Mac, if you allow others to log on, which might not be a great idea in every instance.

Logging Out (and Logging In)

Occasionally you may find it handy to log off your Mac, which allows you to either log on to a different account, let someone else log on to a different account, or simply makes your Mac a little more secure before going to sleep, as someone is required to pick a username and type a password before gaining access to your files.

Tip *There's an easier way to get that level of security. Launch the System Preferences application (Apple ➪ System Preferences) and choose the Security pane. There, select the Require Password to Wake This Computer from Sleep or Screen Saver option. See Chapter 3 for more on security and password issues.*

To log off, simply choose Apple menu ➪ Logout *Username*. A dialog box appears asking if you're sure; click Log Out again if you're sure it's what you want to do. Just as when your Mac is shutting down, you may be asked to save changes in your open documents. Eventually the Finder quits and, after a moment, you see the login window displayed.

To log on to a different account, choose a name, type a password, and click Log In. You can also opt to click one of the shutdown or reset buttons, or you can click the Sleep button to put your Mac into sleep mode.

 Cross-Reference *Mac OS X offers another way for you to make use of multiple accounts, called Fast User Switching, which enables you to switch to one account while another account remains logged in. More on that in Chapter 1.*

Using Your PowerBook or iBook

Exploring Your Portable Mac

Your portable Macintosh, by the very nature of its portability, introduces some tweaks to the typical computing experience. For example, your iBook or PowerBook has a fixed liquid crystal display (LCD) screen that is less adjustable for viewing angle with respect to your keyboard than the display for a desktop model. Similarly, the keyboard is smaller both in the size and number of keys. And rather than a separate mouse and keyboard, tethered by cords or wireless, a keyboard and a trackpad are built in to the case.

Of course, you know these things. The trick, though, is getting these things customized to your liking so that you can enjoy these unique attributes of your portable. You have several options available, from customizing how the trackpad and keyboard respond, to customizing special command keys, to making use of some fun features of Mac OS X — such as Expose and Dashboard — to move around the interface a little faster and get some stuff done on your portable Mac.

In this chapter, you look at some of those options, features, and customizations.

Customizing the Trackpad

If most of your computing life has been spent at a desktop computer, you may find that day-to-day use of a portable requires a little retraining. And the biggest step in that retraining is probably learning to use a trackpad instead of a mouse.

By default, your trackpad is configured to function as a direct (albeit stationary) mouse equivalent. You move the cursor by sliding your finger across the pad area, and you click by tapping the trackpad's button. But Apple decided to make a few additional options available to you through your trackpad, and the way to adjust and enhance your trackpad is through the Trackpad tab of the Keyboard & Mouse pane of System Preferences (choose System Preferences from the Apple menu) shown in figure 1.1.

The two settings at the top, Tracking Speed and Double-Click Speed, are identical to like-named settings you see on a Mac desktop that has a mouse connected to it. (In fact you see both if you have a mouse connected to your portable Mac, as discussed later in this section.) You can use these options to change how quickly the mouse pointer skitters across the screen in response to your finger and how much of a

gap between two clicks the Mac OS allows while still recognizing those clicks as a double-click operation.

The Trackpad Gestures and Trackpad Options section of the Trackpad tab provide access to some options that are unique to using a trackpad. The Gestures, in particular, can make using a trackpad extremely convenient. Select the Clicking option to make a tap of the trackpad area itself (and not just the trackpad's button) into the equivalent of clicking the trackpad's button (or clicking a mouse). If Clicking is selected, you can then extend the gesture support by selecting the Dragging option. If you select Dragging, then double-tapping an item not only selects it, but allows you to drag it around by sliding your finger on the trackpad — all without having to press the trackpad's button.

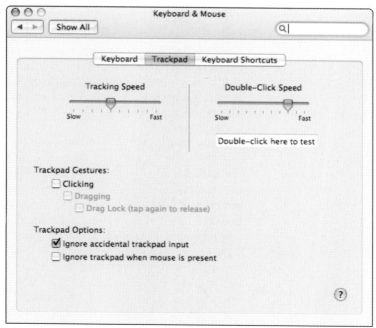

1.1 Trackpad preferences settings are found on the Trackpad tab of the Keyboard & Mouse pane of System Preferences.

Finally, if Dragging is selected, then the Drag Lock option also becomes available. With Drag Lock, you can even lift your finger from the trackpad after something is selected for dragging, put your finger back down, and continue to drag. Until you tap the item again, it's locked in a drag mode.

> **Tip** *You find that if you get used to trackpad clicking and dragging, drag lock may indeed make it easier to you to drag items around.*

Trackpad Options include Ignore accidental trackpad input (selected by default) and Ignore trackpad when mouse is present. The former means that when the palm of your hand or your wrist brushes against the trackpad while typing, that contact is ignored. The latter option is convenient for when you have a mouse (or trackball) attached. No contact on the trackpad is registered until the mouse is detached.

> **Note** *If you're curious as to how the OS determines that the trackpad input is accidental, the math is actually pretty simple. The Mac checks to see if a key had been pressed immediately prior to the trackpad input. If a key has very recently been pressed, the Mac checks how recently. If it was pressed within the same amount of time as a double-click of the mouse, the Mac determines that was too quick and assumes you accidentally brushed the trackpad while typing, so the contact is considered accidental. Obviously, if you're lightning fast from keys to trackpad, you can deselect this option.*

Using the Laptop's Function Keys

Your Mac laptop is a compact computer — something you can pretty much tell just by looking at it. One side effect of its reduced size, though, is the fact that even on the 17-inch (diagonal) PowerBook, there isn't room to hold the full expanse of an 18-inch-wide Apple Pro Keyboard. Don't even think about it on a 12-inch iBook or PowerBook. However, Mac has cleverly disguised most of the features associated with those keys — so while some of the keys may be gone, and some others of them made a little smaller, most of the full keyboard functionality is still there.

The Fn key and your Mac's second keyboard

With fewer keys on the keyboard, some functions have to either be cut or added in a more creative way. Apple opted for the latter (as do most Windows-based computers) by including a modifier key that you don't find present on standard keyboards — the Fn key.

Similarly to the ⌘ key, pressing Fn while pressing other keys results in an action other than typing the character indicated by the key's primary label. (For example, a grouping of keys in the middle of your keyboard can be used as a numeric keyboard if you happen to be adept at entering numbers or calculating figures in such a way.) Figure 1.2 shows the characters typed with and without the Fn key pressed on a G4 PowerBook keyboard — notice how much of the keyboard's right side is a numeric keypad when Fn is pressed. Then, Table 1.1 explains what happens to a particular key when you press the Fn key.

 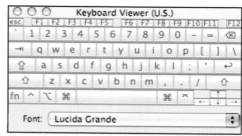

1.2 With Fn is pressed (left), many keys produce different results from what they normally do (right).

Tip

Home and End (which you get when you press the Fn key with the Left and Right arrow keys, respectively) can be handy shortcuts if you get used to them. Different applications use the Home and End keys differently; in Microsoft Word, for instance, the Home key takes you to the beginning of a line of text and the End key takes you to the end of that line; in Safari, the Home key takes you to the top of the Web page you're viewing; End takes you to the bottom of that page. I suggest that you experiment in your favorite applications to see if Home and End can make life any easier for you.

The alternate characters produced by pressing Fn are stamped in small print on your keyboard's key caps. For example, pressing the left-most function key dims the screen, but if you press Fn+F1, whatever function is assigned to F1 in the currently running application takes over (Ctrl+Fn+F1, for

example, toggles full keyboard access and allows you to select almost anything on your screen using just the keyboard).

Understanding function keys

As mentioned, the fact that a Mac portable's keyboard has fewer keys means some of them do double-duty. In fact, most of the Function keys across the top of your Mac's keyboard are used, by default, as hardware controls for items like screen brightness and volume (see Table 1.2).

However, the Function keys (often called the F keys) are also used for other commands, both within applications and more generally throughout the Mac OS itself. For instance, by default the F11 key is used by the Mac OS's Exposé feature to move all open windows out of the way and give you access to the Mac's desktop background. On your Mac portable, to invoke that command you'll need to press Fn+F11.

Table 1.1
Portable Keyboard and the Fn Key

This Key...	Becomes This When Fn Is Pressed...
6	Clear
7	7
8	8
9	9
0	/ (division)
-	= (equals)
U	4
I	5
O	6
P	* (multiply)
J	1
K	2
L	3
;	- (subtract)
M	0
.	. (decimal)
/	+ (add)
Return	Enter
Up arrow	Page Up
Down arrow	Page Down
Left arrow	Home
Right arrow	End

Table 1.2
PowerBook and iBook Function Keys

Key	Function
F1	Controls screen brightness
F2	Controls screen brightness
F3	Controls speaker volume
F4	Controls speaker volume
F5	Controls speaker volume
F6	NumLock
F7	Toggles the video mode between dual monitor and mirrored displays on some PowerBook models
F8	Lowers keyboard illumination (on some PowerBook models)
F9	Raises keyboard illumination
F10	Maximum keyboard illumination
F11	n/a
F12	Ejects discs that have been placed in your CD or DVD drive.

Customizing keyboard combos

You've seen the power both of the Fn key and the "F Keys" across the top of your Mac's keyboard. Those are some great options for improving productivity by learning to use those special keys — but they aren't the only special keyboard combinations you can make use of in the Mac OS X interface. There are quite a few others that make use of the Control, Option, Shift, and Command (⌘) keys on your keyboard. Each of these keys has its own Symbol, too.

Which brings us to an interesting possibility on the Keyboard Shortcuts tab of the Keyboard & Mouse pane of System Preferences, shown in figure 1.3. This tab is one of the most powerful customizing tools on your Mac. This is where you can create your own keyboard shortcuts for use in an individual application or for use in all applications. Additionally, this tab is handy because it unlocks all the secret key combinations on your Mac — all in one central location.

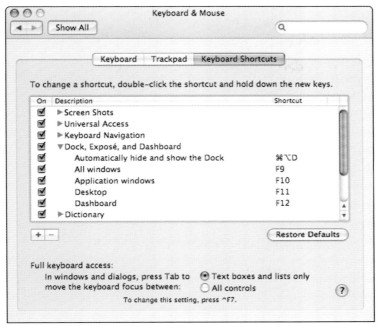

1.3 Here the shortcuts for the Dock, Exposé, and Dashboard are shown.

If you scroll through this list you'll see many different shortcuts that have been predefined and that you can learn and use as you deem fit. It's also worth knowing that it is a simple matter to change one of these keystrokes here. As an example, to change the shortcut for hiding and showing the Dock, follow these steps:

1. **Select the Automatically hide and show the Dock line in the Keyboard Shortcuts tab of the Keyboard & Mouse pane.**

2. **Click in the Shortcut column.** The current shortcut appears as selected text.

3. **Press the key of your new choice.** The change is made, as shown in figure 1.4.

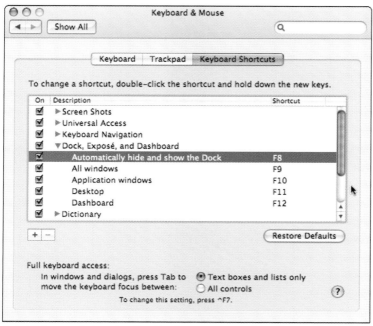

1.4 Hiding and showing the Dock now responds to F8.

Using Exposé

Introduced with Panther (Mac OS X version 10.3), Exposé is one of the coolest approaches to managing open windows on a personal computer that uses a graphical interface. It's designed to take the "window clutter" problem that you've probably experienced on your Mac — so many windows opened and piled up on one another that you can't find the one that you're looking for. Exposé offers a few visual commands to help you overcome window clutter. And it's a feature that's always on, ready for you to use at a moment's notice.

Managing windows

Exposé offers a creative approach to navigating the mess of windows that you often encounter on a busy user's Mac display. By default, Exposé takes over three function keys, F9, F10, and F11, to provide its three functions, as follows (remember that you may need to press the Fn key with F9, F10, and F11 on your Mac portable, depending on the model you have):

✦ **F9** miniaturizes and temporarily realigns all your open windows, in all your running applications, as shown in figure 1.5. As your mouse passes over a window, its name appears.

✦ **F10** miniaturizes and temporarily realigns all the windows in the front-most application, as shown in figure 1.6. As you slide the mouse over the various windows, their names appear.

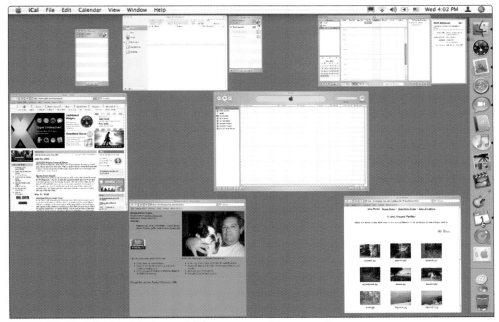

1.5 F9 makes all your windows visible at once, without overlap.

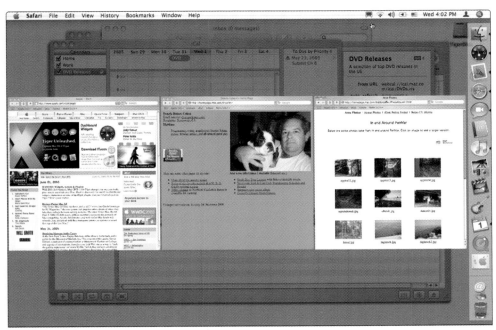

1.6 F10 tiles the front-most application's windows.

If you press F9 and decide that you want to restrict the display to just the current application's windows, you can quickly switch to F10 mode by pressing Tab.

✦ **F11** makes all your windows scurry out of sight, revealing your Desktop so that you can get at the icons there, as shown in figure 1.7. This allows you to quickly get at an item on the Desktop, double-click it to launch it, create a new folder, manage files, and so on.

Tip *For a neat trick try this: From this Desktop-revealing mode, you can drag an icon and exit Exposé (press F11 again), and the drag continues after returning to your normal window stack. This is a very quick way to drag an icon, for example, from the Desktop to an e-mail message as an attachment.*

When you press F11 to make all the windows move out of the way to reveal your Desktop, the edges of the windows are still visible (look closely at the edges of figure 1.7). Clicking one of the window edges is a quick way to exit Exposé, but it won't bring the clicked window to the front — you always go right back to the most recent open window where you were when you entered Exposé. The exception to this is if you use either the Dock or the ⌘+Tab keystroke combination to exit Exposé, in which case you can choose the application you want to switch to upon that exit.

Tip *If you're in F10 mode and want to switch to a different application, ⌘+Tab cycles you through the other running applications, just as if Exposé weren't active.*

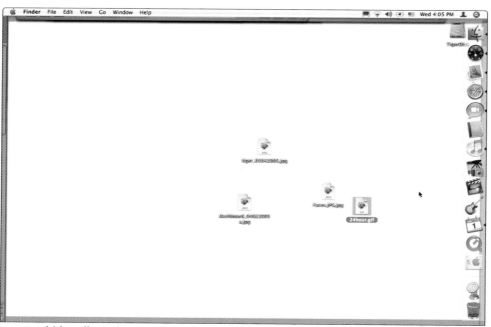

1.7 F11 hides all windows, making your Desktop available.

Quickly tapping an Exposé key once places you in the mode associated with that key until you either press the same or a different Exposé key, or click an object on the display. However, if you press and hold an Exposé key, you exit Exposé only when you release the key.

Assigning hot corners

Not everyone wants to dedicate scarce function keys to Exposé. So, Apple makes it easy for you to redefine the invocation keys, or, if you aren't fond of using keystrokes at all, you can designate different corners of the screen so that when you move the mouse to a particular corner, one of Exposé's functions is invoked. (This also works with Dashboard — discussed in the next section — and Screen Saver functions.) And there are other options — if you have a multibutton mouse attached to your Mac, you can allocate mouse button actions to Exposé.

To set your own hot corners, open the System Preferences application (choose System Preferences from the Apple menu), and then click the Dashboard and Exposé icon to launch the preference pane shown in figure 1.8. In that example, you may see options that are a little different from what you see on your own screen; that's because I also have a two-button mouse attached to my iBook, which results in more options.

Tip *I like to carry a mouse with me in my iBook's travel bag, so I have access to all the options a mouse offers once I get to a desk or table large enough to accommodate the mouse.*

Note *If a multibutton mouse (or trackball) is not attached, the right-hand column of pop-up menus in the bottom well is not present and the bottom well is labeled merely Keyboard Shortcuts rather than Keyboard and Mouse Shortcuts.*

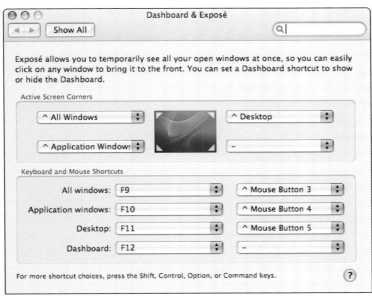

1.8 Select your own Exposé invocations in the Dashboard & Exposé System Preferences.

To set a screen corner, simply choose that corner's pop-up menu, and then choose the command that you want associated with that corner. For instance, if you choose Application Windows, that's the equivalent of Exposé's F9 command, which highlights the open windows of the current application.

Because Mac OS X allows you to specify screen corners for Screen Saver activation and disabling, the pop-up menus in the Active Screen Corners include those options, as well. Note that I elect to include the Ctrl key with the corner options, so that an accidental flick of the mouse pointer past the Apple menu or Spotlight (in Mac OS X 10.4, the Spotlight icon is in the top right corner of the screen) doesn't trigger Exposé.

You can use any of the modifier keys (Shift, Ctrl, Option, or ⌘) in conjunction with corner, keyboard, or mouse shortcuts, and you can even specify a specific modifier key (including Fn) as a keyboard shortcut — your system can even distinguish between the left and right Shift keys. To set a key combination, follow these steps:

1. **Open the pop-up menu first for a particular corner.**

2. **Press that modifier key as you select the Exposé, Screen Saver, or Dashboard command you want to associate with that corner.**

3. **Release the key and mouse button to set them.** Now, when you press the key *and* mouse to that corner, the command you've chosen will be invoked.

Getting Info from Dashboard

Normally present in your Dock, right beside the Finder, is the icon that represents Dashboard. Dashboard is the environment that makes it possible for your Mac to present its *widgets*, which are small gadgets bearing some similarities to programs, services, desk accessories, and Web pages, but aren't really any of those. Dashboard is a separate layer in which the widgets function — you can use copy and paste to move data among your programs and widgets, but you can't drag between widgets and applications or even from widget to widget.

You display the Dashboard, shown in figure 1.9, by either clicking the Dashboard icon in the Dock or by pressing the default hot key, which is F12. (On most iBooks and PowerBooks you'll need to press Fn+F12, because F12 is the hardware eject key for ejecting CDs and DVDs.)

 Note *Click the Dashboard icon in the Dock and you'll see a menu pop up — choose More Widgets and you'll be automatically switched to your default Web browser and taken to Apple's Dashboard download Web page, where hundreds of additional widgets from Apple and other parties are available for download. Widgets have been popular since the release of Mac OS X 10.4 such that many of the little applets are available to download and add to your Mac's Dashboard functionality.*

Notice the circled plus (+) sign in the lower-left corner of the screen (see figure 1.9 again). Clicking this symbol slides your screen up to display the Widget Bar, where all of your installed widgets reside, just waiting to be called upon, as shown in figure 1.10.

1.9 Invoking Dashboard dims your screen and displays the widgets you have opened from previous Dashboard sessions, if any.

1.10 The Widget Bar resides just below the bottom of your screen – displaying it slides everything up.

Tip ⌘+= *toggles the Widget Bar display, for those who prefer the keyboard.*

To close a widget that's running, click the circled X in the upper-left corner of the widget. When the Widget Bar is visible, all running widgets display the close symbol; however, when the Widget Bar is hidden, so are the close symbols. However, you can press and hold Option while moving your cursor over the widget to see the close symbols.

Some widgets, such as the Clock widget, display a small info badge (a lowercase *i*) in their lower-right corner when the cursor is over them (see figure 1.11). That's how you make changes and settings. For example, to set the clock:

1. **Click the Dashboard icon in the Dock or press F12 (you may need to press Fn+F12) to display the Dashboard.**

2. **Locate the Clock widget and hover over it with your mouse.** That causes the "i" icon to appear.

Note *Not all widgets will have the i icon. Third-party widgets might offer a Configure button or a similar option.*

3. **Click the info icon.** That causes the widget to turn its back to you.

4. **Make changes using the controls given to you.** In the case of the clock, you can choose a continent and the city whose time you want to display.

5. **Click Done when you've made the setting changes.** That should flip the widget back around so that you can see the result.

1.11 Many widgets have a settings panel or info display, accessible by clicking the info badge in the lower-right corner.

To open a widget, just click it in the Widget Bar and an instance plops down in the center of your screen. You can drag it to another location if you want. Alternatively, you can just drag the widget in one step from its Widget Bar to position it where you want it on your screen. You can drag multiple instances of a widget into use — for example, you can create a newsroom-style clock display of different time zones by placing three or four clocks, each set to a different locale, side by side, as shown in figure 1.12.

Tip *Refresh a widget's displayed information by clicking the widget and pressing ⌘+R. Even if the information doesn't need updating, you witness an amusing visual display.*

The default Fn+F12 keyboard shortcut for displaying the Dashboard can be changed in the Dashboard & Exposé System Preferences pane, as described previously for Exposé shortcuts.

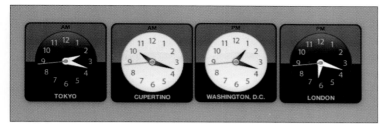

1.12 You can run multiple copies of a widget simultaneously.

Widgets on the Web

If you find widgets on the Internet, like the one shown here, that you want to use with Mac OS X, download them to your Mac and double-click them. The display switches to the Dashboard and a dialog box should appear asking if you want to work with the widget for the first time; click Accept and the widget is run. If you enjoy using the widget, you should copy it to the Widgets folder inside the Library folder found in your home folder. Once there, the widget will be a permanent part of your Dashboard. (If you don't like the widget, you can simply delete it from wherever it was stored when it was downloaded.)

Using and Customizing the Dock

One of the most obvious elements that makes up the unique Mac OS X interface is a translucent strip of icons that, by default, rests along the bottom of your screen. This strip is called the Dock and it is loved by many, derided by some, and accepted by most. Once you get used to it (particularly if you're coming to the Mac from a Windows-based PC or from an older version of the classic Mac OS), you find that the Dock is both multipurpose and useful, as well as relatively unobtrusive (see figure 1.13).

Launching items

As delivered by Apple, the Dock contains a few icons: Finder, Dashboard, Mail, Safari, iChat, Address Book, iTunes, iCal, QuickTime Player, and System Preferences on the application side of the Dock's dividing line and a link to Apple's Mac OS X Web page and the Trash on the document side.

 Note *If you got this version of Mac OS X with a new Mac, you might have some additional icons installed by default; for example, the icons for the iLife applications iPhoto, iMovie, iDVD, and GarageBand.*

As you pass your cursor over a Dock icon, its name appears (handy in case you don't recognize the icon). While an application is starting up, its icon bounces up and down — if you find this annoying, you can turn off the animation in Dock preferences, as described a little later in this chapter. If you turn off the animation, a little black triangle beneath the icon blinks during start-up and then holds solid to show that the application is active.

You can give yourself quick access to your favorite applications by adding their icons to your Dock, making those applications just a single click away. To add an item, all you have to do is drag its icon from a Finder window (or the desktop) down to the Dock:

✦ If you're adding an application, you should drag its icon to the left side of the dividing line in the Dock.

✦ If you're adding a document for quick access, drag it to the right side of the Dock.

To remove an item, simply drag it off the Dock and release the mouse button — it disappears in a puff of smoke. Rest assured that only the Dock icon disappears; the application or document itself is still secure on your Mac's hard drive until you go into the Finder and delete the actual file(s) by dragging it to the Trash and emptying the Trash.

1.13 The Dock is the small strip of icons at the bottom of your Mac's screen.

Managing running items

Along with being available as a quick launcher option, the Dock also shows the icons for applications that are currently running with a small, black triangle beneath them (or to the side, if you've repositioned your Dock as described in the next section). The Dock icons for running applications can provide a lot of additional functionality, if you choose to take advantage.

For example, you can click and hold (or Ctrl-click) a running application's Dock icon to see a contextual menu — among the items in that menu are a list of all the application's windows, and all you have to do is choose that window name and the window appears front-and-center on your screen. Other applications, such as iTunes, provide a subset of their menu commands so that you can control them without bringing the application forward as the active application (see figure 1.14).

Tip *You can place folders of application icons or aliases in the Dock on the non-application side and have quick access through the contextual menu to a large number (or all) of your applications without using up much Dock space.*

Note *Some of the menu items will even change when you press Option. For example, Quit changes to Force Quit when you add Option, letting you terminate a non-responsive application.*

Of course, whenever you launch an application, its icon appears on the Dock so that you can manage it while it's running. By default, when you quit that application, its icon disappears from the Dock. If you want to keep that application's icon in the Dock for launching later, however, follow these steps:

1. **Launch the application that you want to permanently add to the Dock.**

2. **Click and hold the mouse on that item's icon in the Dock while it's running.** The icon's contextual menu appears.

3. **Choose Keep in Dock from the application's contextual menu.** The Dock retains the icon for that application, allowing quick access even after you quit the application or restart your Mac.

1.14 A Dock icon's contextual menu can provide a lot of control.

Setting Dock preferences

The Dock has its own pane in System Preferences that you can use for settings. The most direct ways to Dock preferences are to choose Dock ➪ Dock Preferences from the Apple menu or to Ctrl-click a blank area of the Dock and choose Dock Preferences from the contextual menu that appears. Figure 1.15 shows the Dock preferences pane.

Here are the options:

✦ **Dock Size.** Use the slider to change the size of the Dock. Note that the icons can get very small, but they are limited in how big they can get by the edges of your screen — once the Dock hits the edge, the Dock and icons can't grow any larger using this setting.

✦ **Magnification.** This is an interesting one, particularly on smaller screens; with Magnification turned on, individual icons will be magnified when you pass over them with your mouse. You can turn on the effect by clicking its checkbox, and then use the slider to decide exactly how much magnification you want to experience.

✦ **Position on screen.** Use these radio buttons to choose where you'd like to place the Dock on your screen; the default is the bottom, but you can move the Dock to the left or right edge of the screen, if desired.

✦ **Minimize using.** When you click the minimize button in an open window, that window is placed on the Dock; you can choose the Genie Effect (which takes more processor power) or the Scale Effect (which is less impressive looking).

 Tip *If you press Shift while minimizing a window, you can view the effect in slow motion.*

✦ **Animate opening applications.** Turn on this option if you like seeing your application's icon bounce as the application is launching; if this is turned off, then all you see is the blinking triangle under a launching application icon.

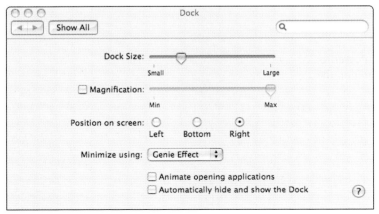

1.15 The Dock's System Preferences pane.

✦ **Automatically hide and show the Dock.** Turn this on if you want the Dock to disappear off the edge of the screen when your mouse point isn't near it; it will reappear when the mouse pointer gets close. This is handy for getting the Dock out of sight so that you can concentrate on the open windows that you're working with.

Tip

Most of these commands are also available via a contextual menu that you can see by Ctrl+clicking the dividing line on the Dock. The contextual menu lets you turn Hiding on or off, turn Magnification on or off, specify a screen position for the Dock, and specify the minimization effect. Additionally, you can click and drag on the dividing line between the application and non-application sides of the Dock to resize the Dock.

As previously noted, Apple places the Dock at the bottom of the screen by default. One reason for this choice is to make it comfortable for those switching from Windows, who are accustomed to having a Task Bar and System Tray at the bottom of their screen. If you enjoy this orientation, feel free to stick with it.

Apple tends to build wide displays these days, however, and particularly if you work on 15-inch or 17-inch PowerBooks, the display is considerably wider than it is tall. Thus, I like to place my Dock on the right edge of the screen, where it is conveniently located but out of the way with respect to the windows I have open in my applications. The orientation you choose is completely up to you, but you might want to experiment with different options to see which works best.

Switching applications swiftly

The Dock is your ally in switching from one running application to another. Just click the desired application's Dock icon and that application, along with all its windows, comes to the front. If you only want a single window to come to the front, just click and hold the mouse button on that application's icon — a contextual menu will appear, enabling you to choose that window's name. This comes in handy when all you want to do is check one piece of information for your current task and don't want to bury your current application's windows behind a plethora of other windows.

Another rapid method for moving among running applications, but without the fine control of selecting just a single window, is to press ⌘+Tab to cycle through your active applications in left-to-right/top-to-bottom Dock order (Shift+⌘+Tab cycles in the opposite order).

Setting Preferences

The System Preferences application in Mac OS X is the epicenter of options and settings for your Mac. It's in this application that you'll do everything from set options for the Dock or colors for your Mac's desktop background to important networking and Internet settings that make it possible for you to get online and access other computers.

To launch System Preferences, choose System Preferences from the Apple menu. The result will be the System Preferences window, shown in figure 1.16. To dig into any particular set of preferences you simply click

1.16 The System Preferences application window.

one of the icons in this window, which then opens that particular preference *pane*. It's in the panes that you'll make settings and choices that affect how your Mac operates.

Administrator versus user preferences

System Preferences tend to fall into two major categories: those that affect all users and those that affect just the current user. OS X addresses this dichotomy by requiring Administrator access to alter settings that affect the way the Macintosh operates, such as a networking setting. That's as opposed to settings that are simply a user's preferences, such a desktop background – those don't require a special password. As a laptop user, you're less likely to be sharing your Mac with other users and thus, more likely to be running with the Mac's sole (Administrator) account. That means your

username and password should gain you access to most any System Preferences pane.

Preference panes that require Administrator access to change settings are indicated with a small padlock icon in the lower-left corner, as shown in figure 1.17. In addition to the Date & Time pane, the Accounts, Network, Sharing, Startup Disk, and Security require Administrator access if you want to make changes.

You don't have to be logged on with an Administrator account to make changes, but you do have to know the Administrator account name and password. When you click the padlock to indicate you want to make changes to the protected settings, an Authenticate dialog box appears that requires you to enter the administrator name and password as shown in figure 1.18.

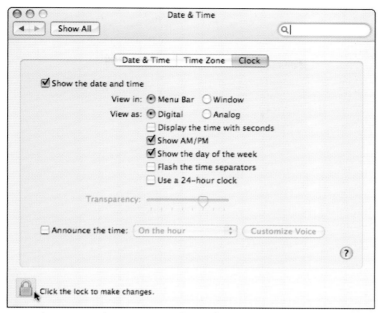

1.17 The Date & Time pane requires Administrator access to alter the settings.

1.18 If you click the padlock, you are asked for an Administrator account and password.

Appearance, time, and date

I touch on different Preference panes throughout the chapters in this book, ranging from the Network pane to the Security pane to the Energy Saver pane, all of which are important to Mac portable users. But, before you get to those more advanced panes, take a look at a few of the more basic panes.

System Preferences offers an Appearance pane, which is where you can make some default choices about how Mac OS X looks and acts. Launch System Preferences, choose the Appearance pane, and you see the options shown in figure 1.19.

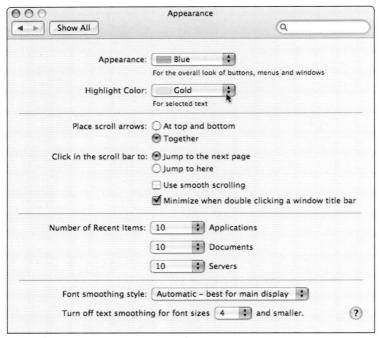

1.19 The Appearance System Preferences pane.

There are many options to choose from in the Appearance pane.

✦ **Appearance.** This option lets you change the overall look of buttons, windows, and menus. Choices from the menu include the default, Blue, and the option Graphite, which makes the interface generally grayer.

Note *Some graphic designers prefer the Graphite appearance to the Blue appearance because the graphite color scheme doesn't compete as much with other colors on the screen in your application windows.*

✦ **Highlight Color.** This setting changes the color that selected text is highlighted. Choices include a number of different colors — choose your favorite.

✦ **Place scroll arrows.** Select At top and bottom if you want your arrows to be on either side of the scrollbar in your document windows. Choose Together (the default) if you want your arrows right next to one another (which takes a little less mousing).

✦ **Click in the scroll bar to.** Choose from Jump to the next page or Jump to here. You can also select options for Use smooth scrolling and Minimize when double clicking a window title bar.

✦ **Number of Recent Items.** Choose from the number of recent items displayed in the Recent Items menu (within the Apple menu). This menu can be used to access the items you've most recently opened and worked with, on the theory that you'll often be opening the same application or document again. These settings enable you to add or take away from the number of recent items that are tracked.

✦ **Font smoothing style.** Choose a font smoothing style based on either the recommendations made in the menu or based on the type of display you have; if you're making this choice for your PowerBook or iBook's main built-in display, you'll probably choose Medium font smoothing.

✦ **Turn off text smooth for font sizes [ ] and smaller.** Choose a point size at which text smoothing will no longer affect the text — if the text is smoothed when it's too small, it will be too fuzzy to read.

Tip *It may not seem like it, but these are actually important options for a Mac portable user. If you're like me, you may find it very handy to have scroll controls bunched together at the top or bottom of scroll bars, as that means less effort on the trackpad to move from the top (or left) of a scroll bar to the bottom (or right) in order to access the different directions.*

On the Date & Time preference pane, you have three tabs to choose from: Date & Time, Time Zone, and Clock.

✦ **Date & Time tab.** You can set the current time and date through the Date & Time tab (see figure 1.20). Use the controls to set the date and time manually or select the Set Date & Time Automatically option and choose a time server computer that your Mac should access. If you have fairly regular access to the Internet, this is the option I suggest; the more accurate your Mac's clock is, the better it will function in a variety of circumstances. Apple's time servers consult the atomic clocks that keep extremely accurate time on the Internet, so it's a good bet that a clock set in this way is extremely accurate and synchronized with many computers and servers on the Internet, which is a good thing.

✦ **Time Zone tab.** Instead of setting the time manually, you can simply set your location on the Time Zone tab and let that determine the time (assuming you also have the Set Date & Time Automatically option checked on the Date & Time tab). Note that not all cities are found in the time zone list, but you should be able to find one that's close to where you are.

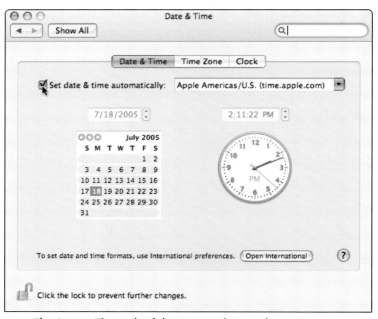

1.20 The Date & Time tab of the Date & Time preference pane.

✦ **Clock tab.** You can make choices about the clock that appears, by default, on the menu bar. You can choose, for example, to make it not appear at all, or you can configure it in a variety of ways to look the way you want (see figure 1.17).

Managing accounts

Mac OS X is designed to allow you to have multiple user accounts on a single Mac — for example, a home computer might have different accounts for mom, dad, and the kids. This multiple user approach is cool because each individual account can have different settings, preferences, and even different e-mail accounts and Web bookmarks — by *logging in* and *logging out* of your own account, you can keep your private documents out of the sight of others and you can keep others from (accidentally or otherwise) deleting your files or changing your preferences. And anyone else who has a user account on your Mac can do the same.

On a portable Mac, multiple user accounts might not seem necessary at first blush, particularly if you don't share your portable Mac with others. If you do share it, such as checking out your portable from your employer for use when traveling, that's a great reason to have multiple accounts.

But, there are other reasons (some of them rather clever) to have multiple accounts, even if your Mac's sole users are you, you, and you. For example, you might just want separate accounts for everyday and business use; it can be a good idea to have a clean account for business presentations, so that you don't have e-mail noises and iCal alert messages popping up while you're giving the presentation. You might also want to

set that specific account's Energy Saver preferences so that your portable doesn't blank the screen or sleep automatically while you're giving a presentation.

 Energy Saver is another important preference pane in the System Preferences application. See Chapter 2 for more discussion of Energy Saver and getting the most out of your Mac's battery life (or, conversely, getting better performance with less "sleep" mode) by tweaking your Energy Saver settings.

Another good reason to have a separate account is for testing or administrative purposes. This can be very handy when a piece of software starts behaving oddly — you can log on with the less-used account name and password and launch the application to see whether the misbehavior persists. If it doesn't, that can help you troubleshoot the problem — an application that misbehaves in one account but not in another suggests that it's encountering a corrupt document or preferences file in the original account.

 One reason to get serious about user accounts is to better manage the security of your files and those of any other users who use your Mac or who access your Mac over a network. Chapter 3 covers that in detail, in particular because security for a portable Mac is very important.

See Chapter 7 for troubleshooting advice.

It should come as no surprise that the Accounts pane (figure 1.21) controls user accounts on your Mac. It has options for various aspects of accounts in these panes: Password, Picture, Login Items, and Parental Controls.

1.21 The Accounts System Preferences pane.

Adding or making more than minimal modification to your own account requires Administrator access. Some changes you can make to your own account without Administrator authorization include changing your password (click Change Password in the Password tab), updating your Address Book Card (click Open in the Password tab), changing the picture associated with your account in the Login window (Picture tab), specifying programs to run and documents to open when you log on to your account (Login Items tab).

A great place to start is by understanding the process of creating a new account. You can create an account at any time, as long as you are an administrative user (or have access to an administrative user's account name and password). Here's how:

1. **Choose System Preferences from the Apple menu and click the Accounts icon.** The Accounts pane appears.

2. **In the Accounts pane, you may need to authenticate; click the Padlock icon if it is closed, and then enter an administrator's account name and password.** If your account is the only one on the Mac then you are definitely an administrator.

3. **At the bottom of the list of accounts, click the plus (+) icon.** A dialog sheet appears (see figure 1.22).

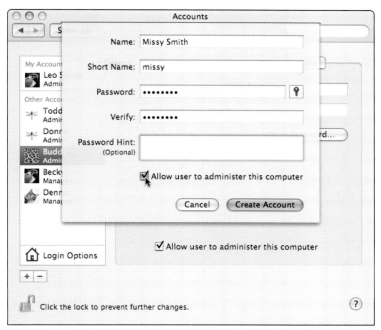

1.22 A dialog sheet appears to enter user information into when you opt to add a user.

4. **Enter a name for the new account; then edit the short name if desired.** The short name can be used for logging into the account both on your Mac and if you ever happen to access this Mac over a network. Plus, the short name is the name that is assigned to your home folder.

5. **In the Password entry box, enter a password for this account, and then enter it again in the Verify entry box.** You can also enter a password hint in the Password Hint entry box if desired.

Cross-Reference *Chapter 3 offers some good information on choosing passwords and securing your account.*

6. **If you would like the account to have administrative privileges, click the checkbox next to Allow User to Administer This Computer.**

7. **Click Create Account.**

Once an account is created, it appears in the account list portion of the Accounts pane. That's when the other tabs come into play — you can select an account in that list and then choose one of the tabs to make changes:

✦ **Password.** On the Password tab, you can change the name of the account or click the Change Password button to make changes to the account's password.

✦ **Picture.** Click the Picture tab and you'll be able to choose a picture to represent this account in various places, including the Login window, e-mail messages (at least, those sent to other Mac users), and in iChat windows, along with other places. You can select an image from within the Picture tabs screen (see figure 1.23) or click the

Edit button to edit the selected image. You can also use the Edit window to choose an image from your hard disk — click the Choose button — or to take a picture of yourself using a digital camcorder or an Apple iSight camera, if one is connected.

✦ **Login Items.** Click this tab and you'll see a list of items that are set to open automatically whenever this account logs into the Mac (see figure 1.24). You can click the plus (+) icon below the list to add any additional applications that you'd like to have open automatically. You can also click the Hide checkbox next to an item if you'd like it to launch, but not appear on-screen when the account is logged into.

1.23 You can choose a picture from Apple's own built-in offerings.

1.24 The Login Items screen lists items that are set to launch whenever this account is logged into.

✦ **Parental Controls.** Click this tab to set options that limit this account's ability to do certain things on the Internet — these are only active if the account that you are selecting is a Standard account (meaning it has not been enabled as an administrator account; see the sidebar "About Account Types" for details).

Parental Control options are ideal for accounts that are used by small children or in a computer lab situation — while those are a little less likely with your portable, you may want to dig in and use them anyway. Here's a quick run through:

1. **To enable one of the Parental Controls for this account, click the checkbox next to it in the list.**

2. **If a dialog sheet doesn't appear automatically, click the Configure button for that option.** Note that this works for all the options except Safari, which is configured differently.

3. **In the dialog sheet, follow the on-screen instructions.** Use the plus (+) icon in the Mail and iChat controls to add the users with whom this user is allowed to communicate and to whom "permission" e-mail should be sent when someone new tries to communicate with the user. If you're setting Finder & System controls, then make choices in that dialog sheet as shown in figure 1.25 (this is also discussed in the sidebar "About Account Types").

4. **Click OK in the dialog sheet to put those options to work.**

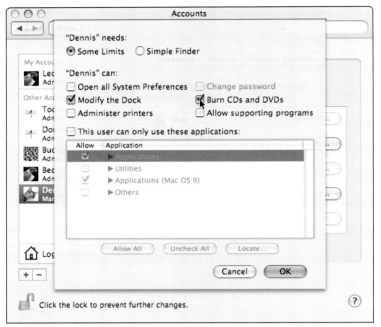

1.25 If you choose Finder & System, you'll have some choices to make in terms of how you're going to limit this user's access in the Finder.

About Account Types

Accounts come in three flavors: Administrator, Standard, and Managed. As should already be clear, *Administrator* accounts have almost unfettered access to make changes to the Mac and all its settings. *Standard* accounts can run all the applications in the Mac's Applications folder and can do pretty much anything that doesn't involve modifying systemwide settings. To create a standard account, all you have to do is make sure the option Allow This User to Administer Computer is not turned on when you're creating the account. (And, in fact, you can turn the option off at a later date once the account is created by accessing the Password tab for that account.)

Managed accounts are subsets of a standard account where you can use the Parental Controls tab to limit access to applications, e-mail, Web pages, iChat usage, Dock modification, CD/DVD burning, and the range of words that can be looked up in the Dictionary application. In particular, turning on the Finder & System parental control enables you to select from a number of options as were shown in figure 1.25. To create the most basic account, choose Simple Finder in that window, which limits users to only the applications that you place in the Dock for that user. This is great for really young kids or for public access Macs that you don't want to offer any options for changing preferences.

As mentioned, Safari works a bit differently. With the Safari parental control active in this Account pane, you then do the following to manage Web sites for this user:

1. **Turn on this user's Safari parental control; then close System Preferences.**

2. **Log into this user's account.** See the Fast User Switching instructions in the next section for a quick way to do this.

3. **Launch Safari and enter the URL for an approved site.** If the site isn't yet a bookmark in Safari, you'll see a message telling you that the site can't be displayed (see figure 1.26).

4. **Click the Add Website button if you'd like to allow this account to access this Website.** In the

Authenticate dialog box, you are asked to enter your user name and password. Once the site is added, this user will be able to access the site in the future.

Fast User Switching

Mac OS X offers a feature called Fast User Switching, which is a fun way to enable multiple people to use a Mac at nearly the same time. If, for example, you and your significant other are traveling together and have one portable Mac between you, use the Fast User Switching feature to move from one user account to another quickly. Each user can access his or her own applications and Desktop without logging off of one account before logging on to another.

1.26 With the Safari parental control turned on, new Web addresses have to be approved by an administrative user.

To use Fast User Switching, you first need to turn it on. Follow these steps:

1. **Choose System Preferences from the Apple menu, and then choose the Accounts icon in the System Preferences window.**

2. **Click the Login Options icon.** Toward the bottom of the screen, you see an entry called Enable Fast User Switching.

3. **Click to place a checkmark next to Enable Fast User Switching.**

4. **Choose from the menu how you want the Fast User Switching icon to appear in the menu bar.** The icon can be just an icon, or it can be the short name or full name of the current user. (This is handy for quickly showing you what account you're logged into.) Whenever you want to switch between user accounts, you can simply access the menu bar item.

To switch between accounts, follow these steps:

1. **Click the Fast User Switching icon (or the current username) from the menu bar to see a menu.** The menu lists the users on your Mac (see figure 1.27).

2. **Select the user account you want to switch to.** A login window appears that enables you to login to that account.

3. **Enter the login information.** When you're successful, the screen changes to that new account, complete with all the customizations you'd expect when logging on as that user.

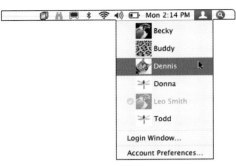

1.27 Use the menu bar icon menu to switch between users.

In the Fast User Switching menu, you see checkmarks for any user that is currently logged on to the system; to switch back, select that user again in the menu and type a password for that account. The switch should take place quickly.

Caution *You can only shut down or restart your Mac while other users are logged on through Fast User Switching if you are an administrative user and you authorize your Mac to shut down the other user accounts before restarting. If you do that, changes in open documents could be lost in the other user accounts. If possible, have other users log out before you shut down or restart your Mac. As an alternative, put your Mac in Sleep mode, which may be low-power enough for your needs.*

Cross-Reference *The Login Options window offers a few other options that might be of interest, including some choices that govern what the main Login window looks like when you start up your Mac. These relate to the security of your Mac's data, and are discussed in Chapter 3.*

Setting Up Your Portable Mac

✦ ✦ ✦ ✦

CHAPTER 2

In This Chapter

Portable ergonomics

Using your portable as your desktop

Working with two computers at once

Using .Mac sync tools

Traveling with your Mac

✦ ✦ ✦ ✦

Part of the reason for the rise in the popularity of Apple's portable line of Macs is the fact that they now have the power and capacity to be seriously considered as desktop replacements. Years ago, portable Macs sacrificed too much performance in favor of portability, making it difficult for anyone using a Mac to its fullest — particularly users who work with graphics and multimedia — to use a portable Mac exclusively. Instead, the portable Mac was often considered a second computer for the business user or delegated for certain tasks like writing and Internet communications.

Today, your portable can serve as an adjunct to your desktop computer, especially if you happen to have a really nice, fast desktop machine — or if, for example, it's necessary to leave your desktop computer connected to your network at work, running important applications, and so on. If so, you can synchronize your PowerBook or iBook easily with your desktop and get quite a bit of productive work done on your portable.

If, however, you want to explore using your portable as your only Mac — a desktop replacement — then I have some advice on how to accomplish that. I've used a portable computer as my main computer more than five years — moving from a PowerBook G3 to a PowerBook G4 to an iBook G4 — and it would be difficult for me to go back to a regular desktop at this point. The portability and easy access to my important files is too critical. Of course, there are drawbacks and compromises to using your portable Mac every day at your desk, so this chapter considers those issues — and how to work around them.

Also, as part of setting up your portable, you should understand how to keep the portable safe when you transport it, as well as how to work best with your portable when it's on battery power or anytime it needs power away from the confines of your home or office.

Portable Ergonomics

All of the hours and days that people spend sitting at computers these days has driven a keen interest in the ergonomics of the workplace, including how your computer should be configured and positioned. I learned early on when I switched to using a PowerBook most of the time that I wanted the experience in my office to be different from my home computing, if only because I was in my office much more. The primary reason? Back pain and strain. Sitting over a portable computer can force your neck to angle down to look at the screen, while the smaller keyboard is hard on the hands.

Most suggestions for desktop computing ergonomics come down to a few basics. I'm not a doctor (and if you have any problems with pain when computing you should consult one), but to avoid a doctor visit when working at your portable for long periods of time, try to adjust your portable setup with these ergonomic guidelines in mind:

✦ **Keep your display at eye level.** When possible, you should be looking directly at a computer monitor, with the top of the display area about even or just a little higher than a spot that you see when you look directly ahead at the display. You should never have to bend your neck (that is, lower your chin) to look down at a display.

✦ **Keep your display directly in front of you.** You should be looking directly at a computer monitor,

not to one side. I like to equate this with driving a car on an interstate highway while looking out the driver's-side window. That would hurt after a while, right?

✦ **Keep your elbows at approximately a 90-degree angle.** This is nearly impossible to do when you are situated with your portable's display at eye level in front of you. So, your best bet is to plug in a USB (or wireless) keyboard and not use the Mac portable's keyboard. The keyboard should then be positioned slightly lower than the typical desk height.

✦ **Keep your knees at 90-degree angles when sitting.** That essentially means that you need a desk that fits your height and an adjustable chair. When you adjust the chair, you need to be able to adjust the keyboard's height, as well.

You can also attach an external mouse, use special accessories to raise the display, and add external displays so that you're using something other than your portable's display when you're working long term in the office.

Input peripherals

The first step in making your portable-as-desktop experience a little better is to get an external keyboard and mouse. This is true for two reasons: First, an external keyboard and mouse are usually more comfortable and less cramped than the portable's keyboard and trackpad. Second, and more importantly, getting an external keyboard and mouse frees you to raise your portable's display to a more ergonomically appropriate height.

Adding a keyboard and mouse to your portable is easy. All modern Mac portables have built-in USB ports that recognize nearly any USB keyboard and/or mouse attached to your portable Mac. (With some Windows-compatible keyboards, you may have to flip a switch on the keyboard or deal with an odd keystroke or two, although many will remap the Windows key to the Apple command key.)

Note *USB stands for Universal Serial Bus, and it's a technology that's used by Macs to connect everything from keyboards and mice to printers, scanners, and external storage devices. Earlier PowerBooks and iBooks support the USB 1.1 standard, which tops out at 12 megabits per second (or about 1.5 megabytes per second), which is fine for many peripherals but not ideal for external hard disks and such. USB 2.0 is much faster — up to 480 megabits, or about 60MB/sec — making it handy for external storage and other high-speed devices.*

The easiest external keyboards to work with are Apple models, partly because they offer a passive USB hub within them that allows you to connect your mouse to the keyboard and, usually, another peripheral that doesn't require USB power. This can be a particular benefit with Mac portables, because they tend to have fewer USB ports than Mac desktops; when you fill one port with a keyboard it leaves only one more port for the mouse, unless you have a USB hub or a keyboard that supports USB devices.

Note that with many PowerBook models, you need to open your portable before plugging in a USB keyboard; if you plug in the keyboard while the Mac is in Sleep mode, it will start up the PowerBook in a *headless*

mode, which means the PowerBook is in a mode to power an external display, not its built-in LCD. If you want to use an external keyboard and the PowerBook's internal display, plug in the keyboard *after* waking the PowerBook from Sleep.

Tip *While the design of the Apple mouse is attractive, I personally recommend that you at least take a look at some of the two-button mice offered by other manufacturers. For example, the Microsoft line of USB optical mice tends to be relatively inexpensive and high quality. Mac OS X automatically recognizes a second mouse button, using it the same way you would use a Ctrl+click with a single-button Apple mouse.*

If your Mac offers Bluetooth wireless support, you might opt for a wireless keyboard and/or mouse. When using Bluetooth devices, make sure they're charged and powered on. Follow these steps:

1. **Choose System Preferences from the Apple menu.** The System Preferences window opens.

2. **Click on the Bluetooth icon to open the Bluetooth pane.**

3. **Click on the Settings tab and make sure the Bluetooth Power is turned on.**

4. **Click on the Devices tab and check if your keyboard (and/or mouse) is discovered.**

5. **Select the device from the list, and click Set Up New Device.** The Bluetooth Setup Assistant dialog box appears (see figure 2.1) to walk you through the steps of adding it as an input device for your Mac.

Bluetooth isn't the only type of wireless; you can also get RF (radio frequency) keyboards and mice that will work with your Mac to enable you to work with wireless devices. However, Bluetooth, if your Mac supports it, is a better option because it doesn't require a USB port. In order to use an RF keyboard, you still need to plug the wireless receiver into a USB port on your Mac. Bluetooth also enables you to lock ("pair") your Mac to a specific device, and the signal is weak enough that it generally won't bleed over and affect any computers close to you that also have Bluetooth (in a café, computer lab, office cubicle, etc.).

2.1 Setting up a Bluetooth keyboard in System Preferences.

Bookendz

A company called Photo Control (www.photo-control.com) offers the Bookendz series of docks for PowerBooks and iBooks. These docks enable you to slide your Mac into the dock's cradle, which then offers connectors for the devices that you would use with your portable; a printer, network cable, external input devices, and so on.

The idea is that you don't have to plug and unplug all those devices whenever you want to move your portable; you simply slide into the dock to which those devices are already connected. It's not a bad idea, and some models offer interesting solutions, such as the iBook dock that features a built-in VGA adapter for your desktop display.

Raise the computer

One thing that connecting external input devices does is free you to move the PowerBook or iBook itself a little farther away from your hands; since you don't have to type on it and use its trackpad at your desk, you can raise the Mac — and, hence, the display — to a more ergonomic height. In fact a number of devices exist to help you do that, including the iCurve from Griffin Technology (www.griffintechnology. com), shown in figure 2.2.

2.2 The iCurve is an attractive stand that raises your computer — and, hence, the display — and offers space underneath for placing your external keyboard when not in use.

Another popular model is the iLap (www.raindesignllc.com), which has the advantage of being flexible for use on your desk when you still want to type on your portable, or when you want to use your Mac on your lap, but still improve your ergonomics. Macally (www.macally.com) offers the iceStation, which is adjustable and can raise an iBook or PowerBook's display quite a bit higher than most other solutions — to a good height for a long session at your desktop.

By placing your portable on a stand of some sort, you can raise the LCD display so that it's in a more ergonomic position, enabling you to look directly at it instead of looking

down on it. Of course, you don't have to opt for a special PowerBook or iBook holder that's specifically designed for the purpose; in the past, I've used a wire in box-type basket from the office supply store to raise the portable to a better height. And, with a wire or mesh design, you even get some airflow under the machine. Similarly, you can find office-supply display mounts or even desks that work for raising a PowerBook nearly as well as they work for placing a CRT or external LCD in a good place.

Connecting external displays

So you've seen how you can raise your Mac so that it's ergonomically a little more appropriate for sitting in front of, but one of the most interesting options for desktop computing with a portable is plugging in a larger display that can be dedicated for the purpose. All modern PowerBooks and all second-generation iBooks (white models) have external video ports; the only thing you need to worry about is whether your Mac supports the same technology as the external display that you're working with. Here's a quick look at the external video technologies that are found on different Mac portable models:

✦ **VGA (Video Graphics Array).** This is the technology that has been used on PowerBooks for a long time, through some of the PowerBook G4 models. With a full-sized VGA port on the back or side of the Mac, you can plug an analog CRT or VGA-compatible LCD directly into the portable, making it easier to work with an external display or an overhead projection for presentations.

✦ **DVI (Digital Video Interface).** Later PowerBook G4 models offer a DVI port, which connects directly to DVI-compatible LCD screens. Few CRT-style displays offers a DVI connection, as DVI is more common on newer LCD displays, but it's a relatively inexpensive prospect to get a DVI-to-VGA adapter so that you can connect your portable to an older analog external monitor.

✦ **Mini-VGA or Mini-DVI.** On certain PowerBooks — particularly the smallest 12-inch PowerBook G4 models — Apple gives you a special video port that requires an adapter to connect to a CRT or LCD computer monitor.

✦ **Apple Video Out.** On many iBook models and certain PowerBooks, Apple gives you a special video out port. Depending on the adapter you connect to it, it can either handle an external VGA display or a composite or s-video signal that can be connected for display on a TV or video equipment (see figure 2.3).

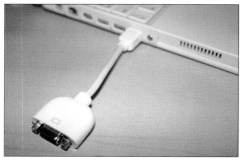

2.3 Here's a VGA adapter connected to an iBook's Apple Video Out port.

Once you connect your Mac to an external display, you can generally use that display in one of two ways. With almost any iBook or PowerBook, you can use the external display in a mirrored image mode, where what's displayed on your PowerBook is also shown in the external display. This can be handy for either using your PowerBook with a much larger display at your desk or using it to give a presentation or teach a class by mirroring to a projector. To do this, you simply plug the display into the VGA, DVI, or adapter port on your Mac. Then, in the Displays pane of System Preferences, you'll see your mirroring options (see figure 2.4). You can tweak the resolution of the external display, if desired.

 The Displays pane will change names in its title bar to reflect the type of monitor that it's running on; with PowerBook and iBook displays the name will often be Color LCD; if the display is recognized by your Mac the name of the pane might be DELL D1028L or similar.

In the second case, you can use the display that's built into your PowerBook and the external display together doing something called *spanning*, which expands the screen area that you have to work with by allowing each display to be independent, but letting your mouse pointer move from one to another. With my PowerBook, this is my favorite way to compute — I like to put Mail and iChat applications on one screen where I can always see them (usually the PowerBook's display off to one side) while using the other display for writing and other work.

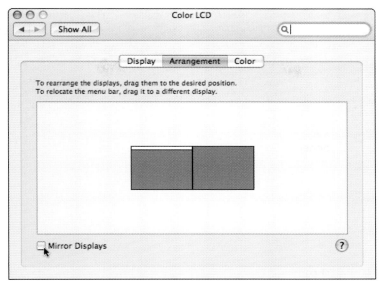

2.4 With multiple displays you have the option of mirroring the image from your PowerBook to the external display, which is handy for presentations or playing back multimedia.

Note *An iBook doesn't offer you the luxury of screen spanning, at least not by default. However, many iBook models can be set into a mode that allows them to span — the only problem with this approach is that it could damage your iBook and, if it does, your Apple warranty doesn't cover it. If you're still interested, you can head to* www.macparts.de/ibook/, *which offers a special download and tells you how to convert your late-model iBook so that it can use screen spanning.*

When you have the option to span displays, the Displays pane in System Preferences will be a little different. First, you see the Arrangement tab; this tells you the external display is recognized (see figure 2.5). On the Arrangement tab, you can click and drag the display representations around until you have them in a logical space relative to one another — so that you can mouse off the right side of one display and it appears on the left side of the other, for example. Notice also that if you decide spanning isn't the solution you are looking for, you can switch back to Mirroring by simply selecting the Mirror Displays option.

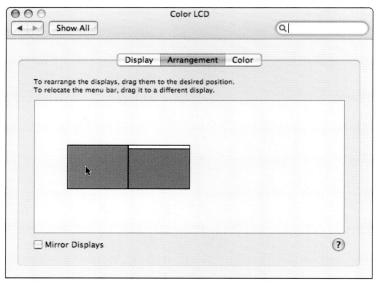

2.5 When you opt for screen spanning, you can arrange representations of the displays so you can use them more effectively.

The Second difference is that multiple displays will result in multiple Display pane windows — one for each display that's connected. When you've got both displays active, you see a window in each when you access the Displays pane of System Preferences; the individual windows enable you to set the resolution and color levels of each display separately.

You may find that screen spanning alone makes it worth it to think in terms of using your portable as a desktop replacement, because it already has one display built in. By adding another one, you can significantly increase the display space you have to work with and set yourself up for a better ergonomic experience because you're looking at high-quality displays (hopefully) at comfortable heights and angles.

Move It

What's the best ergonomic advice you can get? Get up and move around. At the very least you should make a habit of looking away from your computer screens every so often and, at regular intervals, you should get up and stretch, walk, and do at least a little something active to give your thinking, mousing, typing, and hunching-over muscles a rest. If you can't seem to remember to get up and move around, you might consider a little application such as Dejal Time Out (www.dejal.com/timeout/), which reminds you to take a break every hour or so, or get serious with commercial software like Stretch Break Pro (www.safecomputing.com/stretch_break_ pro.html), which includes some visuals of stretches you can do.

Working with Two Computers at Once

So what if using your portable as a desktop isn't an option? Or maybe you don't want it to be, because your desktop is so much more powerful than your portable and you end up using it a lot of the time. Fair enough. But if you're like me, the idea of not having your e-mail and contacts and data files on the portable once you're away from the office gets you a little worried.

Apple has been working recently to help Mac users synchronize data more easily among a number of different Macs. Through the .Mac subscription service and Mac OS X 10.4, you can synchronize a number of different items, including your bookmarks, Address Book, and your iCal calendars. Using an IMAP or .Mac e-mail account, you can leave your e-mail on the server and access it from multiple locations.

If you don't opt for some of those fancier synching services, you've still got options. The brute force method is to connect your portable and your desktop through a network or similar connection — or through target disk mode, which treats your portable like an external FireWire disk — and copy items from one to the other. The next section takes a look at some third-party tools that make that easier to synch your computers.

Target Disk Mode

Before digging into synchronization approaches and software, I'd like to touch on *Target Disk Mode*. Almost any Mac that has FireWire ports can be placed in this special mode that causes the Mac to act as an external hard drive when connected to another Mac. The advantage is that you can easily access the files on that Mac, make changes, and even synchronize lower-level preferences and other files without as much concern over passwords and file privileges or ownership as you have when you're working over a network connection.

Plus, with your portable Mac running in Target Disk Mode when connected to your desktop Mac, you may not even have to worry about synchronizing files, because you can simply work with the files that are already on your portable. If you've got your presentation files or Word documents or even your digital photos on your iBook or PowerBook, for example, you can connect it to your desktop through Target Disk Mode, work on those files, save them to the iBook or PowerBook, and then disconnect. You're ready to go because those files are already on the portable.

Here's how to get Target Disk Mode working for you:

1. **Shut down the Mac that you want to put into Target Disk Mode so you can use it as an external hard drive.** This is probably your portable, although you can put almost any FireWire-capable Mac into this mode.

2. **Start up the Macwhile pressing T.** After you hear the start-up tone and wait a moment, you see a FireWire icon appear on the Mac's screen. It floats around the screen as a screensaver of sorts.

3. **Connect a FireWire cable from the FireWire port on your portable to a FireWire port on your desktop.**

4. **Using the Finder, go to the Desktop.** After a moment, you should see a FireWire icon appear that represents your portable Mac (see figure 2.6).

2.6 Using a FireWire cable and the Mac's built-in Target Disk Mode, you can use your Mac as an external hard drive.

5. **Double-click the Mac's icon on the desktop or single click it in the Finder window sidebar.** That should open it for access, just as if it were an external hard disk that had been mounted by your Mac's file system.

When the Mac is in Target Disk Mode, you have access to nearly any file or folder on the Mac, including those in other users' account folders as well as in important system folders. It's worth noting that the Mac OS doesn't govern your access to files on external drives in the same way that it does for the boot drive, so you should be careful with what you synchronize, what you copy, and what you delete. I recommend that you stick to the files in your own home folder, and even with items such as your Library folder (where preferences, application support files, and your e-mail database are stored), you should work carefully.

To get out of Target Disk Mode, follow these steps:

1. **On the desktop, select the icon for the computer connected as a drive.**

2. **Choose File ⇨ Eject or, in a Finder window Sidebar you should be able to click the small eject icon (see figure 2.7).**

2.7 Eject a Mac in Target Disk Mode as you would any external hard drive.

3. **Press the Power button on your portable Mac and it should shut down.**

4. **Unplug the FireWire cable from between the two Macs and then press the Power button on your portable to start it up again.** You should hear the chimes, and your Mac starts up as it normally does.

Synchronizing with a desktop Mac

If you've got a desktop Mac and you need to synchronize its contents with your portable, the fundamental issue is knowing what you need to synchronize and how often. For me, working with my notebook as my desktop is essential because I like to be up-to-date with my multiple e-mail accounts, and it's tough to synchronize all that data from one Mac to another. But it's not impossible, by any means.

The most basic approach is to simply connect your Macs through a network or a FireWire cable and Target Disk Mode. You can then copy files from your Documents folders or similar folders in your home folder so that you have access to them in both places. Synchronization can be considerably more complex, however.

You Synchronize

One interesting third-party utility for synchronizing your Mac is You Synchronize (www.yousoftware.com). It is an inexpensive tool that takes file synchronization between two Macs very seriously. The tool enables you to choose a local folder (the one of the Mac where you're running the software) and a remote folder that you'd like to synchronize between the two Macs. Figure 2.8 shows the You Synchronize setup screen.

Before you can put the synchronization into motion using this software, there are a series of decisions to make regarding how that synchronization is done. You make these choices from the Type menu in the Settings section that is shown in figure 2.8. Choices include:

✦ **Two-Way Synchronization.** In this case, no files are overwritten in either the local folder or the remote folder. Instead, all of the different files are added to both and then synchronized with the latest versions.

✦ **Local Replaces Remote.** This gives the Mac you're running the software on precedence in terms of replacing one folder and its contents with another folder. If you'd like your Documents folder on your portable to be identical with the

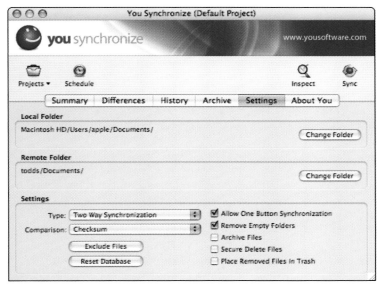

2.8 To set up synchronization software, you'll need to take some important steps.

one on your desktop Mac (and you're running the software on your desktop) then you'd choose this option. It destroys any unique files in that folder on the portable.

✦ **Remote Replaces Local.** Obviously this is the opposite approach, enabling you to replace the files on your desktop (if that's where you're running the software) with the files on your portable in that particular folder.

This synchronization task doesn't have to synchronize your entire home folder — in fact, that may not be the best idea, as the home folder on each individual Mac will have subtle differences, particularly in your Library folder, where preferences and applications support files are kept. Instead, it's best to focus on your Documents folder and other folders that hold the important files that you work on with productivity applications.

 Caution — *Be very careful if you try to synchronize preferences and application support data between Macs that have different versions of Mac OS X installed — even slightly different versions. You may find that applications stop working because of differences or changes in their low-level support files if you opt to overwrite them from another Mac. For example, some applications use the ByHost folder in your personal Library folder's Preferences folder. That special ByHost folder is for preference files that are specific to a particular Mac; if you synchronize those preferences files to another Mac, they won't work correctly.*

You Synchronize has the ability to synchronize files and maintain their Created and Modified dates, which is one of its main selling points.

If you simply copy files from one computer to another, that may change their modified dates; however, it can be handy to have those dates intact when you need to know at a glance the last time you truly opened and modified a document. And as with other synchronization tools, You Synchronize allows you to skip certain files when synchronizing and schedule automatic sync operations. It uses a database to track files that you've synched in the past, and it automatically creates and archives files that have been synched previously but don't show up in the latest synchronization operation, giving you an opportunity to retrieve files that have been deleted from the watched folders.

Synchronize! X Pro

You Synchronize isn't the only option. Another tool that's highly thought of is Synchronize! X Pro (www.qdea.com). While a bit more expensive than You Synchronize, it is still reasonably priced — especially when you consider it is a full-featured backup utility that can synchronize folders, manage scheduled backup operations, and even create bootable copies of a hard drive and Mac OS X installation so that you can use an exact copy of one Mac's files on another Mac. (This is impractical for day-to-day use but it's handy for moving from one Mac to another or creating an extensive backup to an external hard drive.) The same company makes Synchronize! X Plus, a less-expensive tool that focuses on folder-to-folder synchronization.

FolderSynchronizer

Another great option is FolderSynchronizer (www.softobe.com). This product is the least expensive of the three products mentioned here. It offers many of the same features as Synchronize! X Pro, including the ability to create bootable backups, synchronize multiple folders, and even automatically mount and access network volumes for synchronization purposes.

Using .Mac Sync Tools

Another salvo in Apple's bid to get us all to subscribe to the .Mac service is that service's ability to help you synchronize data and preferences on multiple Macs. Using the .Mac service as an intermediary, you can synchronize data in your Address Book, in iCal, your Keychain (a database that stores passwords and security information), and even from within Mail 2.0. Many of these features have been added or augmented in Mac OS X 10.4, and going forward, this sort of synchronization is a focus for Apple.

Setting up .Mac Sync

With .Mac, what you're doing is tying two different Macs (or more) to the same .Mac account. That's the first step for synchronization. To get things started, follow these steps:

1. **Choose System Preferences from the Apple menu.**

2. **Launch the .Mac pane by clicking the .Mac icon.** The .Mac pane appears.

3. **In the Account tab, type your .Mac account name and password.** Do this for every computer that you want to synchronize using the .Mac service. They'll all need access to the same account.

Once you get all the computers you want to synchronize logged in through the .Mac pane, you are able to activate synchronization for a number of different Mac applications and services. Once all the Macs are synchronized, the same data on all of those Macs that are managed by the same .Mac account is available to you. This is particularly handy if you personally have more than one Mac (such as a desktop in the office and a portable that moves around with you), since it gives you an automatic way to synchronize important data on those machines.

To get a quick look at everything that you can synchronize via the .Mac service, follow these steps:

1. **Open System Preferences.**

2. **Launch the .Mac pane.**

3. **Click the Sync tab (see figure 2.9).** There you'll see all the items that can be synchronized between your .Mac-enabled Macs.

4. **Click the checkboxes next to the items that you want to synchronize.**

5. **After you make those choices, you can click Sync Now to begin the synchronization process immediately.** You'll see the process begin with a dialog box indicating how things progress.

In the course of the synchronization, dialog boxes appear that ask you how you want to proceed – you can overwrite data that's stored in your .Mac account, you can merge this Mac's entries with the .Mac data, or you can replace your Mac's data with data from .Mac. Make that choice and click Sync (see figure 2.10).

2.9 The Sync options in the .Mac pane of System Preferences.

2.10 During the Sync process you are asked how you want to proceed with certain types of data.

As the Sync actions take place, warnings may appear that tell you when a large number of items will be changing — that's your Mac's way of getting you to reiterate that you're sure you want the operation to go forward just in case you've chosen the wrong type of synchronization. For example, if you have your Address Book contacts overwritten on your local Mac by the data stored in your .Mac account, you may lose quite a bit of important info. In the warning dialog boxes, double-check your selections. When you're comfortable, click Allow.

Also, your Mac notifies you when there appears to be a conflict, such as two different contact cards that appear to be for the same person but have different information. When you encounter such a dialog box, simply choose the card you want to use and click Sync to continue the process.

When the .Mac Sync process is complete, your Mac's internal data has been synchronized with your .Mac account on Apple's servers. That's one step in the process. The next step is to move to your other Mac (or Macs) and do the same thing — set them up to access that same .Mac account (open the .Mac pane in System Preferences and enter your .Mac account name and password); then set them up to synchronize to the data that's stored with that .Mac account, as we just discussed. What's good to remember here is that you're ultimately synchronizing the data with the .Mac account — a copy is kept there — regardless of how many Macs are used in this process. Any Mac that you own or use can be linked to that .Mac account and be synchronized.

So how do you know which Macs are synchronized? Head to the Advanced tab of the .Mac pane in System Preferences (see figure 2.11), and you'll see a list of all the Macs that are currently registered to sync data with your .Mac account. What's more, you can also see when the most recent synchronization was just to give you a sense of how up-to-date your data might be on your connected Macs.

Tip

On the Sync tab in the .Mac pane, don't forget about the Synchronize with .Mac option; select the option and choose a frequency for updates. (It automatically syncs every time you change information in a managed application if you're currently connected to the Internet.) That way your synced data stays up-to-date all the time.

Using Your iDisk and iDisk Sync

On the topic of using the .Mac service to work with two or more computers, one solution to keeping your important files in sync is to make use of your iDisk for those files. For example, if you find that you're spending a lot of time working on a presentation, a series of design files, or a folder full of Word documents, you can store those items directly on your iDisk instead of on your Mac's hard drive. That way, you can quickly pick up where you left off when you switch Macs.

What's an iDisk? It's a bit of storage space on Apple's .Mac server that is assigned to your .Mac account when you subscribe to the service. On your Mac, it looks like an

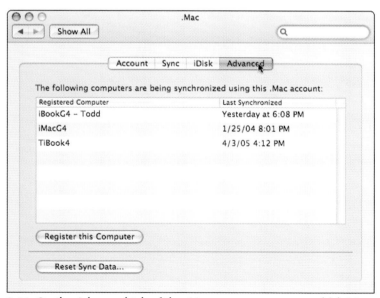

2.11 On the Advanced tab of the .Mac pane, you can see which Macs are registered to sync data using your .Mac account.

external hard drive or a network volume — if you have an active Internet connection you can log on to it and access the folders and files on that iDisk. Then you can load files from it or save files to it, and then eject it when you're done working with it. Those files remain on the iDisk, stored safely on Apple's servers until you log on again to access them. Not only does this make those files accessible to multiple computers, but it means they're stored offline and off your Mac, so that they can be accessed from another computer if anything ever happens to your Mac — or even your whole home or office.

 Cross-Reference *Chapter 3 covers using .Mac and your iDisk to automatically back up files.*

Accessing your iDisk

To use your iDisk for storing files, begin by making sure you have your .Mac account information in the .Mac pane of System Preferences. If it's entered and accurate, then using your iDisk is simple — just click the iDisk icon in the Sidebar of any Finder window. After your Mac is connected to the .Mac servers, the iDisk comes alive and you can access the folders stored on your iDisk (see figure 2.12).

You should use the folders pretty much as they're labeled. The Movies, Music, and Pictures folders are used not only for your own organization, but they're also used automatically by the .Mac HomePage tool (shown in figure 2.13) if you decide you want to use multimedia files Web pages created with HomePage — for example, if you opt for one of the QuickTime templates available using the HomePage tool, HomePage looks in the Movies folder on your iDisk for the movie files that you can use for that page.

The Public folder is also important; it's a special folder that others can access through a Sharing page that you publish on the Internet using the HomePage tool. Your Public folder can also be made accessible to other Mac users who can access it by choosing Go ➪ iDisk ➪ Other User's Public Folder. Because other people can access this folder, it's a good idea to put only files in it that you *want* other people to access.

2.12 My iDisk is active and ready to be put to use.

Note *By default, any file that you place in your Public folder can be accessed immediately by anyone who knows your .Mac username. You can change access to your Public folder by choosing the iDisk tab in the .Mac pane of System Preferences and choose Password Protect Your Public Folder at the bottom of the window.*

The Software folder is a special folder that doesn't count against the space that Apple allows for your account; instead, it's simply a convenient way to access software that Apple has made available to you for downloading, including Apple software and some updates, as well as software bonuses that Apple makes available from time to time for .Mac subscribers.

Using iDisk Syncing

The problem with trying to use your iDisk for important documents can be the fact that you may not always have Internet access, particularly on your portable Mac. The solution to that is iDisk Syncing. iDisk Syncing creates a local version of your iDisk and stores it on your Mac's hard drive. That's the version that you use whenever you want to access a file or save one to it.

When a change is detected on your local version (or at the online iDisk storage space), then the files are synchronized between the online and local versions. This is handy for portables, because it means you can access the contents of your iDisk even when you're not connected to the Internet. It also makes it a little easier to use

2.13 The HomePage tool will automatically create photo albums (for example) from subfolders within the Pictures folder on your iDisk.

an iDisk with two (or more) Macs — if they all have iDisk Syncing turned on for the same .Mac account, then they all have access to the same files.

To turn on iDisk Syncing, open the .Mac pane of System Preferences and click the iDisk tab. There you see the option to turn on iDisk Syncing by clicking Start. When you do, your Mac begins the process of copying the contents of your iDisk to your local Mac. The first time this happens you may be in for a relatively long wait, depending on how many files you have stored on your iDisk. Note also that, in this dialog box, you can choose whether you want the synchronization to happen Automatically or Manually (see figure 2.14).

You'll notice that the iDisk tab is also handy for quickly seeing how much space is being taken up on your iDisk, which includes any items you've uploaded and any e-mail and attachments you have in your .Mac account. Apple very conveniently offers a Buy More button, which you can use to access Apple's site and pay them for additional storage space, if desired.

Now, when you use your iDisk, you find that it's more responsive in the Finder because you're actually just copying files from one part of your Mac to another. If you've set your iDisk to synchronize automatically, you see that happen whenever you connect to the Internet; copy a file to your iDisk and, after a moment, an indicator appears at the bottom of a Finder window to let you know that those files are being synchronized.

2.14 I've turned on iDisk Syncing and opted to have it synchronize automatically.

If you select manual syncing you need to do so every so often; otherwise, either your iDisk or your Mac (or both) ends up with files that the other doesn't have. To sync, click the two round arrows that appear next to your iDisk in the Finder window Sidebar; in fact, you can click this at any time that you're connected to the Internet and you want to synchronize immediately, regardless of whether you select the Automatically or Manually sync option in the .Mac pane (see figure 2.15).

2.15 Click the curved-arrows icon to immediately synchronize your files.

If you decide that the iDisk Syncing approach isn't working for you, return to the iDisk tab in the .Mac pane of System Preferences and click Stop in the iDisk Syncing section. That causes your iDisk to go back to its default online-only mode, and the files that were previously saved on your Mac are turned into a disk image that you can access if needed.

Creating and using disk images are discussed in more detail in Chapter 6.

Traveling with Your Mac

Well, it's portable for a reason, right? If you're going to be moving your portable from place to place on a regular basis, it's a good idea to invest in some technology and some techniques that you can use to get the most out of your Mac while you're moving it around. In this section I discuss the case that you put your laptop in, power adapters and related accessories, and some techniques for getting more battery life out of your Mac when you're on the road.

Choosing a laptop case

A case for your portable Mac should combine safety and security with your own personal style. The first thing it should be, though, is specifically designed to carry a laptop computer; if you don't yet have a bag that's designed for transporting a computer, look into one immediately, as they're extremely important for protecting your investment.

The first decision to make is the type of bag you're interesting in — different types offer different levels of protection for the computer as well as different features and styles. Here's a quick look:

✦ **Laptop sleeves/thin bags.** A laptop sleeve (see figure 2.16) is usually just a thin, padded laptop case that's designed to project your portable when it's carried within another bag. A laptop sleeve usually doesn't offer much in the way of pockets or room for additional items, although some thin bags that might qualify as sleeves will include an extra feature or two.

Courtesy Waterfield Designs

2.16 A laptop sleeve is a great idea, particularly if you want to use your own backpack or carry-on for transporting your portable. Shown here is the Sleevecase from Waterfield Designs.

Sleeves made specifically for PowerBooks and iBooks are offered by several companies, including

- Acme Made (www.acmemade.com)
- Booq (www.booqbags.com)
- Willow Designs (www.willowdesigns.com)
- Pinder (www.pinderbags.com)
- Waterfield Designs (www.sfbags.com)
- Sumdex (www.sumdex.com)
- Ogio (www.ogio.com)

✦ **Backpack/messenger bag.** Most bags in these styles offer a number of different straps, multiple compartments, and because they're designed for activity, the best of these bags offer good padding and protection for your portable Mac. Usually the ideal in this situation is a bag that features a special laptop compartment that absorbs shocks or allows your portable to float, or includes a laptop sleeve for added protection.

Some cool backpack/messenger bags are offered by

- Waterfield Designs
- Sumdex
- Booq
- Tom Bihn (www.tombihn.com)
- Timbuk2 (www.timbuk2.com)
- PacificDesign (www.pacificdesign.com)
- Kensington (www.Kensington.com).

✦ **Laptop briefcase.** If you need a more formal look, laptop briefcases are readily available. These keep your computer safe while allowing you to take care of the files, paperwork, and accessories that you need for a business trip or sales call.

Briefcases are made by numerous companies including

- Kensington
- Pacific Design
- Sumdex
- Samsonite (www.samsonite.com)

My favorites, though, are the offerings by Shaun Jackson Design (www.sjdesign.com), which fold out into laptop desks, complete with a cool pad bottom and sidesaddle pockets. The Laptrap is a well-received contender (see figure 2.17).

Courtesy of Shaun Jackson Design

2.17 The Laptrap is a popular briefcase-turned-mini-office option for your PowerBook or iBook.

✦ **Carry-on case.** The last category I identify is the laptop case on wheels — a number of cases are available that take the classic carry-on dimensions for a rolling bag and add features that make it attractive for carrying your portable. Targus (www.targus.com), for example, makes rolling carry-ons that put your business on one side and your clothes on the other, so that you can still use your carry-on in a meeting. Carry-on and rolling bags are offered by many of the manufacturers already mentioned, as well as many others.

> **Tip** *If you like to carry the least amount of stuff possible for a given situation, look into the different systems offered by Booq, Sumdex, and others that enable you to pull a smaller laptop sleeve from your larger travel bag once you get to your destination.*

The bag you choose needs to fit your style and be appropriate for the situations into which you're taking your portable; otherwise, you may find yourself in situations where you decide not to use it. The most important thing you should do to increase the life of your portable is to get it some padding when it travels and separate it from other hard, sharp, or loose objects in your bag that can damage it or wear away at its shiny exterior.

> **Tip** *Those stories you've heard about laptops beings stolen after leaving the X-ray machine at airport security have been largely debunked as urban legends — but there's something that comes out of those stories that can make sense. Your laptop may be a bit more secure if it's in a bag that doesn't scream, "I'm a laptop bag." That extra-thick laptop briefcase is a dead giveaway, while certain backpack, messenger bags, and even a dusty canvas bag from your public radio station might be an interesting solution — as long as you've got a laptop sleeve that's taking care of your portable.*

Portable accessories

Along with a nice, safe bag for your portable you need some accessories to slide into that bag. Here's a look at some key possibilities:

✦ **Power adapter.** There's nothing wrong with the one that comes with your Mac, except that it won't work in a car or plane. Instead, you might want to opt for a notebook adapter that offers support for all sorts of power situations. Kensington has a few Mac-compatible offerings (they have to fit the power port on the back or side of your Mac) that can be used for airplanes, trains, or cars, and then switched back to AC power for the hotel room or boardroom. Targus and Macally also offer a universal power supply that can handle auto/air/AC. You'll find other vendors that offer just auto/air

Keeping It Clean

You'll be putting your portable Mac into a few more nontraditional situations than you're likely to do with a desktop Mac, which tends to get placed on a desk and left there. With your portable, there are all sorts of trauma that it's capable of experiencing.

One phenomenon with the PowerBooks and iBooks of the past few years is that their keys and displays tend to touch when the clamshell is closed. Over time, the result is small marks on the display from the oils of your hands that accumulate on the keys. You can fight that by cleaning the display regularly, either with wipes designed specifically for the task such as those made by Klearscreen (www.klearscreen.com), or you can use a soft cloth (such as those designed for cleaning camera lenses) made slightly damp. Note also that when you clean the screen, you want to support the back of the display at all times and avoid allowing any liquid to drip or run under the edge of the display near its casing.

Another approach is to use a specially designed screen or keyboard cover. Acme Made (www.acmemade.com) offers the iCover, for example, which slips over your portable's display while still allowing it to close; this protects the screen from the keyboard as well as protecting the top of the screen's case. Or, try the keyboard cloths distributed by Dr Bott LLC (www.drbott.com) or by Macally. These covers and cloths also allow the clamshell to close, but they act as a barrier between the keyboard and display.

adapters that you can slip into your bag right next to the brick you got from Apple.

✦ **Travel kit.** If you need to take your iBook or PowerBook overseas, you can be compatible with world power systems by using a kit offered by Apple through the Apple Store, as well as through authorized dealers. Macally also offers a converter kit.

✦ **Security.** Kensington makes a number of interesting notebook accessories that you might find handy, such as the Microsaver Security Cable that loops through your portable's security hole (all modern models have them) and then locks to a desk or other sturdy furniture or something like a hook in the wall.

✦ **Extras.** Kensington also makes the FlyLight, a device that connects to a USB port and provides a flexible light that can be looped around and pointed at the keyboard. And, Kensington offers retractable Ethernet and modem cables that are handy for traveling; similar items are available from Targus, Belkin (www.belkin.com), and IOGEAR (www.iogear.com).

Getting better power management

When you're working under battery power, you want to conserve battery life. Depending on the PowerBook or iBook model, you have a practical limit of about two to four hours of battery life. (Some iBooks boast more than that, but it's tough to squeeze all that time out of the battery.)

The first thing you can do to add a little life to your batteries is take full advantage of the options in the Energy Saver pane of System Preferences. (Choose System Preferences from the Apple menu, and then click the Energy Saver icon in the System Preferences application.) When you work with a portable Mac, you find that the Energy Saver pane has some interesting options. In particular, the Settings For menu gives you the ability to make different choices as to how power is managed when your Mac is plugged into a Power Adapter versus when it's running on Battery.

Battery settings

To make some choices about how your Mac manages its energy needs when it's not plugged in, choose Battery from the Settings

for menu. You can, of course, set up your Power Adapter options at any time, as well, but, by definition, choosing Power Adapter settings won't affect battery life, which is what this section is about.

With Battery selected, the idea is to choose settings that are optimal for increasing that battery life. Choose Better Battery Life from the Optimization drop-down list as shown in figure 2.18, and you set Energy Saver at roughly the best level you can expect. If you like, you can click Show Details, and then tweak anything that you'd like to have a little different. For example, I like to set the Display sleep to something above the default one minute because I sometimes find that the screen dims as I'm reading a page full of text when it's set to the default. (The screen dims when you go a certain amount of time without touching a key; so, having this setting too low will save some energy but might get in the way of your work.) Otherwise those settings are pretty good.

Options

The Options tab has some interesting entries, including settings that govern when and how the display changes its brightness level and whether or not you're willing to

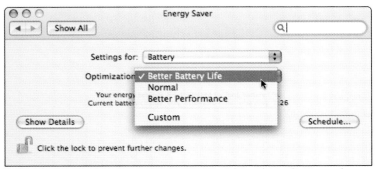

2.18 Choose Battery from the Settings for drop-down list to make separate choices for how the Mac will run on battery.

allow processor power to be reduced when you run on battery. If you have Battery selected in the Settings For menu, you'll see a special command, Reduce the Brightness of The Built-In Display When Using This Power Source. Turn that option on and your iBook or PowerBook's display will dim somewhat when you're on battery power, so that battery life is extended.

Other settings on the Options tab include the Wake options, which enable you to decide what will rouse your Mac from sleep mode — you can have your Mac wake automatically when it detects an incoming call on its modem or when an administrator attempts to access it via Ethernet (this second option only appears when you're setting up Power Adapter settings). The Other options are a bit more random; Restart Automatically After a Power Failure is pretty self-explanatory. The Show Battery Status in the Menu Bar option can be used to determine whether or not you have a battery indicator icon in your menu bar — it's there by default, but you can turn it off here, if desired.

> **Tip**
>
> *While you're actually running on battery power (that is, if you don't have the AC adapter plugged in) the Energy Saver tab will show the estimated battery charge and running time. For example, I noticed that simply by changing the processor setting in the Processor Performance menu to Highest, I shaved about 40 minutes off the estimated battery time, which means the Mac runs a little faster, but it'll run out of battery power much more quickly. In that case, running a little bit slower might be preferable.*

Energy saving tips

Energy Saver isn't the only place where you can save a little energy. Here are some more tips for saving battery life while commuting.

✦ **Put your Mac to sleep when you're not using it.** Sleep is a low-power alternative to turning your Mac on and off repeatedly.

✦ **Turn your display brightness down to as dark as you can stand it.** The less light used on your Mac's LCD, the longer the battery will last; sometimes the power savings can be dramatic.

✦ **Turn off AirPort, if possible.** It takes a bit of energy to power that AirPort card, which eats into your battery time. The same is true for Bluetooth. You can turn either wireless technology off using its menu bar icon menu.

✦ **Turn off AppleTalk and other networking protocols.** In fact, in the Network pane of System Preferences, remember that you can select Network Port Configurations from the Show menu and turn off various ports; turn off any ports you don't plan to use.

✦ **Turn off all network services, if you can.** In public places it's possible that others would attempt to access your Mac via file sharing, Web sharing, or Bonjour iChat if you have those services running — and that network activity takes up battery life.

✦ **Remove discs from the CD/DVD drive, particularly anything that you're not using.** Even if you're not using the disc, occasionally the drive will spin, which costs you power. If you do need to use a particular reference CD or DVD, consider using the Disk Utility application to create a disk image of the disc, which you can store on your Mac and then mount and access when you need its data.

> **Cross-Reference** *Disk images are discussed in detail in Chapter 6.*

✦ **Avoid external devices.** This is particularly true for devices that rely on USB, FireWire, or the PC card slot on a PowerBook for power.

✦ **Use as few applications as possible.** The more applications you have running, the more likely your Mac is to need to swap large chunks of those applications to the hard drive when you switch between them. The result is more hard drive access time, which eats into battery life. You might plan ahead a little bit and try to use only a few applications when you're on battery power, such as just doing some word processing or getting through your Mail inbox.

✦ **Save files less frequently.** This is a gamble, as it's important to save changes so that you don't lose data. However, the less you save files, the fewer times your hard drive is accessed (all other things being equal).

✦ **Have more than one battery.** The final trick is to have more than one battery in your bag, fully charged, so that you can swap one for the other when it gets low. Note that modern Mac portables need to be shut down before you can swap their batteries if they aren't on AC power. With them shut down, you can change the batteries and start back up again.

The Battery Status icon

The last little item I'd like to cover briefly is the Battery Status icon that appears, by default, in your menu bar. (Recall that you can turn this on and off in the Options tab of the Energy Saver preference pane.) It may look deceptively simple at first, but it's worth exploring a bit as it can help you quickly make some choices that can save battery life.

First, the indicator by default is a simple icon; when your Mac is plugged in, the icon is a battery with a small lightening bolt (see figure 2.19); when your Mac is not plugged in, the icon is a battery that shows a level indicator. The indicator is a handy visual for getting a sense of how much time you have remaining in battery life.

The menu itself can be used for a number of reasons. As shown in figure 2.19, you can check the menu when you're connected to a power adapter to see how much longer it will be before the battery is fully charged. When you're working on battery power, that same area of the menu will tell you how much time you have remaining before the battery is depleted.

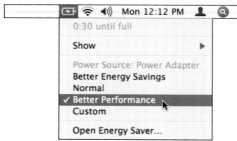

2.19 The Battery Status menu offers information and options.

The Show submenu enables you to choose the information that you'd like to see on the menu bar itself; instead of just the battery icon, you can have the icon appear along with time remaining (Show ➪ Time) or the percentage of battery life remaining (Show ➪ Percentage).

Within the menu are a number of options, such as Better Energy Savings, Better Performance, and so on. Those items are the presets that can be found in the Energy Saver preference pane; you can use this menu to quickly switch between them. Note, in particular, the Custom option. If you've made any preference settings in the Energy Saver pane, then choosing Custom from this menu should put those options into action.

Finally, the menu offers a quick access command to open the Energy Saver pane so that you can check settings or make changes. Choose Open Energy Saver from the menu to automatically launch the System Preferences application and open the Energy Saver pane.

Tip

If you happen not to like the location of the Battery Status menu bar icon (or any of the icons, for that matter) you can change it; hold down ⌘, and then click and drag the icon to another location on the menu bar.

Security Basics for Your Portable Mac

I f your iBook or PowerBook ever gets in the wrong hands, it's important that your personal or business information isn't compromised. Security precautions and portability go hand-in-hand because a portable Mac is much easier to lose or have stolen than a desktop Mac. Also, for many of us, the data on the computer can be more valuable and irreplaceable than the computer itself, so implementing a backup strategy and keeping your data secure are important.

Your Mac OS X Password and Security

One of the most important setup tasks in getting an iBook or PowerBook ready for the road is securing it from access by unauthorized users. These Macs' portability makes them targets for theft and loss, and a Mac in the wrong hands may offer up personal, financial, and other data that you'd prefer not to share with others. Fortunately, it's relatively easy to secure your Mac and its contents from prying eyes, even if the iBook or PowerBook gets lost or stolen. It just takes a little vigilance.

Choose a good password

The first step in securing your Mac is to choose a good password for your Mac OS X user account; more than likely you selected one via the Setup Assistant that runs when you use your Mac for the first time. When you choose a password, consider some of these key rules:

✦ Your password should be at least eight characters long.

✦ Your password should not be composed of words found in the dictionary; nonsense is better.

✦ When possible, use a combination of letters and numbers to make up your password.

✦ Change your password frequently, particularly if other people use your Mac and/or you travel with it quite often.

Tip

If you use your Mac in an office setting, it's good to change passwords every few weeks. Employees come and go, so a trusted colleague may be working for someone else the next time you see him or her at a conference.

The best passwords are a string of characters and numbers that mean something to you — which helps you remember the password — while meaning nothing to other people. For example, you could use a phrase such as "It was the Fourth of July when I fell for Sally" to create the password iwt4o7wif4s or something similar. That might be easy for you to remember but hard for someone else to guess.

A truly secure PowerBook actually has a number of passwords. As you'll see in later sections, it's possible to scramble your documents and data so that someone without the proper password would need to set up

some serious encryption-cracking tools to get at your files. And, the PowerBook offers a low-level password that gives you the ultimate security for a lost or stolen PowerBook, making it nearly impossible to access the drive directly.

Note

Encryption is the process of storing files in a format that appears to be nonsense, but that can be decipher by someone who has the right tools. In the case of your Mac, we'll explore some different utilities within Mac OS X that enable you to use a password to encrypt documents that are stored on your hard disk so that their contents can't easily be accessed by someone who gets his hands on your Mac portable.

The first password you need to change to make your Mac more secure, however, is your everyday Mac OS X user account password — the one you use to log on to your Mac when you want to get some work done. Here's how:

1. **If you haven't already, log on to your user account (or any Administrative user's account).**

2. **Open the System Preferences application (choose System Preferences from the Apple menu), and then click the Accounts icon.** By default, your account is selected in the Account list, and the Password tab is shown.

3. **Click Change Password to type a new password.** When you do, the dialog sheet shown in figure 3.1 appears.

3.1 You can type a new password using the dialog box that appears when you click Change Password in the Accounts pane in System Preferences.

It's also helpful to know that you don't have to come up with that extremely clever password on your own; you can get Apple to help you with it. Here's how:

1. **Open the System Preferences application if you closed it after the previous set of steps.**

2. **Type your old password in the Old Password field.**

3. **Click the small key icon to the right of the New Password field.** The Password Assistant dialog box appears. (Shown in figure 3.2; note that this feature requires Mac OS X 10.4 or higher.)

4. **Choose a password type from the Type menu.**

5. **When you're done creating a new password, close the Password Assistant.** The password is entered in the New Password field for you.

6. **Type that password again in the Verify field.**

7. **Type a hint for yourself in the Password Hint field.** This is optional. If you have trouble getting the right password when you're logging on, the hint appears after three failed attempts — or you can see it by clicking Forgot Password in the login window.

8. **Click Change Password.** Your password is changed.

3.2 The Password Assistant can help you create more secure passwords.

In the Password Assistant dialog box, you can use the Type pop-up menu to choose the different types of passwords that the Password Assistant will help you with. You can take a few different approaches:

✦ If you already have a password in mind, choose Manual from the Type menu, and then type the password in the Suggestion entry box. As you type, the Assistant responds by showing the length of the password and the Quality of the password. The more obscure and difficult to guess, the better the Quality rating will be.

Note *If your password is difficult for your to remember — so much so that you end up writing it down and putting it in your wallet or on a sticky in your laptop bag — then it's less secure than one that you can remember fairly easily but that otherwise follows the rules.*

✦ If you can't think of your own password, use the Type menu to choose a type of password. The Memorable passwords tend to be a little less secure, but they're randomly generated and easy to remember because they mix real words with numbers and symbols. The other types of passwords tend to be high quality because they are collections of letters, numbers, and/or symbols — they just might be more difficult to remember.

Tip *You don't have to use the first suggestion that appears in the Suggestion entry box. Click the down arrow next to the Suggestion entry box and you'll see a menu of other suggestions.*

Administrative Accounts and Security

On the screen for each user is the option to Allow User to Administer This Computer. By default, the original account you create on your Mac through the Setup Assistant is an Admin account. If you're particularly paranoid about security, you can create a user account for which this option is turned off and then use that account for day-to-day work.

If, while working in a regular account you encounter the need for an Administrator's password, then you can type your original username and password. By working in a regular account, you don't allow access to any administrative functions to anyone who sits down and begins using your Mac while that account is active. Instead, anyone accessing an Administrative function from a regular account is forced to type a username and password for a valid Administrator account before going forward.

Setting logon options

Once you have a secure user account password, you need to make sure your Mac is configured to use that password. By default, your Mac may be set up to bypass its password screen and automatically log you on to the account that was created when you went through your Mac's Setup Assistant. That may be convenient, but it's not really the best idea if your goal is security for the important data on your portable.

To check whether the password screen is bypassed, you can check it in the Accounts pane of System Preferences. Follow these steps:

1. **Choose System Preferences from the Apple menu, and then click the Accounts icon in the System Preferences window.** That causes the Accounts preference pane to appear.

2. **Click Login Options.** You'll see the window reconfigure with a series of options.

3. **If the Automatically Log In As option is selected, deselect it and turn the option off (see figure 3.3).**

Other options in the Login Options window are interesting for security. Under Display Login Window As, you can choose to show a List of Users (the default) or just the Name and Password. If you choose the Name and Password option, someone accessing your Mac's logon screen won't see a list of the

3.3 Turning off automatic login is an important security measure, as it requires anyone who starts up your Mac to log on with a valid user account.

existing users — and, hence, won't be able to simply select a user and then start guessing his or her password. Instead, any potential user needs to know a valid username first that can be typed into the Name field.

Another option under Display Login Window As that is interesting for security is the ability to turn on and off the Password Hints option. If you feel strongly that you can remember your password and no one else accesses your iBook or PowerBook, just deselect that option.

> **Tip** Need to know how to change a password that you've forgotten? If you can, log on as a user who has Admin privileges, and change the password for the account that you've forgotten. If you don't have a user with Admin privileges, you need to restart your Mac from a Mac OS X installation CD, and then choose Reset Password from the Utilities menu. See Chapter 7 for more on recovering from a forgotten password.

Require your password often

After establishing a better, more secure user account password, you are ready to enact more security measures. A good place to start is in the Security pane of System Preferences. Launch System Preferences (or, if it's already open, click Show All to view all of the preference panes), and then click the Security icon. That reveals the Security pane (see figure 3.4).

In the Security pane, you see important security items under the heading For All Accounts On This Computer. Here's a look at those items:

✦ **Require Password to Wake This Computer From Sleep or Screen Saver.** I pretty much always have this one turned on, particularly on my Mac portables. That's because it's a great first line of security for situations where you don't want others to have even casual access to your files. With this option turned on, you can put your Mac to sleep with the Sleep command from the Apple menu (or allow it to go to sleep or into screen saver mode) and your Mac is instantly password protected, requiring your login password before it will allow you or another user access to your account and any open applications and/or documents.

✦ **Disable Automatic Login.** This option forces a user to use the logon window to access the Mac from startup, restart, or after an account is logged out.

Setting Up a Screen Saver

In order to use a screen saver for security, you need to turn the screen saver on first. You do that via the Desktop & Screen Saver pane in System Preferences. Open the pane, and then click the Screen Saver tab. Select a screen saver from the list. Use the Start Screen Saver slider to determine how long the computer should be idle before the screen saver kicks in. There you'll also find the Hot Corners button, which you can use to activate the screen saver when you place your mouse point in one of the corners of the screen. When combined with the Require Password to Wake option, using a hot corner for the screen saver means instant security for your account.

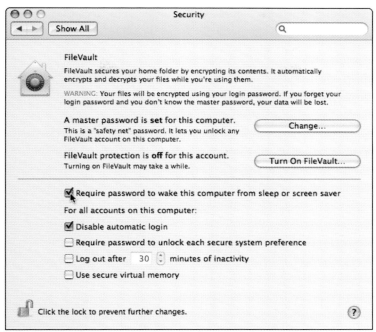

3.4 The Security pane of System Preferences gives you options focused specifically on keeping you data private.

✦ **Require Password to Unlock Each Secure System Preference.** This option slows the access to your Mac down somewhat, but it means you have to type the password for an Administrative user in order to change important settings in the System Preferences application.

✦ **Log Out After ___ Minutes of Inactivity.** Select this option and choose a length of time if you want accounts to be automatically logged out when the computer is not in use. (Note that applications with unsaved changes or those that have other issues can blog the Log Out After command from finishing the log out process.)

✦ **Use Secure Virtual Memory (Mac OS X 10.4 and higher).** When this option is active, items that are swapped to temporary files as you're working in multiple applications are stored in a secure, encrypted manner.

With all those options turned on, you can be assured that your Mac is reasonably secure for day-to-day use. But you're not totally secure yet.

While the casual unauthorized user will be deterred by requiring logins and password-protecting sleep or screen saver waking, someone who gains access to your Mac and who wants to get at your data has other options. That person may still be able to restart it in Target Disk Mode, for instance, which allows unfettered access to your files. And, an unattended Mac can be restarted with a Mac OS X installation disc, which gives the user access to the Reset Password utility — your passwords can be changed and your files accessed.

Fortunately, there's a way to lock people out of these features, too, with a special Open Firmware password.

Later in this chapter you see how to encrypt the data on your hard drive so that it's not easily read even if the Mac is taken apart and the hard drive removed.

Set Your Open Firmware Password

After you press the power button on your Mac, a small set of instructions is responsible for starting up the computer, testing its vitals, and then handing control off to the Mac OS. Those instructions, called *Open Firmware* on a modern Mac, are stored on a special type of static memory chips that maintain data even without electrical power. And aside from getting your Mac started up and tested, Open Firmware also checks to see if you're holding down any special keys on the keyboard. Certain keys send a signal to the Mac that you want to start up the Mac in a different way than usual.

That's why — even if you're diligent with your account password — it's still possible for someone to gain access to your Mac. One technique is to restart with a Mac OS X installation disc and use the Reset Password function to change an accounts password. (All you do is insert an optical disc in the drive and restart the Mac. After the startup tone, press and hold C and the Mac attempts to boot from the disc instead of the internal hard drive.)

Or, a person can press and hold T to boot your Mac into Target Disk Mode, connect it to another Mac through FireWire, and access your files.

 Target Disk Mode is discussed in Chapter 2.

Fortunately, there's a way to lock down your Mac so that these startup keys are ignored and a special password is required to change a setting in Open Firmware, including these startup options. It's called, appropriately enough, the Open Firmware Password, and you set it using a special utility application.

 It's imperative that you remember this password once it's set. Not even Apple can retrieve it if you forget it.

Here's how to set this special Open Firmware password:

1. **Launch the Open Firmware Password application that's located in the Utilities folder inside your Mac's main Applications folder.** The Open Firmware Password window appears.

2. **Click Change to move to the next screen.**

3. **Select the Require password to change Open Firmware settings option and then type a password twice in the entry boxes provided and click OK.** Figure 3.5 shows a new password being created in the Open Firmware Password window.

3.5 Use the Open Firmware Password utility to change the password that blocks access to startup keyboard shortcuts.

4. **Type the name and password for an Administrator on this computer and click OK.** If the admin account name and password are accepted, a message appears saying that the password has been updated.

5. **Choose Open Firmware Password ⇨ Quit Open Firmware Password to quit the utility application.**

Once you successfully set the Open Firmware password, you have another layer of security active. Now, the keyboard shortcuts for starting up from a CD/DVD or starting into FireWire Disk mode are disabled. To change the way the Mac starts up, you must use the Startup Disk pane of System Preferences and type an administrator's account and password.

To boot into the open firmware operating system itself (where there's actually a text prompt), restart your Mac and press and hold ⌘+Option+O+F. At the Open Firmware prompt you'll need to type your Open Firmware password before you can move on to any other commands.

Manage Your Keychain

If you're like most computer users, you have many passwords that you use with your Mac — both within the operating system interface and on the Internet — and you find it's tough to keep up with them in a secure way. With your PowerBook or iBook, if you have your passwords written down any-where in the vicinity, such as in your wallet, in the computer bag itself, in your luggage, and so on, then you increase the risk that someone who gains access to your portable can access the data it contains.

Apple's solution to that issue is called the *keychain*, a technology built into Mac OS X that can help you manage your mountain of passwords by giving you a central repository that you can access with a single password in order to unlock all of your other pass-words. Ultimately, your keychain is a special, secure database that stores automatic login information for certain resources (such as local network logins and some Web-based login information) as well as any scrap of information that you'd like to keep pass-word protected, such as login information, credit card numbers and details, and so on.

Understand your keychain

A keychain is created for you when your user account is created, and this default *login* keychain has the same password as your user account. When you log in to your user account, the keychain is unlocked and left unlocked; your applications can access passwords that they store in the keychain, so that, for example, Mail can access e-mail servers or a stored password can be accessed by Safari. That sort of thing is handled automatically; the only indication that you sometimes get from an application is a request, in the form of a dialog box, to access that item (see figure 3.6).

3.6 Occasionally a dialog box appears while you're working that asks if an application can have access to your keychain.

If you see this dialog box, you can choose to deny the application access to your keychain database, you can give it one-time access, or you can tell it that that application can always access that particular item.

As you work in your applications, you find different opportunities to store passwords in the keychain. Figure 3.7 shows an example in Safari; in general, you work with the keychain by selecting an option in a dialog box where you typed the password for network or Internet resource.

3.7 In this example, Safari allows the password for an online account to be saved in the keychain.

As long as you're logged in to your account and your keychain password is the same as your user account password, then your applications have access to those keychain items. This is worth noting because if you change your user account password, your keychain password is not changed along with it. As a result, you'll be asked by your applications for your keychain password (see figure 3.8) as well as permission to access the keychain. Your keychain password, in that case, will be the password that you had for your user account when the user account was created.

3.8 Occasionally you'll see a dialog box that asks for the password to your keychain, particularly if your keychain is locked or if the password is different from your login password.

Manage your keychain

You can manage your keychain in a hands-on way, and there are some benefits to doing that. To get to your keychain and its preferences, launch the Keychain Access application found in the Utilities folder inside your Mac's main Applications folder. When you do, the Keychain Access window appears, as shown in figure 3.9.

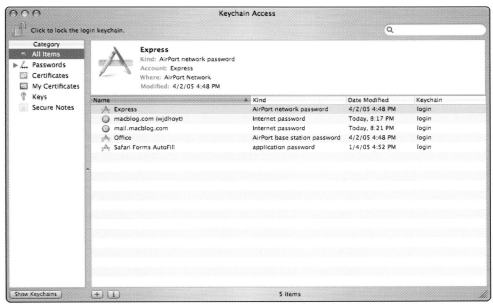

3.9 The Keychain Access application is used to manage your keychain.

The first thing to notice about the Keychain Access application is the padlock icon at the top-left of the window. If it's open, then your keychain is open, meaning applications can access the keychain and its contents, in some cases without your typing a password or making any choices. If the padlock is locked, then your keychain password is required before any of the items on that keychain can be accessed.

So, one thing you can do with your keychain in Keychain Access is lock it if it's unlocked or unlock it if it's locked. To do either, click the padlock icon. If the keychain is unlocked, then it will be locked immediately; if the keychain is locked, a dialog box appears that requests your keychain password. If you type it correctly, the keychain is unlocked.

Once you unlock your keychain, it stays unlocked until you log out of the account (or switch to a different user account). So, if your Mac stays logged on to your account and is accessible to other users, they can conceivably use data stored on your keychain, such as Internet account names and passwords.

It's more secure to lock your keychain when you're not using your Mac, but leaving it logged on to your account. The easiest way to do that is to set the keychain to lock automatically. Choose Edit ➪ Change Settings for Keychain. In the dialog box that appears (see figure 3.10), select the Lock after ___ minutes of inactivity and/or Lock when sleeping option(s). In the blank, type the number of minutes or use the arrow controller to change the number of minutes you want your Mac to wait before locking your keychain.

3.10 The Change Keychain Settings dialog box can be used to automate the locking of your keychain.

The Keychain Access window is designed to give you quick access to different categories of items that can be stored on your keychain, each of which is shown in the Categories list. By default, the All Items category, which shows you all of the keychain items you have stored at once, is displayed. But the Categories list can also be used to show specific items, such as passwords that have been stored for various reasons. Click the disclosure triangle next to Passwords in the list to see the types of passwords — AppleShare, Application, and Internet — that are stored.

 Note *AppleShare passwords are generally stored when you log on to network resources, and Internet passwords are stored when you use a Web browser, FTP application, e-mail application, or something similar to access an Internet server. An application password is used to get into the secure portion of an application — for example, you might password-protect documents or diary entries in some applications, or use a password to get into your financial software. If the application is capable of it, you might be able to automatically store those passwords in your keychain.*

You've already seen how you can use options within your keychain-aware applications to add passwords to your keychain; you can also add them manually. Follow these steps:

1. **Choose File ⇨ New Password Item if you have an Internet or similar password that you want to store.** A dialog sheet appears.

2. **In the dialog sheet (see figure 3.11), type the name or URL for the item, the account name, and password.**

3.11 You can create new password items from within Keychain Access.

3. **Click Add.** The item is added to your keychain for safekeeping.

Note *Not every Internet password that you type results in your being able to log in automatically using your browser. The keychain can only communicate with Web sites that use the browser's own authentication methods; in most cases, if you find that you're actually typing the username and password for a site on the Web page itself (instead of in a dialog box generated by your Web browser) then you probably can't use the keychain for login, but simply for safely storing the password so you can refer to it later.*

If you ever need to jog your memory about this (or any other) account password, it's simple — just double-click the item to open its information window. Then, select the Show Password option on that screen. Most likely, a dialog box appears asking you to allow Keychain Access to access your keychain. Type your keychain password and click Allow Once or Always Allow. If the dialog accepts your password, you're returned to the information window for that item and you should see the password now in plain text (see figure 3.12).

Along with passwords, another important use of your keychain is to store secure notes that can only be accessed by someone who has your keychain password. A note can be used for a variety of reasons — it can be a list of passwords you lock away, credit card or financial information, or even a small diary entry or other pasted text that you just want to keep to yourself. Whatever it is, to create a secure note, follow these steps:

1. **Choose File ⇨ New Secure Note.** A dialog sheet appears.

2. **Type a name for the note in the Keychain Item Name field, and then type your note.**

3. **Click Add.** The note is added to your keychain (see figure 3.13).

Back in the keychain window, double-click a note to view it, and then select the Show note option to see the portion that is secure (see figure 3.14). Keychain Access consults your keychain and asks you for your keychain password. Type it and choose either Allow Once or Always Allow; the contents of the note appear in the text area.

3.12 You can use a keychain item for a quick reminder of the password you stored.

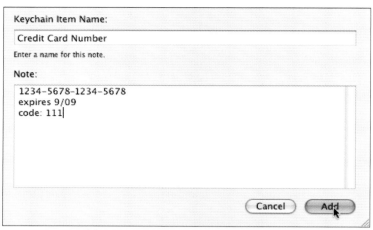

3.13 You can add secure notes to your keychain that can only be accessed by someone with your keychain password.

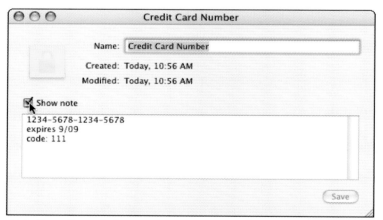

3.14 Once the note is stored, you can access its contents only if it's been authorized through your keychain password.

The keychain also manages other items, such as information that your Mac uses to access encrypted Web sites and keys that can be used for sending encrypted messages.

Cross-Reference

Because some aspects of the keychain are little more focused on security when you're literally on the Internet, they are covered in more detail in Chapter 6.

Encrypt Your Home Folder

Ready to take file security to yet another level? How about securing against data access even if someone not only gains access to your portable Mac, but also is able to remove the hard drive? By encrypting the contents of your home folder using FileVault, a feature built in to Mac OS X, you can all but ensure that anyone but the most intrepid hacker is unable to read the data files that can be accessed by spelunking into your Mac's case. And, frankly, even that intrepid hacker would have an extremely difficult and likely unsuccessful job on his or her hands. This is because encryption essentially turns your files into a completely unintelligible string of characters based on an *encryption algorithm* (mathematical formula) that's set in motion by your personal password. That's another reason why the password should be a good one that is not easily guessed.

If there's a downside to encrypting your home folder, it is this: If you forget your password — and you forget the safety Master Password that Apple builds in — you've all but lost your data. The other issue to at least be aware of is the home folder encryption uses your login password as the key to decryption, so the whole encryption scheme is only as secure as your logon password.

The entire scheme is also based on the security of a Master Password, which you set the first time you attempt to initiate FileVault. Pick the most un-guessable password you can come up with. See the section "Your Mac OS X Password and Security" earlier in this chapter for advice.

Caution *I recommend you back up any and all important files in your home folder before encrypting because it's really uncool if something happens to your Mac during the encryption process and you can't get your important documents back. Also, note that your home folder should have the same name as your accounts' official short name (which is specified when creating your account and used to name your home folder) or you may run into trouble with FileVault.*

One point is worth noting before you attempt to encrypt your home folder — you need enough free space on your hard drive to create an entire copy of that home folder. If your home folder takes up 50MB, then you'll need at least 50MB of free space. If it takes up 5GB, you'll need at least 5GB free. If you're not sure how much space your home folder takes up, locate its icon in the Finder, highlight that icon, and choose File ➪ Get Info. In the General section you can see how much space your home folder takes up by looking at the Size entry (see figure 3.15).

If you don't have enough room or if you're simply surprised to find that your home folder is taking up a ton of space (like I was) then consider moving some items out of your home folder's hierarchy, such as movie, music, or photos that don't really need encryption. You can move them elsewhere on your Macintosh HD (or whatever name you've given your Mac's internal hard drive) or, perhaps, to the Shared folder instead of your main Users folder.

3.15 Check the size of your home folder in the Get Info window, and then make sure you have enough room on your hard drive.

Turn on FileVault

Once you know you have enough space and you're otherwise ready to encrypt your home folder, here's how:

1. **Make sure no other users are logged in to your Mac using the Fast User Switching feature.** You can't turn on FileVault unless you're the only active user.

2. **Launch the System Preferences applications (choose Apple menu, System Preferences) and click the Security icon.** That opens the Security pane.

3. **If a Master Password has not yet been set, click the Master Password button.** That reveals the Master Password dialog sheet.

4. **Read about the Master Password; then type one in the Master Password field; type it again in the Verify field.** If desired, type a hint for yourself if you forget the password that will jog your memory without revealing the password.

5. **Click OK.**

6. **Click Turn On FileVault.** A dialog sheet appears requesting your user account password.

7. **Type your user account password and click OK.** Another dialog sheet appears warning you about FileVault.

8. **Read the dialog sheet, and then click Turn On FileVault.** You can also choose to turn on Use Secure Erase if you want your unencrypted files erased securely by your Mac. (The files will be overwritten after being erased, which makes them very difficult to recover.)

When you click Turn On FileVault, your Mac logs out and the FileVault dialog box appears showing the progress of the operation. After what may be a while, you return to the login window and asked to log in again. When you log in, you are working with an encrypted home folder; in fact, if you check out your home folder icon, you see it has a new icon that looks a little like a combination safe in the shape of a house.

Note that FileVault makes it impossible for you to log in to your account from a remote Windows computer and access files through file sharing when you're not logged in to your Mac; that's because your Home folder is, for all intents and purposes, one large, encrypted disk image. That image is *mounted* (meaning that it's made available for access by the Mac's underlying file system) when you log in to your account with the appropriate password.

> **Cross-Reference** *Interestingly, although FileVault is a relatively new feature in Mac OS X, this is mostly a clever use of Apple's existing disk image technology that you can use for a variety of reasons. For more on disk images and encryption, see the section "Other Encryption Solutions" in this chapter, as well as more discussion of disk images in Chapter 6.*

Turn off FileVault

If you find that FileVault is unworkable or if you simply don't need the extra level of security or the file sharing hassles, you can turn it off. Follow these steps:

1. **Make sure no one else is logged on to the computer using Fast User Switching.**

2. **Open the Security pane of System Preferences and click Turn Off FileVault.**

3. **After confirming that you want to turn off FileVault in the dialog box that appears, your account logs out and the FileVault dialog box appears.** You see the progress of decrypting. When FileVault is done, you return to the logon screen, and you should be able to log on to your newly decrypted home folder.

FileVault password recovery

So what happens if you encrypt your home folder and then forget your login password? That's when the Master Password kicks in.

Generally speaking, when someone on your Mac forgets his or her login password, one solution is to log on using another administrator-level account and change the password. But with FileVault, one admin user can't change the password of a user who has FileVault active. That's because you sever the link between the user's login password and FileVault password, which means you can't access your files even if you logged in.

Instead, you need to attempt to log in to your account — and fail. After three attempts, you are asked for the Master Password. Type that (or have someone else type it if it's a password you don't know or control) and click Log In. You are then walked through the process of changing the password for the encrypted account. This messes up the account's access to its keychain, which uses the same (forgotten) password as the logon, unless you change it.

> **Note** *As you can see, the Master Password is pretty powerful. You need to make sure that it's a high-quality password that is not easy to guess or defeat — otherwise, there isn't much point in going to the trouble of encrypting your home folder.*

Other Encryption Solutions

FileVault is handy because it's built in to your Mac, but it isn't the only solution to maintaining data integrity. Another clever way to add encryption to your overall security arsenal is something already mentioned. In fact, it's the same technology that FileVault is based on — an encrypted *disk image*. A disk image is really just a special kind of file that, when double-clicked, appears to mount a volume on your Mac as if you'd inserted a CD or DVD or attached an external hard drive. (Mounting simply makes the disk's contents available for access in the Finder.) The difference is that, once unmounted, the disk image continues to be a typical file that can be stored, transmitted to others, burned to disc, or, in this case, encrypted so that it can only be accessed via password.

Using the Disk Utility that comes with Mac OS X, you can create an encrypted disk image that's then used for storing files that you want to secure using a password. Here's how:

1. **Launch Disk Utility, which you find in the Utilities folder inside your main Applications folder.**

2. **Click the New Image button in Disk Utility's toolbar. A dialog sheet appears.**

3. **In the dialog sheet, type a name for the disk utility, and choose a place for it to be stored.** Then, choose a size for the image from the Size menu.

4. **In the Encryption menu, choose AES-128 and choose Sparse Disk Image from the Format menu.** A sparse disk image only takes up as much storage space as is required by the files you add to it; a read/write disk image takes up the amount of space you specify in the Size menu, regardless of the storage requirements of the files on the disk.

5. **Click Create.** The Disk Utility progress dialog box appears. Soon after, the Authenticate dialog box appears (see figure 3.16).

3.16 The Authenticate dialog box is used for creating a password to secure your encrypted disk image.

6. **Type a password for the disk image's encryption in the Password field, then repeat that password in the Verify field.** You also have the option of adding this password to your keychain so that the disk image can retrieve the password from your keychain instead of asking you for it every time you mount it.

7. **Click OK after typing the password twice.** That's it. The progress window continues until the image is created and mounted.

With a disk image, you see two things — the disk image file, and, when mounted, the disk image itself (see figure 3.17), which appears on your desktop by default as well as in the Sidebar of Finder windows. It's the disk image where you drag any files that you want to store; the disk image file is what you double-click to mount the disk image.

To unmount the disk image, simply select it in the Finder and choose File ➪ Eject, or click and drag the disk image (not the disk image file) to the Trash.

secure_backup.sparse image

secure_backup

3.17 The disk image file (top icon) is what you double-click in order to mount the disk image, which is the volume you work with as if it were a removable disk.

Tip *As you're dragging, you see the Trash icon turn into an Eject icon, which is a helpful reminder that you're dragging the right item.*

Now, the next time you double-click the disk image file to mount its disk image, a password will be required. If you access the disk image from your own account, and you stored the password in your keychain, then the disk image will use your keychain to retrieve the file. If not, you need to type the password before you can access the disk image and retrieve the files; otherwise, it remains encrypted.

Backing Up Your Files

Backing up important documents is a key part of data security for any computer user; for those of us who rely on a portable

computer to conduct personal or professional business, backup is critical. Fortunately, it doesn't have to be terribly difficult or time consuming, particularly if you come up with a system for managing it.

The key to successful backup is two-fold: redundancy and distance. The process of backing up files gives you, by definition, copies to which you can refer if you have trouble with your Mac or trouble with that file. A backed-up document can even be handy in cases where you have no trouble with the file except that you saved over it or made a change that you later regret. If you have a previous version available as part of your backup scheme, you can grab it and start over.

The other thing that's important to do with a backup is to get it away from your computer. Putting discs of important data in fireproof safes or safety deposit boxes is always a good idea. Backing up to an online service can be a handy way of accomplishing both, which is one reason that Apple includes the option with its .Mac subscription service. By backing up online, you have both redundancy and distance; but the data isn't so far away that you can't get to it quickly over an Internet connection. The downside is that online storage is a lot more expensive than recordable CDs or DVDs, so it's only ideal for data that you're in serious need of backing up.

So, one good choice is .Mac and the Backup software that comes with it. If you don't want to pay for the .Mac subscription, however, you can opt for third-party backup software, or you can cobble together a system for yourself using the Mac OS and a tool such as Automator, a new tool in Mac OS X 10.4 that enables you to create automatic workflows to make your Mac take steps on its own, such as perform backups.

Backup and .Mac

Backup is software that comes with your .Mac subscription; if you are a subscriber and haven't yet downloaded it, you can get at it in a few different ways — log on to www.mac.com and click the Backup icon, or access your iDisk and open the Software folder. The Software folder is actually a link to downloadable items that Apple offers — it doesn't take away from your storage space on your iDisk. In the Apple Software folder you should find a Backup, which you can copy to your hard drive by clicking and dragging it to the Desktop or another Finder window. Double-click the disk image file and you gain access to the Backup disk image; you should see the Backup.pkg file that you can double-click to install the software.

 Note The version of Backup at the time of this writing does not offer encryption of the data that you back up from it, even if you've encrypted your home folder. So, be aware that with very sensitive information, it's theoretically a bit less secure sitting on your iDisk. You may want to opt for a third-party backup system in situations where you need top-notch file security.

When you launch Backup, it checks for a valid .Mac account (which you need to have typed in the .Mac pane of System Preferences) and it may ask for your permission to access your keychain in order to get your iDisk password (or, failing that, it just asks for your iDisk password). Once it's connected to iDisk you see the main Backup pane (see figure 3.18).

Backup understands fairly well how your Mac is organized, so it's able to be fairly specific about the items it suggests that you

back up. In the Backup window, it offers a list of QuickPicks that are both convenient and suggestive. You'll notice that Backup is trying to help you pick and choose what important files you opt to back up, because it knows that the typical iDisk doesn't have a lot of space to burn.

Note At the time of writing, the standard .Mac account offers 256MB of space to be shared among all its tools — as you can see in figure 3.18, I paid extra to upgrade mine to 512MB.

Begin by selecting the categories of items on your Mac that you want to back up. To learn more about what's being backed up in a certain category, select it and click the information icon at the bottom of the Backup window. A drawer appears (that's the window portion that slides out from the side of the Backup window), showing you the items that Backup intends to back up.

If you don't see a category, click the plus (+) icon at the bottom of the Backup window and an Open dialog box appears; here, you can select a particular folder that you want to back up or you can even add a particular file that you want Backup to track. (For example, you might want to back up your accounting software's main database file on a regular basis.)

Once you have Backup configured with the items you want to back up, you can immediately initiate that backup by clicking Backup Now. Backup begins the process of synchronizing your files between the iDisk and your Mac. Note that this means that items that have changed on your Mac are replaced on your iDisk, including any changes you made since the last time you backed up.

3.18 The Backup application enables you to quickly select key items you'd like to back up.

This type of synchronization backup isn't always a good thing. It can overwrite files that you may prefer to have multiple versions of in different states of completion. For example, you might want to be able to access your backup version from last week because you accidentally deleted important parts of a Word document and then saved those changes. If your backup solution is exclusively the synchronization approach, then your older versions are overwritten during the backup process. So, it's a good idea to back up both online in this fashion and to disc, as described in the next section.

Along with manual backups, you can use Backup to perform scheduled backups as well. To do that, click the calendar icon at the bottom of the Backup window (actually, it looks a little like a calculator). A dialog sheet appears that you can use for scheduling your backups (see figure 3.19).

Choose whether you want to update the backup weekly or daily, and then set a time. Note that you need to be logged on to your account and your Mac needs to be turned on at that time, so take that into consideration. Click OK in the dialog sheet and your schedule is in place.

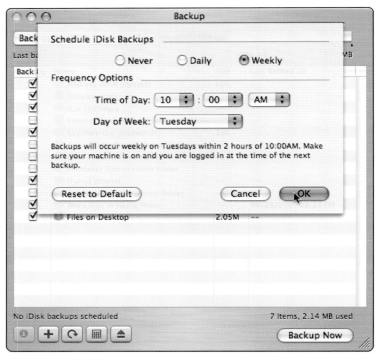

3.19 Backup can schedule itself to back up your files weekly or even daily.

Tip

Curious as to whether a backup occurred? Backup keeps a log. Choose File ➪ Show Log to see the log of backup operations and make sure that the most recent one happened as you expected it to.

Backup to drive or disc

Backup can also back up your files either to a hard drive or to a removable optical disc if your Mac supports burning data to recordable CDs or DVDs. To configure a backup, choose the appropriate entry from the unlabelled menu at the very top of the Backup window. It may say Back up to iDisk initially. You can also, depending on the options

your Mac supports, choose View ➪ Back up to CD, View ➪ Back up to DVD, or View ➪ Back up to Drive.

Note

You only see options that your Mac supports; if your Mac doesn't have a DVD-R drive, you won't see the Back up to DVD option.

These options are all very similar; compared to back up to iDisk, you immediately find that you have a few more options in the window (such as backing up your entire iTunes library or all of your e-mail), primarily because Backup assumes that you have a lot more storage space available on a hard drive or on removable discs. Figure 3.20 shows the default options for backing up to a large external Firewire drive.

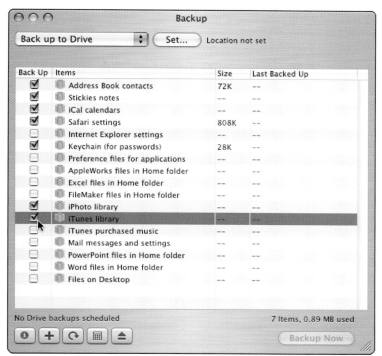

3.20 When you opt to backup to CD/DVD or hard disk, you'll see a few more default options than you did when backing up online.

For starters, look at how to back up to CD or DVD:

1. **In the Backup window, choose Back up to CD/DVD from the unlabeled pop-up menu.** You can also choose View ➪ Back up to CD/DVD if you prefer.

2. **Place checkmarks next to the items that you'd like to back up.** As you check items, note that the bottom of the window shows you the estimated number of discs required, as shown in figure 3.21.

3. **To add folders that aren't in the list, click the + icon.** A dialog sheet appears.

4. **In the dialog sheet, navigate to the folder that you'd like to add to your list of items to back up, highlight the folder name (or a particular document, if desired), and click Choose.** The dialog sheet disappears and you are back in the main window, with the new folder or item listed and checked.

5. **When you've made all of your selections, click Backup Now.** A dialog box appears.

6. **In the dialog box, give this backup set a name and click Begin Backup.** You see the Burn Disc dialog box.

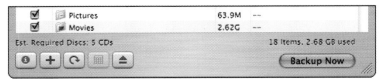

☑	🖼 Pictures	63.9M	--
☑	🎬 Movies	2.62G	--

Est. Required Discs: 5 CDs   18 Items, 2.68 GB used

(ⓘ) (+) (↻) (▦) (⏏)   (Backup Now)

3.21 The bottom of the Backup window shows you estimates of the discs required to store the items you want to back up.

7. **Enter a blank disc if you haven't already and, when the Burn button becomes active, click Burn.** The Backup window reconfigures to show your progress while your files are gathered and the burn process begins so that your files are written to the disc.

> **Note**
>
> *Backup is able to use more than one CD or DVD disc if you choose more files than will fit on that single disc; it can split a file over two discs if necessary. As the backup process goes forward, you'll be prompted to insert others. Feel free to choose as many files as you want using the plus (+) button at the bottom of the Backup window.*

If you choose Back up to Drive, the only difference is that you need to set the location for your backup files by clicking the Set button near the unlabelled menu at the top of the window. Here's how:

1. **In the Backup window, choose Back up to Drive from the unlabeled pop-up menu.** You can also choose View ⇨ Back up to Drive.

2. **Place checkmarks next to the items that you'd like to back up.** As you check items, you'll see the total number of items and the storage space that they consume appear at the bottom right of the Backup window.

3. **To add folders that aren't in the list, click the + icon.** A dialog sheet appears.

4. **Navigate to the folder that you'd like to add to your list of items to back up, highlight the folder name (or a particular document, if desired), and click Choose.** The dialog sheet disappears and you are back in the main window, with the new folder or item listed and checked.

5. **When you've made all of your selections, click the Set button.** A dialog sheet appears.

6. **If you already have a backup location defined, you can click Open; otherwise, click Create.** The dialog sheet changes to a Save As dialog sheet.

7. **In the Save As dialog sheet, give your backup set a name (it will be a single file on the drive) and navigate to the drive and folder where you'd like the backup set stored; then click Create.** You're returned to the Backup window.

8. **Click Backup Now.** The Backup window will reconfigure itself and you'll see the progress of your backup operation. When it's done, you'll be returned to the full Backup window and you should see the message "Last backup successful" at the top of the window under the unlabelled pop-up menu.

Note *It's not terribly useful or safe to back up to your Mac's internal hard drive because that doesn't quite meet redundancy and distance requirements. However, this approach is great for backing up your files to another computer on your local network if you have a LAN, or to an external hard drive that you connect to your Mac for this purpose. Ideally, that external hard drive should be something that you leave behind, in a safe location. If not, you might want to send key files to your iDisk and back up all of your documents to a hard drive for additional redundancy.*

As with online backup, you can also schedule a backup using the small Schedule button — the one that looks like a calendar page — if you want to back up to a hard drive. (Backup won't allow you to schedule a backup to an optical disc, based on the assumption that you may not be there at the prescribed time to insert one or more discs.) Again, your Mac has to be turned on and you need to be logged on to your account at the time that the backup is scheduled if it's going to happen successfully.

Restore from backup

If you get in a situation where you need to access your backed up files, you do it by switching Backup to its Restore mode. Here's how:

1. **From the unlabeled menu in the Backup window, choose Restore from iDisk, Restore from CD/DVD, or Restore from Drive in Backup, depending on which you want to do.** You can also choose those same options from the View menu, if you prefer.

2. **Then, you select the items that you need to restore in the QuickPick list; to select all items, choose Edit ⇨ Check All from the menu.**

3. **With the items selected, click Restore Now.** Backup accesses the hard drive or iDisk in question (it may prompt you for a CD or DVD) and then locates your backup set. When it does, it starts asking questions about any files that you opted to restore, particularly if a matching file already exists on your hard drive (see figure 3.22).

3.22 When you restore files, you may be asked whether you want to overwrite existing files.

4. **Choose whether you want to overwrite the file or not.** Note the option Apply to All, which you can use so that you don't have to answer for each item.

That's really all it takes; follow the prompts in the case of CDs or DVDs that need to be swapped, but otherwise Backup automatically restores the files from your backed-up versions. When it's done, check your hard drive and you should see copies of the files that you've overwritten and/or restored.

Note *Backup doesn't have an option for extracting an individual file for recovery; however, if you know there are certain individual files that you specifically need to track in Backup, add those files as individual items in the list (for example, your accounting software database or client list documents). If you don't have the specific file in your list, use the dialog box shown in figure 3.22 to replace only the file that you're looking for.*

Other backup solutions

A number of third-party backup solutions exist, but only the high points are listed here because I recommend a .Mac account for your portable computing anyway, and Backup is a solid solution, particularly for an individual user. That said, there are stronger backup applications worth considering, depending on your needs. Here's a quick look at the options:

✦ **Dantz Retrospect (**www.dantz.com**).** This commercial option is one of the more respected in the industry for completeness. The company offers a number of different versions from Dantz Desktop (for individual users) to Dantz Workgroup and Dantz Server. With Dantz, you're encourage to rotate your backup media, create multiple incremental backups, and take other important steps that ensure redundancy of your data, making it that much more likely that you'll recover from trouble. And the network versions are great for small or medium-sized offices where you want both server computers and individual computers — including portables that connect to your network — to be backed up.

✦ **Intego Personal Backup X** (www.intego.com)**.** This is another commercial offering, aimed squarely at the individual user. Personal Backup will help you back up and synchronize between two different volumes, or it will back up to disks or even to an iDisk. It will also create compressed disk images that you can use for archival purposes and it will clone your Mac system so that it can be booted from another disk.

Note *While the backup approach taken by Apple's Backup is something of an online solution — meaning you always have a recent backup at your disposal — creating archives of your files can also be useful. You may, at some point, want to access a particular file as it was six months or a year ago — again, accounting software and databases come to mind. That's what an archive is for — it's a snapshot of your important files at a moment in time, which you store away until it's needed.*

✦ **Synchronize X (**www.qdea.com**).** Another option that has grown up with Mac OS X is Synchronize, which is shareware (try-before-you-buy) software available online. But don't let the shareware moniker fool you — this is full-featured stuff, particularly the Pro version. Either version offers automatic backup or synchronization, while the Pro version can also create a bootable backup of your Mac system.

 Cross-Reference *For more on synchronization of files, see Chapter 2. For more on bootable backups, see Chapter 7.*

✦ **Dobry Backuper**
(www.dobrysoft.com). It has kind of a cutesy name, but this inexpensive shareware option is a great personal backup option. It works much like Apple's Backup with the exception that you choose all your own folders and files for backing up; the software also compresses items as they're backed up so that they take up less space on the target disk.

Homegrown backup solutions

If you're not up for buying a .Mac subscription or some third-party software, that doesn't mean you should do no backup. You've still got options.

My first suggestion is to use the disk image instructions earlier in this chapter and create a special spare disk image that you can fill up with files that you want backed up. You can then take that disk image file and copy it to either a recordable disc or to an online site; if the disk image is encrypted, you can feel pretty good about copying the disk image file to any FTP location that your ISP provides for you, for example. (As a precaution, endeavor to make sure that FTP location isn't publicly available.) Or, if you have access to an external hard drive or a network, you can copy the disk image file to one of those locations.

 Cross-Reference *As detailed in Chapter 6, Disk Utility will create a recordable disc from a disk image, so you can create your disk image with that in mind.*

Of course, what's cool about Backup and similar applications is that they automatically find files that are important to you. However, if you use the Mac OS X home

folder hierarchy as it's created, you should have relatively little difficultly backing up important files — it may be as simple as backing up your Documents folder or your Photo folder and so on.

For a more sophisticated approach, you can use a tool like Automator (found in the Applications folder on your Mac if you have Mac OS X 10.4 or higher installed) to create your own impromptu backup script.

Here's one approach, which uses Mac OS X 10.4's new Spotlight search feature to gather files that have been recently modified on your Mac and then back them up to an external hard drive or a network volume:

1. **Launch Automator by double-clicking its icon in the Applications folder.** The Automator window appears (see figure 3.23), complete with a Library of items on the left side; the right side of the window is used to build your workflow, which will be the steps that Automator will undertake automatically when you run your creation.

2. **In the Library list, select Spotlight.**

3. **Click and drag the item called Find Finder Items from the Action list to the main Workflow area.**

4. **In the Find Finder Items workflow item, select where you want to search for files that have changed from the Where menu.**

5. **In the Whose menus, choose Date Modified from the first menu, and then choose a time frame, such as Within Last Two Weeks (see figure 3.24) from the second menu.**

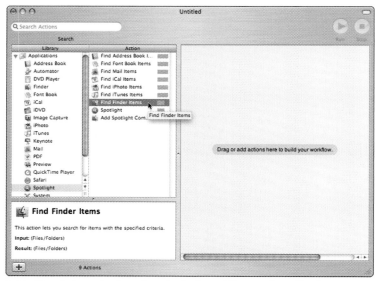

3.23 The Automator interface includes a Library of applications; select one and a list of actions appear that you can drag into the workflow area.

3.24 In Automator, you can find files that have been recently modified.

6. **Choose Finder in the Library.**

7. **Locate the Copy Finder Items action and click and drag it to the workflow area.**

8. **In the To menu of the Copy Finder Items action, choose a location for the files you're going to back up.**

9. **Click the Run button at the top of the Automator window to see the workflow in action or choose File ➪ Save to name and save the workflow.**

This very simple example gathers all the files that have been changed in the last two weeks and copies them to a new location; you can then burn that folder to a disc, transfer it to another computer or to a network volume, and so on. You should also experiment with Automator if you go this route — there are a number of other options you can add to this script to make it more complex and complete, such as automatically creating a compressed archive, or mounting a disk image.

> **Note** Save an Automator workflow as an application so that you can simply double-click it in the Finder to launch it. Choose File ➪ Save As in the Automator menu bar; then, in the Save As dialog sheet, give the workflow a name and choose Application from the File Format menu. Click Save to create an application icon for this workflow that you can use as you would any other double-clickable application.

Getting the Most from Your Portable Mac

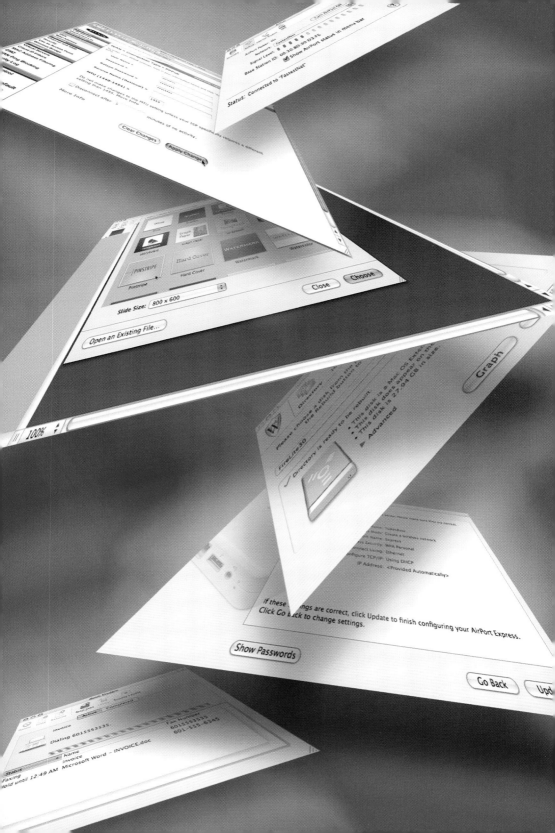

Online on the Road

◆   ◆   ◆   ◆

◆   ◆   ◆   ◆

Among the advances that really excite me about the here and now of portable Macintosh computing are the many options available for connecting to the Internet. Access to the Internet plays a big part in work for many of us, as evidenced by the proliferation of high-speed Internet options at hotels and motels around the United States and the world — not to mention the coffee shops, airports, and other public spaces that offer high-speed Internet access for free or for a fee. The fact that such access seems to be barreling toward ubiquity means that the always-on future is closer than ever.

Of course, it's not just everywhere yet that you can get a high-speed WiFi connection from the comfort of the reclining chair in your hotel suite; there are still plenty of reasons to use the modem that's built in to all modern Mac portables, or to take advantage of some of the growing alternative Internet options, like those provided by mobile phones or mobile data carriers.

This chapter explores all these options, including accessing wired and wireless Internet, creating your own wireless network, and getting Internet access in a pinch from your mobile phone. You end the chapter looking at the Locations feature in the Mac OS, which enables you to create different presets of Internet settings based on the different places you take your portable Mac.

Connecting via Modem

In larger metropolitan areas (and, in my experience, in college towns) you're likely to find broadband Internet access available in a variety of motel and hotel situations, as well as in coffee shops and perhaps in libraries, convention centers, public spaces, and so on. And broadband access — much of it wireless — is likely to proliferate at an impressive speed over the next few years. That doesn't preclude the need, however, for modem-based Internet connections at least in remote areas or in roadside motels, bed-and-breakfasts, or any number of places where you may travel with your PowerBook or iBook and not have access to a high-speed Internet connection.

Choose an ISP

If you regularly travel with your Mac portable for business, pleasure, or both, I recommend a modem-based solution (often called "dial-up") for at least secondary access to the Internet, even if you often find yourself in locations that offer high-speed access. You never know when that high-speed access advertised on a motel's door is actually going to mean Web access built into a TV set-top box, for example (unless you ask at check-in) or when the publicly available service might be down for repairs. If access to the Internet is mission-critical for you, then a modem-based account is part of the solution.

> **Tip**
> Of course, most hotels will tell you the type of access they have on the Website or when you call to make a reservation if you make a point of asking. If you're on a driving trip, however, or take a few driving days in the country after your business trip in the city (for instance), having a modem-based backup solution is still something I recommend.

In order to get modem-based Internet access, you need to make arrangements with an Internet service provider that offers national service. This might be the same company that offers broadband access to your home or office — check with them to make sure that can't also give you a modem-based account for dial-up access when you're traveling; sometimes that's a possibility for free or for a lower-than-normal fee. Or, if you don't have access to such a service, consider signing up for a modem-based account from a Mac-specific service such as Ninewire or FasterMac.net, or a national ISP such as AOL, Earthlink, Internet Express, Juno, or NetZero. All of those national services offer Mac-compatible services although it's worth noting that, with the exception of FasterMac.net, their Web accelerator services tend to be Windows-only.

> **Note**
> For what it's worth, "Web accelerators" are a bit more marketing hype than reality in my experience. A modem simply offers less bandwidth than higher-speed connections, but it can be a great fallback when you don't have another option.

Configure for dial-up

Once you've chosen your ISP and signed up, the next step is generally to learn the local phone numbers for access, and then configure

AOL on the Road

The AOL service has a Mac version that not only gives you access to the AOL service itself, but it also enables you to run other applications — Web browsers and e-mail programs — on top of the AOL application while it's active. AOL also has extensive national service numbers and the ability to dial up and find those locations through an 800 number, which is handy when you're traveling by road and aren't sure where you're going to stop. Also, from the TCP/IP tab in the Network pane you can set up your modem specifically for an AOL dial-up connection, which you may want to do particularly when you're headed out on the road.

your Mac to access the ISP. For dial-up connections, that means configuring your modem in the Network pane of System Preferences. Here's how:

1. **Open the Network pane and, in the Show drop-down menu, select Internal Modem.** You'll see the window reconfigure to show the tabs that are appropriate for modem configuration.

2. **Click the TCP/IP tab and make sure that Using PPP has been selected in the Configure IPv4 menu.** If something else has been selected, switch it to Using PPP.

3. **Click the PPP tab.** You see some blank entry boxes where you'll put information about your ISP.

4. **Type the account name, password, and telephone number that you want to use to connect to your ISP (see figure 4.1).** If your ISP offers a secondary number for your area, then enter it in the Alternate Number entry box. (You can also enter a Service Provider name — this isn't used to complete the connection, but it's used to give this configuration a name, as you'll see later when we're dialing out.)

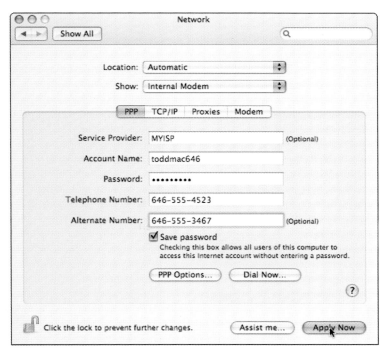

4.1 Setting up a modem to dial out to an ISP.

5. **Click the Save Password check-box if you'd like your Mac to remember your password.** If you leave this unchecked, you'll need to enter your account password every time you attempt to dial out the modem and connect for Internet service.

6. **When you're done, click Apply Now to apply your changes.**

Those are the basics for a typical dial-up connection. However, you can dig deeper if you'd like. Click PPP Options to view a series of options that govern how this PPP connection is made. A dialog sheet appears with two sections — Session Options and Advanced Options. Perhaps the more interesting are the Session Options (see figure 4.2), which govern how long your Mac stays connected before it asks you if you'd like to continue the connection, how long it waits before signing off automatically, and whether you want to configure the modem to dial automatically when Internet data is requested.

Here's a quick look:

✦ **Connect Automatically When Needed.** Turn on this option if you want your Mac to dial its modem whenever there's a request for Internet data. For example, if you tell Mail to check for new e-mail messages, but your Mac isn't currently connected, then it will attempt to dial out automatically.

✦ **Prompt every __ minutes to maintain connection.** Turn on this option if you'd like your Mac to remind you that it's connected to the Internet; this is particularly handy if you're paying toll for a long-distance call or if you get charged for the time you spend online by your hotel. Note that you can specify the number of minutes in the entry box.

✦ **Disconnect if idle for ___ minutes.** This allows your Mac to automatically disconnect the modem connection if it senses that you haven't used it in the given amount of time.

✦ **Disconnect when user logs out.** This may be a personal choice for you — if you have multiple users on your Mac, you might want to turn this option off so that others can use the same connection. If you forget about your connection, however, you may end up staying connected to the Internet for a while after you've logged off. (Or, you may find that you are disconnecting abruptly from your ISP, which can lead to extra charges or other problems, such as delays that keep you from signing back on quickly.)

✦ **Disconnect when switching user accounts.** This is similar to the Disconnect When User Logs Out option, but it deals specifically to Fast User Switching; if you want others to be able to access the modem connection when you're using Fast User Switching to allow access to another account on this Mac, then turn this option off. (I generally keep this one off so that my travel companions or family members can use Fast User Switching to switch to their accounts and check their e-mail or surf the Web without forcing another dial-up session.)

✦ **Redial if busy.** Turn this option on and specify how many times the modem should redial and how many seconds it should wait between redialing attempts if the modem encounters a busy signal when trying to connect to the remote computer.

The Advanced Options section offers additional esoteric configuration choices, most of which you probably won't need unless directed by your ISP or your system administrator. For a typical dial-up connection, the defaults will work fine. Click OK in the dialog sheet when you're done setting options.

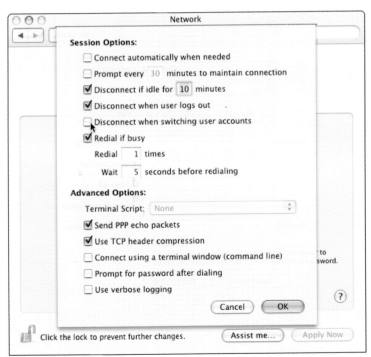

4.2 The Session Options enable you to determine how and when your Mac will sign on and off automatically.

Make the connection

Once your Mac is configured for dial-up, you're ready to make the connection. The easiest way to do that, at least the first time, is by clicking Dial Now in the Network pane. That launches the Internet Connect application, which is the program that's responsible for making your modem dial out and connect (see figure 4.3).

> **Note** *Internet Connect is a special little "dialer" application that is used to complete many different types of connections including modem connections, AirPort connections, and others. Notice that the Internet Connect window is labeled Internal Modem because that's the device that Internet Connect is working with in this instance.*

4.3 The Internet Connect application is where the modem dials the number for your ISP.

If the configuration looks correct in the Internet Connect window and your Mac is connected to a phone line that's also plugged into the correct wall socket (or, in many hotel rooms, the telephone data port on the side of the phone) for access, then you should be able to click Connect and begin the process of dialing out. When you do, you should first hear the dial tone and then hear your Mac's modem dialing (as long as you don't have your Mac's volume

set to mute). Then, you see messages in the Status area of your Internet Connect window. When you successfully connect, a Connected message and small colorful indicators appear that indicate that data is flowing to and from the ISP.

To end the connection, click Disconnect.

> **Caution** *If you're in a hotel room or office building and you aren't sure where you should plug your modem cable, ask the front desk or an IT person. If you plug your modem into a digital phone jack (one that would be used for a PBX phone system) then you could easily damage your modem and potentially even your Mac's internal circuitry. If you're traveling outside the US, make sure you're plugging your modem into an RJ-11 port (that's the typical US phone connector) that's designed for an analog modem, such as a data port that's found on the room's telephone.*

See the Configuration menu? You'll notice that your current configuration is named for the Service Provider that you entered in the Network pane — if you entered one. If you didn't, then it may just be called Main Number. If you entered an alternate number previously, then you can choose the Alternate Number entry from the Configurations menu if you'd like to attempt to dial that number instead of the main number.

You can use the Internet Connect window to change the number that you're dialing if necessary; you may find that you need to type a different number when you arrive at a travel destination, or you may need to switch from a seven-digit to a ten-digit number in different locales. To change the number that's dialed, simply type the new number in the Telephone Number field in Internet Connect and click Connect.

By changing the number, you've created yet another configuration that Internet Connect can store for you. The next time you choose Internet Connect ⇨ Quit Internet Connect, a dialog sheet appears. It asks if you want to save the new configuration and give it a name (see figure 4.4).

4.4 After changing a phone number and then attempting to quit the dialer, Internet Connect asks if you want to save the configuration change with a new name before it quits.

To edit existing configurations, use the Configuration menu and choose Edit Configurations. In the Edit Configurations dialog box you can edit the description, username, password, and phone numbers for any configurations that aren't the initial configurations stored in the Network pane.

You can also create new configurations for your modem connection — a new number or even a different username and password — by clicking the + icon at the bottom of the list of Configurations. Click OK after you make your choices.

Once you settle into Internet Connect and you create the configurations you need, it isn't necessary to open it every time in order to connect to your ISP. Instead, you can select the Show modem status in menu bar option, which is found both in the Internet Connect window and on the Modem tab of the Network pane in System Preferences. With that option selected, a new Modem Status menu appears on the menu bar (see figure 4.5) that enables you to quickly

A Handy Comma

When you travel you may encounter circumstances where you need to dial an additional number or series of numbers to either get an outside line or to make a long-distance call. To dial those numbers, type them in the Internet Connect window. What's good to know is that a comma (,) adds a slight pause to your dialing, which can be handy in various situations. So, if you need an outside line before making a call, you might type something like 9,5556757 in the Telephone Number field. Or, if you need to dial a long-distance code, you might type something like 1010811,,16465553454 in order that the code is dialed and Internet Connect waits long enough for the code to be recognized by the long-distance service.

Note also that another good reason to use the comma is to put a phone company code in front of a number, such as *70, to cancel call waiting in many locales. (Check with your local phone company to see if they have a different code.)

connect, disconnect, or choose from different configurations. You can also open the Internet Connect application from that menu if you need quick access to it.

4.5 The Modem Status menu on the menu bar gives you quick access to connect and disconnect options.

> **Tip**
>
> *In preparation for a trip, it's always a good idea to first make a list of the dial-up phone numbers you may need for the locations you plan to be. (It's also good to look ahead and make sure your ISP offers dial-ups in a particular area so that you aren't surprised when you're Net stranded in some locale.) If you're not sure exactly where you'll end up, most national ISPs have toll-free numbers that you can dial in order to get a local dial-up number. Have those on hand, too.*

Manual dialing

Got a ton of codes and numbers you need to dial in order to reach your ISP? If you can't seem to get the connection to work with a series of numbers and commas (see sidebar), then there's another interesting option — Manual Dial. In this case, you connect your Mac to the phone line, but then you pick up the phone (or an extension) and dial the number yourself; when you hear a computer carrier, you tell your Mac to pick up and complete the connection. This

can also be handy in situations where you're traveling internationally and your Mac doesn't recognize the dial tone.

Here's how Manual Dial works:

1. **Make sure your Mac's modem is connected properly to the phone line and that you also have access to the phone (or an extension on the same phone line) so that you can dial numbers manually.** You may need to use a line-splitter for this purpose so that your Mac and a phone can be connected to the same line.

2. **In Internet Connect, choose Connect ⇨ Manual Dial.** A dialog box appears which allows you to change your Mac's modem script. The default should work okay, although you can experiment with different Apple Internal scripts if the default doesn't work the first time.

3. **Click Manual Dial and a dialog box appears that prompts you to pick up the phone and make the call.** Dial the phone.

4. **When you get through to the ISP and the phone is ringing, click OK.** Internet Connect attempts to pick up the connection from there.

More modem options

Most places in the U.S. have standard dial tones and have moved on from pulse dialing, but you may happen to encounter an area of the country — or another country, particularly in less industrialized parts of the world — where your modem can't dial out because of the dial tone or type of phone line that you're connected to. If that's the case, you can configure some additional options for your modem.

In the Network pane of System Preferences, make sure your modem is selected in the Show menu, and then click the Modem tab. That brings up a screen that looks like figure 4.6. There you'll see two options discussed here, along with a few others that might be interesting.

Note *Disconnect any active connection before changing these settings.*

Those options include:

✦ **Enable error correction and compression in modem.** This is typically turned on and results in better performance, but if you're having trouble with your connection, you can try turning off this option and connecting again.

✦ **Wait for dial tone before dialing.** Turn this option off if the phone line you're connected to has a non-standard dial tone, a stutter tone, or any other anomalies that seem to be keeping your Mac from recognizing the connection and picking up to dial.

✦ **Dialing.** These radio buttons enable you to choose Tone or Pulse. Tone is the standard for touch-tone phones (which means the vast majority of them in the US), while pulse is used for rotary phones. If it seems that your Mac is dialing out but never making a connection, you might try pulse dialing, particularly if you suspect you're dealing with antiquated phones lines (for example, if the phone in your motel room has a big dial on it).

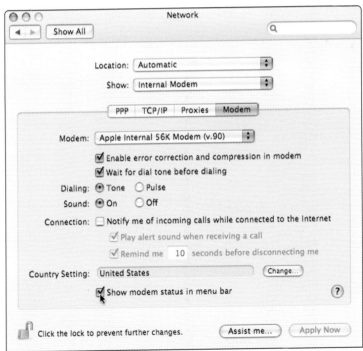

4.6 There are many modem options to choose from.

✦ **Sound.** You can turn the sound on and off depending on whether you'd like to hear your Mac dial through its speakers or not.

✦ **Connection.** These special options can (in some cases) use the call waiting feature on your phone line to let you know when someone is trying to call the line that you're using for a modem connection. These features rely on a modem that adheres to the v.92 specification, which includes all PowerBooks and iBooks made after about 2002; earlier models may have a v.90 modem, which works better if you turn off call waiting when you dial out.

✦ **Show modem status in menu bar.** Turn this option on if you'd like to access your Modem status (and dial it) from a menu bar icon.

When you're done making changes, click the Apply Now button in the Network pane and those changes are made to your modem settings.

Tip *Planning a trip to Azerbaijan or Tibet? One handy site I've found for world travelers is the Worldwide Phone Guide (*http://kropla.com/phones. htm*) which offers information and advice about the phone systems in countries around the world, including whether an adapter or other device is recommended in order to complete a modem connection.*

Connecting to High-Speed Access

For the most part, there are two different approaches to achieving high-speed access via Ethernet. (Wireless access is covered in the next section.) For digital subscriber line (DSL) connections and a very few cable modems — normally this means connections that take place at home or in your office — you may need to use Point to Point Protocol over Ethernet (PPPoE) language in order to make the connection. As with PPP for modem connections, PPPoE is something you can configure from the Network pane of System Preferences.

For other connections, you generally need only to configure your Built-in Ethernet port for Using DHCP and then connect an Ethernet cable from the broadband modem or — in an office, hotel, or similar environment — from the high-speed data port to your Mac's Ethernet port.

Configuring PPPoE connections

You'll use PPPoE for connections that require it — generally, that's DSL modems that are sold and service leased by telephone companies and/or local and regional ISPs. Like a modem-based connection, these technologies require you to connect to the ISP before your service is active; generally you don't need a phone number, however, just a username and password.

Here's how to configure a PPPoE connection using a broadband modem and
your Mac:

1. **Connect your Mac to the broadband modem using an Ethernet
   cable.** This is generally done using
   a standard Category 5 Ethernet
   cable, which may have come with
   the broadband modem.

   > Tip
   > *I've encountered a situation or
   > two with older iBooks that
   > needed to be connected to a
   > broadband modem using a
   > crossover cable, which you
   > might try if you're having no
   > luck getting your modem to
   > work using regular Ethernet
   > cable.*

2. **Open the System Preferences
   application (choose System
   Preferences from the Apple
   menu) and select the Network
   icon.** That opens the Network pane.

3. **On the Network Status screen,
   locate the Built-in Ethernet
   entry and read what it says.** If it
   says "The cable for Built-in
   Ethernet is not plugged in," then
   you need to troubleshoot the connection and make sure you have a
   good Ethernet cable connected to
   your Mac and to the broadband
   modem. If the entry says anything
   else, you should be able to
   move on.

4. **Open the Show menu and
   choose Built-in Ethernet.** The
   window reconfigures to show you
   the Ethernet options.

5. **Click the PPPoE tab and click to
   place a checkmark next to the
   Connect using PPPoE option.**

Doing so activates the options on
the screen (see figure 4.7). Also,
unseen on the TCP/IP tab, turning
on the Connect Using PPPoE
checkbox automatically changes
the TCP/IP settings to Using PPP.

6. **Type the account name and
   password for your account in
   the appropriate entry boxes;
   also, if your ISP requires it, you
   can type the name of the
   Service Provider and/or a
   PPPoE Service Name.**

7. **Click the Save Password checkbox if you would like your Mac
   to remember your account password.** Otherwise you'll need to
   enter it every time you decide to
   connect to your ISP.

8. **Click Apply Now.** That records
   your changes.

On the PPPoE tab, you can click PPPoE
Options to dig deeper into the settings.
There you'll find settings that are similar to
the Session Options for PPP modem connections that were discussed in the section
"Configure for dial-up" earlier in this chapter. In particular, you can set your Mac to
connect automatically when an Internet
application requests data, and you can set it
to disconnect after a certain amount of time.
Make your choices and click OK in the dialog box.

> Tip
> *The PPPoE tab offers the Show
> PPPoE status in menu bar
> option, which is also found in
> Internet Connect. Select it for
> quick access to PPPoE Connect
> and Disconnect commands in
> the menu bar.*

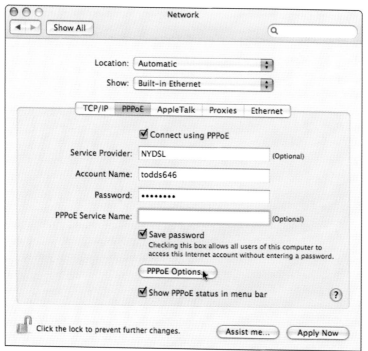

4.7 The PPPoE tab is where you type log-on information for a PPPoE-based broadband connection.

Connect via PPPoE

You can complete your PPPoE connection and begin using your broadband modem by opening Internet Connect and selecting Built-in Ethernet from the toolbar. That reveals the settings that you entered in the Network pane of System Preferences. When you're ready to make the connection, click Connect, as shown in figure 4.8.

You see the Status area change to reflect the fact that your Mac is connecting to your ISP, and then you see a connected message with indicators showing data being sent and received. To disconnect, click Disconnect.

4.8 The Internet Connect application is used to complete a PPPoE connection.

With the Show PPPoE status in menu bar option selected, you can also turn on a PPPoE connection from that menu bar item's menu. Simply click the menu bar item's icon and then choose Connect from the menu (see figure 4.9). As the connection is established, the menu bar item expands to show that status; once connected, that's indicated in the menu bar by bold dots in the PPPoE icon.

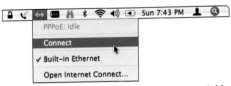

4.9 The PPPoE status menu lets you quickly connect and disconnect.

While you're connected successfully, you can reselect the menu and choose Disconnect in order to stop the current connection.

Tip *As discussed in Chapter 5, you can configure a router or AirPort base station to connect through a broadband modem to your ISP, thus offering PPPoE-based connectivity to all computers that are connected to that router on your network. You do that by accessing the PPPoE tools that are built in to the Web-based configuration tool for a third-party router or through the AirPort administration utilities offered by Apple's devices, which are discussed later in this chapter.*

Configuring for an "always-on" connection

The other approach to broadband Internet access is the sort that doesn't require that you sign on and off; instead, you configure your Mac for access to the ISP, and the

service remains on via your broadband modem or similar device even if your Mac is asleep or disconnected. Whenever you reconnect, your Mac will once again locate the router and, if appropriate, receive an IP address. It's then ready to connect.

An "always on" connection is very much like connecting to a local area network, except that the "router" for your broadband Ethernet connection might be at the cable company's headquarters, for instance, or perhaps it's in the basement of your apartment building or somewhere in the IT center of the hotel where you're staying. Like a LAN, your Mac can be connected at any time and simply request an IP address from the router or, in the case of certain broadband connections in your office or home, you may have a fixed IP address so that your Mac can be used as a server on the Internet as well as a client.

Here's how you connect:

1. **Connect the Ethernet cable from your broadband modem (or from the wall connector for a wired building).**

2. **Open the Network pane of System Preferences and check the Network Status screen to confirm that your Mac has detected the Ethernet connection.** Note that it might tell you that you have an active Internet connection; you may not need any further configuration.

3. **Select Built-in Ethernet from the Show drop-down menu; then click the TCP/IP tab if it isn't already selected.**

4. **On the TCP/IP tab, your selection depends on whether or not your Mac will be receiving a dynamic IP address from the ISP's router.**

   - If so, then choose Using DHCP in the Configure IPv4 menu.

   - If not, then choose Manually and type the IP address, Subnet Mask, Router, and DNS Servers as specified by your ISP. You may also want to type your local domain in the Search Domains field.

   Note *If you can't select anything but Manually or Using PPP, that's because PPPoE has been activated. Click the PPPoE tab and then click the remove the checkmark labeled Connect Using PPPoE.*

5. **Click Apply Now.** With these configuration steps taken, you should be able to attempt to connect to the Internet by launching a Web browser or checking your e-mail in the Mail application, for example. That should cause your Mac to attempt to connect and, if necessary, to retrieve an IP address from the DHCP server.

   Tip *Sometimes your Mac may default to a self-assigned IP address before it retrieves one from the DHCP server. If that happens, you can attempt to convince it to reset and then retrieve a DHCP address by opening the TCP/IP tab (make sure Built-in Ethernet is selected in the Show menu) and choosing Off from the Configure IPv4 menu, and then click Apply Now. Wait a moment and return to the TCP/IP tab and choose Using DHCP. Click Apply Now and close System Preferences.*

With an "always-on" connection you shouldn't have to change any other settings, even if you get up and move around with your Mac or disconnect it for a while and return. The only reason you might have to reconfigure is if you use different types of Ethernet-based broadband connections in different locations — for example, if you have PPPoE at home and a DHCP server at work. If that's the case, see the section "Creating Locations" later in this chapter.

Connecting to Wireless Hotspots

The world isn't quite blanketed with wireless Internet access yet (often called *WiFi* access), but that day isn't too far away, especially for some larger cities. In locales all around the world you can find public and fee-based WiFi networks that are compatible with the AirPort or AirPort Extreme card. And these networks are generally pretty easy to connect your Mac to once you've found them.

Note *WiFi is a common term for the same sort of wireless networking technology that Apple calls AirPort. These wireless approaches are all based on the IEEE 802.11 specification, but given cuter names, since people don't want to say "IEEE 802.11" too often. If you're in an area where WiFi is offered, it should be AirPort-compatible, at least in most cases.*

Tip *Want help finding WiFi spots? The service JiWire.com offers a Dashboard widget for Mac OS X 10.4 and higher. JiWire offers a database of thousands of WiFi-enabled locations in nearly 100 countries.*

In order to make the connection to an available wireless router, you may not need to do anything special at all. To see if your Mac is already configured for AirPort access, simply click the AirPort menu bar icon (see figure 4.10) and look to see if the name of the wireless network appears in that menu. If it does, select the network and then launch a Web browser window.

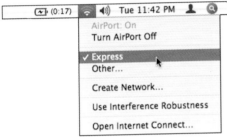

4.10 If you have an AirPort card and it's active, then the AirPort menu bar icon can be used to detect wireless networks that are in range.

If you don't see the wireless network in your AirPort menu and you're expecting to see one, make sure that AirPort is turned on. You can do this from the AirPort menu bar item, by selecting Turn AirPort On. (It's in the same place that the command Turn AirPort Off appears in figure 4.10.)

If AirPort is turned on, follow these steps to make sure it's configured to find new wireless networks:

1. **Launch the Network pane of System Preferences.**

2. **Choose AirPort from the Show drop-down menu.**

3. **Open the TCP/IP pane.** Make sure that the AirPort is set for Using DHCP in the Configure IPv4 menu. If it isn't, that might explain why you have trouble finding open networks.

Tip *If you can't change settings on the TCP/IP tab, click the PPPoE tab and make sure that the Connect using PPPoE option is deselected.*

4. **If you made a change, click Apply Now in the Network pane.**

5. **Return to the AirPort menu bar icon and see if you see the wireless network's name appear; if you do, select it.** If you don't see the network's name, but AirPort is turned on and you've set TCP/IP to Using DHCP, then either you aren't in range of the network or there's something wrong with the wireless router.

When you select a new network in the AirPort menu bar item's menu, you may encounter one or more steps before you can get connected and surfing:

✦ **You may need to type a password.** If so, you need to find out what that password is from whoever manages the network — if this is a public business, ask the staff or management; if you connect to a hotel's wireless Internet service, you may need to ask the front desk or concierge; if you connect to a business office's wireless, you may need to ask a manager or IT representative.

✦ **You may need to arrange payment.** Open a browser window. In many cases, this results in a custom Web page appearing on your Mac — this will be the home page for the service to which you've just connected. If the service is free, you should be up and running — just type a URL and go. If the service is a pay service, make arrangements to pay, either by typing your personal codes (if you already subscribe to the service provider you've encountered) or by following the on-screen instructions so that you can enter a credit card number and other information that's requested.

Once you connect to a wireless network, you should see the AirPort menu bar item's icon show the relative quality of the connection; four bars is full quality with good signal strength and minimal interference, three bars about 75 percent, and so on.

For more detailed connection specifics, you can choose Open Internet Connect from the AirPort menu bar icon menu to see the Internet Connect application's AirPort tab; you can also change wireless networks on that screen or turn off the AirPort card (see figure 4.11.)

Note The biggest problem you're likely to encounter with a public wireless network is it may affect your ability to send e-mail messages using Mail unless you know the SMTP server associated with the specific ISP that is offering the wireless service.

When you're done working on a public wireless network, simply turn off AirPort through the AirPort menu bar item menu, or you can put your Mac to sleep and walk away. That's

4.11 The AirPort tab in Internet Connect shows you signal strength and enables you to switch networks or shut off AirPort.

usually all it takes to get on and off a public network — and it's part of what can make traveling with a portable Mac so much fun.

Tip There are some security steps you should take on public networks. Open the Sharing pane of System Preferences and turn off all services for the duration of time that you spend on a public network, unless you're using a service with someone on that network for specific tasks. (Remember that you can always use iChat for sharing files with a user who has iChat or AIM chatting capabilities.) Chapter 4 discusses some of the sharing options in detail.

Creating Your Own Wireless Network

Whether at home or on the road, you can use an AirPort base station or AirPort Express device to create a wireless AirPort network so that you can share files among multiple Macs or route Internet access to one or more Macs over a wireless AirPort connection. Indeed, the AirPort Express device is extremely portable and can be handy for just such a circumstance — turning a broadband connection in a hotel room or suite into a wireless network that you can use for maximum flexibility for your Mac portable and/or to offer wireless access to others with whom you're meeting and working. And, of course, the AirPort Express is great for houses or apartments and offers the special capability, called AirTunes, which enables it to stream audio from iTunes software to an audio receiver that's connected to your AirPort Express.

Regardless of whether you choose an AirPort Extreme (which is Apple's more expensive and slightly more sedentary AirPort router), an AirPort Express, or a third-party wireless router (with which your Mac should be fully compatible if it's 802.11b or 802.11g compliant), the configuration approach is the same. You need to connect the router to your broadband Internet connection (the AirPort Extreme and some third-party routers can also be connected to a phone line for a modem-based connection), and then configure the router to connect to the Internet as if it were a lone computer. Then you can configure the router to allow wireless (and sometimes wired) access to your Mac portable and any others that you'd like to enable for this network.

Here's how all this comes together:

1. **With your AirPort base station or third-party router in hand, connect it to the Ethernet cable that's wired to your broadband modem.** If you're in an office, hotel room, or wired apartment building, then connect your router to an Ethernet cable that's wired to an Ethernet drop point (usually a wall socket, sometimes an Ethernet router).

2. **Now, run the configuration software for your wireless router.** If it's an Apple router, that usually means the AirPort Setup Assistant and/or AirPort Admin Utility; if it's a third-party router, you'll probably configure using your Web browser and the router's built-in Web-based configuration tools.

3. **With the wireless router configured, you can connect your Mac (or Macs) to the router.** See the previous section "Connecting to Wireless Hotspots."

AirPort Base Station setup

If you're setting up an AirPort Base station or an AirPort Express device, you can do so by launching the AirPort Setup Assistant. Here's how:

1. **Locate the AirPort Setup Assistant application, which is in the Utilities folder inside your Mac's main Applications folder, and double-click its icon to launch the Setup Assistant.** The first screen you'll see is the welcome screen.

2. **Read the Welcome Screen, and click Continue.** That brings you to the Introduction screen.

3. **On the Introduction screen, select the Set Up a New Base Station option and click Continue.** Note that you can only go on from this page if a new base station is recognized; if you previously configured the base station, you need to select the Change Settings On An Existing AirPort Base Station option and click Continue.

4. **If you're setting up a new base station, you see the Network Setup screen.** If the correct network has been detected, click Continue.

5. **On the second Network Setup screen, select the Create a New Wireless Network option and click Continue.** Your other option, Connect to My Current Wireless Network, is what you choose if you want to use this base station to extend the range of your current wireless network. After you click Continue, you move to the next screen.

6. **On the third Network Setup screen, type a name in the Wireless Network Name field (this is the name for the network that will appear to other computers) and type a name for the AirPort device itself (which shows up in iTunes and whenever you opt to configure the base station).**

7. **Click Continue.** The Network Setup screen appears.

8. **On the next Network Setup screen, you can select the type of security you want to use for your network.** If you don't want this network to be publicly accessible, choose WPA Personal if you're using strictly Macs with AirPort cards, or 128-bit WEP for networks that support PCs and others.

9. **Type a password in the Wireless Network Password field and repeat it in the Verify Password field; then click Continue to move to the Internet Setup screen.** Note that for a WEP-based network that is accessible by other platforms the password should be exactly 13 characters long.

10. **On the Internet Setup screen, you may see the Internet connection that the AirPort Setup Assistant believes it detects; if you see changes that need to be made, you can make them on this screen, and then click Continue to get to the AirPort Express Setup screen.** If you don't see the assistant's best guess, then you'll see a list of options from which you can choose, such as cable modems, PPPoE connections, and so on. Step through the assistant to configure that connection according to your instructions from the ISP or your IT manager.

11. **On the AirPort Express Setup screen, type a password for the base station itself in the two fields, and then click Continue to move to the Summary screen.** This is the password you'll use to access the base station to make changes in the future — it should be different from the network password because you need to share the network password with others and this is an administrative password to secure the base station from tampering.

12. **When you reach the Summary screen (see figure 4.12), review everything being summarized; if it looks right, click Update.** When you update, information is fed to the base station and it's restarted.

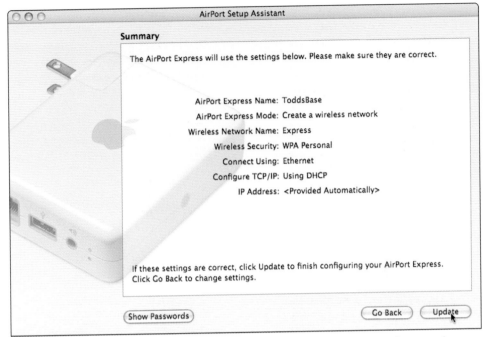

4.12 The AirPort Setup Assistant is summarizing the items it's going to configure and change.

AirPort Express and AirTunes

If you have an AirPort Express base station, if offers a fun extra feature — it can be used with iTunes to stream music from your AirPort-enabled Mac to the AirPort Express device. The device, in turn, can be connected to a home stereo receiver or a similar component so that songs can be played from your wireless Mac through your stereo.

You'll need the stereo connection kit from Apple (or a similar third-party offering) so that you can connect your AirPort Express to your stereo. Next, open iTunes and look for a menu at the bottom right of the iTunes window where you can select where the audio output will be played (see figure). The default option is Computer, but having a recognized AirPort Express device on your network gives you the additional option of choosing the base station that you recently configured.

Once the base station restarts, you should see it appear in the AirPort Status menu bar item's menu, if that menu is active. If not, you can open the Internet Connect application and click the AirPort tab and see if the network is recognized there. When you select the network in Internet Connect or in the AirPort Status menu, you will then be asked for your WEP or WPA Personal password if you opted for one. If the password is accepted, you're ready to surf.

Third-party wireless

If you opt for a router other than an Apple AirPort model, then you need to consult its configuration instructions for the exact method used to get the router connected to the Internet and sharing data with your AirPort-compatible portable Macs. The general approach is to log into the router's browser-based configuration screen, and once you set it up for Internet access, set it up for wireless access as well (see figure 4.13).

The router will likely offer you various options in terms of managing the connections and speed; my suggestion is to begin with special features turned off — such as interference blocking or high-speed burst modes — and then experiment with them by turning them on one at a time if you're curious to see if they increase speed. Also, remember that AirPort Extreme is 802.11g-compatible in case your router offers a variety of speeds.

You will also likely have the option of choosing security settings for your wireless network; if that's the case, look for WPA (no server), if possible, as it's the easiest to get to work with your Mac. If your only option is a WEP mode, then you may need to type the series of letters and numbers that are generated by the router. (Again, consult the router's instructions.) At some point, in the security configuration, the router will generate and show you this key code. You need to retype it in your Mac's password dialog box when you attempt to access this

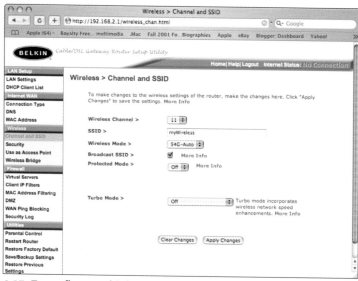

4.13 To configure a third-party router for wireless you'll probably access its browser-based configuration screen.

wireless network for the first time. Store the WEP hex password in your keychain for easy access in the future (see figure 4.14).

4.14 When you attempt to sign into a wireless network that has WEP security, you'll need to enter a long code of letters and numbers. Click the Show Password checkbox if you'd like to see what you're typing.

Once those choices have been made, save them to your router, which may need to be restarted with its new configuration intact. Now you should be ready to connect and get some wireless computing done.

Connecting via Your Mobile Phone

Attempting a connection from your PowerBook or iBook over a mobile phone can be a mixed bag. In the United States, only a relatively few mobile phone services currently offer any level of broadband connection over wireless phones, although that's changing, particularly with the popularity of newer digital networks that support high-speed connections.

For broadband Internet connections via your mobile phone in the US, you'll probably need CDMA (code division multiple access) service — specifically, CDMA 2000 that supports either 1xRTT or 1xEDVO technology.

(On some phones you'll see a little 1x or similar on the display screen.) 1xRTT offers throughput of about 30 to 50 Mbps (about the speed of a decent modem connection) while 1xEDVO hovers between 100 to 300 Mbps, which is closer to DSL and cable modem speeds. Verizon, Sprint, and Alltel are a few of the CDMA carriers.

Other carriers opt for GSM (Global System for Mobile communication), including T-Mobile and Cingular Wireless. They offer data services including GPRS (general packet radio service), which is around 30 to 50 Kbps. Soon you may be seeing newer technologies, such as EDGE (Enhanced GSM Environment), which will push 50 to 200 Kbps, but this technology is still in rollout phase.

A secondary option with some mobile phones is to use the phone as a modem, generally dialing out to an Internet service provider just as you would with a regular telephone modem. If there's a difference, it's the fact that these connections tend to be extremely slow. Still, they're an option when you need to send and receive e-mail or get something similar done quickly, such as check a Web site or conduct an iChat session.

Note *You may have options for connecting your phone to your Mac. The typical approach is through a USB cable that connects to the phone on one end and a USB port on your Mac on the other. For Internet/modem purposes, the phone is often automatically recognized by your Mac. If your phone is Bluetooth-capable, you may be able to pair the phone with your Mac in order to use it for data communications — at least, in some cases. See Chapter 6 for more on pairing phones through Bluetooth.*

Mobile phone broadband

If you have a service that offers broadband access and a phone that's compatible with both it and your Mac, then getting online is probably not that difficult. First, though, confirm that your phone can accept data connections and that your wireless plan includes access to the broadband data offering. (You may have to pay for extra minutes or extra service, depending on the carrier.)

With a USB-based phone, you need to connect your Mac via USB to the phone using a special communications cable. (That cable is likely sold by the manufacturer of the phone or by special mobile phone manufacturers.) When you plug the cable into a live phone and into a USB port on your Mac, your Mac should automatically recognize the phone. To check, open System Preferences and select the Network pane. If the phone is recognized, System Preferences may pop up a dialog box to let you know it's been noticed. If it does, it's a good sign that the phone is compatible with your Mac.

Next, look for the phone on the Network Status screen, and see if it seems to have retrieved a valid IP address. If that also seems to be the case — and the IP addresses isn't self-assigned — then you can launch a Web browser application and see if the phone happens to get service. (If you don't see the phone on the Network Status screen, try closing and re-opening the Network Preferences application and then choosing the Network pane again.) In many cases, phone-based broadband is just about that easy; it's designed to work almost as easily as wireless AirPort or WiFi connections.

Note *If you don't get this kind of instant-on reaction, it's possible that you are either not in a service area that offers mobile phone-based broadband or you haven't configured the phone (or your service account) to offer it. Double-check with the service provider and find out if there are any special codes to be dialed and so on.*

An alternative to using your cell phone for broadband access is to use a special PC card adapter that will work with your PowerBook to offer high-speed wireless data connections. While most such cards don't explicitly offer Mac compatibility, some of them can be made to work with a Mac and third-party software such as Smith Micro's QuickLink software (www.smithmicro.com), which enables you to connect to certain PC cards and mobile carriers (like the Sony-Ericsson models offered by Cingular).

A do-it-yourself open source driver is available for the Sierra Aircard 750 (www.xochi.com/aircard/), which is another popular PC card offered by T-Mobile and others. If you use Verizon as a carrier, you may be in luck, as Apple actually includes (in Mac OS X 10.3.5 and higher) a driver for the Sierra Wireless PC5220 card that's offered in some cities for broadband access; what's more, the card has it's own menu bar icon that you can use to manage your connection. The site www.evdoforums.com can be helpful in finding information and drivers for certain 1xEVDO compatible wireless cards.

> **Note** With a PC Card, you'll likely see a dialog box soon after you insert the card that tells if it's recognized or not. You can then access the Network pane of System Preferences either for confirmation of the connection or to configure the connection according to your mobile carrier's instructions.

Mobile phone as modem

More commonly available is the option of using your mobile phone as a modem, either to dial your phone carrier's data service or to call a third-party ISP for a connection that's similar to a landline dial-up connection. This approach tends to be extremely slow — much slower, in most cases, than using your Mac's modem over a standard phone line — but it may be your best option for checking e-mail when you're away from WiFi and other options.

To use your mobile phone as a modem, you'll need:

✦ A phone that's capable of being a modem

✦ A data connection cable (Bluetooth may also work if the phone offers Bluetooth connectivity for data connections)

✦ A modem driver for the phone installed on your Mac

✦ A phone number and account information for your ISP, or a dialing code and log-on info for your mobile service provider's data service

Mac OS X comes with some mobile phone modem scripts that are preinstalled, including a number of Sony-Ericsson models, a few Nokia models, and some options for particular carriers such as Sprint PCS Vision and Verizon Support. (In Mac OS X 10.4 and higher, there's a General Mobile Phone entry as well, which works with my Motorola 26x series phone.) You can also find third-party modem scripts from a variety of locations — one site that collects some great information about mobile phone modem scripts is www.taniwha.org.uk.

Here's how to get started:

1. **Connect the data cable between your phone and Mac's USB port, or pair the phone using Bluetooth.**

2. **Switch to the System Preferences application and launch the Network pane.** At that point, your phone should be recognized as a networking port if it's connected and compatible (see figure 4.15). Click OK.

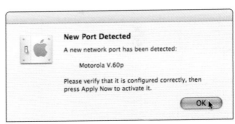

New Port Detected

A new network port has been detected:

Motorola V.60p

Please verify that it is configured correctly, then press Apply Now to activate it.

OK

4.15 When you launch the Network pane, you may find that your phone is recognized.

3. **In the Show pop-up menu, choose the phone's entry; you should be able to set up the phone as a modem.** Type an account name and password, if appropriate, along with a phone number. (See the instructions earlier in the chapter for a modem-based connection.)

One way to connect through your mobile phone is to call out to a third-party ISP; another is to dial a special number, such as #777 or similar, that connects you to the mobile phone company's own wireless Internet service. Consult your mobile carrier's tech support Web site or customer service department for details.

4. **On the Modem tab, open the Modem menu and select the modem script that is the best fit for your mobile phone.** In most cases, you should also deselect the Wait For Dial Tone Before Dialing option.

5. **Click Apply Now to apply your changes.**

To connect, you need to launch the Internet Connect application; on the tab for your mobile phone, make sure the phone number and user information are correct and then click Connect (see figure 4.16). If you're lucky, the stars are aligned, and you really have the data service that you think you do, you should see the connection go live and you'll be able to get some Internet computing done.

4.16 Use Internet Connect to dial and complete the connection through your wireless phone.

Creating Locations

Although some people purchase laptop computers because they're small and don't take up a lot of space when they're not in use, most laptop users take their show on the road — at least occasionally. Your itinerary might include using your Mac on an AirPort network at home, on the corporate intranet at the office, over a modem (possibly through a cell phone) while visiting clients, and through the wireless network at your local coffee house.

Apple introduced networking *locations*, which are network setting collections that can be loaded with a single menu selection and a couple of mouse clicks back in the dark ages of Mac OS 8. The move to OS X made the use of locations an even simpler process — a single menu selection to swap out the old settings and swap in the new.

Network settings are a system-wide setting, shared by all users of the computer. Thus, not surprisingly from a security standpoint, only users with Administrator access can define a location or modify a location that has already been defined. However, you do not require Administrator access to switch from one defined location to another.

Figure 4.17 shows you how to switch from one location to another; just choose the desired location from the Apple menu's Location submenu.

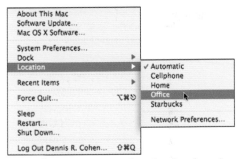

4.17 Choose your new location by choosing Location from the Apple menu.

Creating a network location is easy. Proceed as follows:

1. **Choose the Location ➪ Network Preferences from the Apple menu.** The Network preference pane, shown in figure 4.18, appears.

Tip

If you'd like to skip these steps, click Assist Me at the bottom of the Network System Preferences window and an Assistant will walk you through the process of defining your new location.

2. **Choose New Location from the Locations menu.** A sheet drops down asking you to name your new location, as shown in figure 4.19. Type a descriptive name.

3. **Choose Network Port Configurations from the Show menu.** You'll see a list of ports that have checkmarks next to them; those are the ports that are enabled for this location.

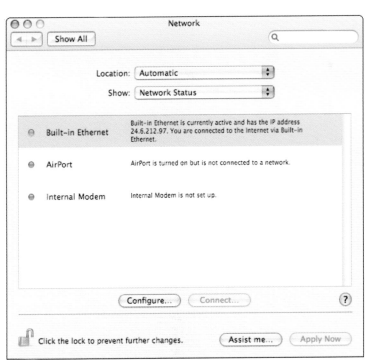

4.18 Here's the Network preference pane; note the Location menu says Automatic.

Name your new location:

Untitled

All users of this computer will be able to choose this location in the Apple menu without entering a password.

Cancel   OK

4.19 Enter the name you'd like for your new location in the dialog sheet that appears.

Cross-Reference *See Chapter 5 for a discussion about how to select and order the network ports you want to use for this location.*

4. **Click to place checkmarks next to the ports that you want to have active.** If you know that you're always only going to use AirPort in your Home location, for instance, you can disable the other ports by removing their checkmarks.

5. **For each of the ports you enable in Step 4, choose that connection type from the Show pop-up menu, and set its values as described earlier in this chapter (Ethernet, Wireless, Modem, and so on).** Once you've selected the port in the Show menu, you will see the TCP/IP, PPP, and other tabs that you can use to configure that port for Internet access.

Congratulations, you just created a location and established its settings. The next time you're at this location with your laptop, all you need to do is choose the Location submenu from the Apple menu, and you'll be online and productive.

Networking Your Portable Mac

When you're in the command and control center of your office, home office, recreation room, or wherever you have established as your home base, you'll almost assuredly want to set up some sort of Internet access, as was described in Chapter 4. After that, depending on your needs, you may want to consider setting up a network.

If you have more than one computer, then a small office network is generally a necessity and a home network is increasingly a luxury that's easily afforded. With the AirPort wireless technology that's built in to your Mac portable, you have a wireless network that is both practical and an enjoyable way to make use of your Mac's portability while getting a little work done on the kitchen table or answering a little e-mail from the front porch.

In this chapter, I cover setting up a local area network, connecting your computers, and sharing files. I touch on both wired and wireless approaches to networking and also discuss connecting your network to the Internet so that all of your computers can gain access.

The Networking Basics

Mac OS X uses the same protocol for sharing files on a local area network (LAN) as it does for accessing the Internet. The Transmission Control Protocol/Internet Protocol (TCP/IP) language is that protocol — it's the fundamental language that computers use to talk to one another on the Internet as well as, in the case of Mac OS X, on a network of computers that are all connected in your home or office.

How networking works

Before computers can speak TCP/IP to one another, they need to be connected and aware of one another. For your LAN, that means either connecting your Macs to a central Ethernet *hub* or *switch*, or if your Macs have AirPort cards installed in them, you can "connect" them to a wireless hub or AirPort base station. When you connect to such a device, your Macs are then able to recognize one another and begin sharing files or otherwise take advantage of being connected to one another for applications like iChat or networked games.

As you saw in Chapter 4, for a broadband Internet connection, the configuration is similar; usually you just use an Ethernet cable to connect your Mac to the broadband (DSL or cable) modem device provided by your Internet service provider (ISP). If you have a broadband modem and a LAN — and you want high-speed access for all your networked Macs — then you need to add a *router* to this mix. A router is a device that enables you to connect your LAN to the Internet through that broadband modem.

So, getting connected over a network or a high-speed connection takes three steps:

1. **Create the connection using cables or a wireless method.**

2. **Configure your Mac to speak TCP/IP.**

3. **Turn on the services you want to use — for example, File Sharing — and complete your Internet connection and launch your client applications for accessing the Web, e-mail, and so on.**

Begin by getting connected.

Types of network connections

As you've seen, modern Macs have Ethernet ports built into them, and most of them either have AirPort wireless cards installed in them or a slot that enables you to install AirPort. So, one question you might have is, which is better?

 Note Ports *are numbered connection openings for network communications.*

For starters, Ethernet is generally faster. At the very least, modern PowerBooks and iBooks support 100BaseT connections, which is technology that enables data to move at up to 100 megabits per second (Mbps), or about 12.5 megabytes per second. Starting with PowerBook G4 models introduced in late 2001 (the PowerBook G4 550MHz and later), the Ethernet port is cable of 1000BaseT, also called "Gigabit" connections. In megabits, that's 125 megabytes per second.

Along with speed, Ethernet is a bit more secure, since the data that you're sending around your network isn't flying through the air and, thus, it's a little more difficult to "hack" into an Ethernet network. (It's certainly *very* difficult to do from the curb outside your house.) With wireless networks, you need to be more vigilant about creating and using passwords to secure the network from unauthorized access.

Of course, AirPort wireless networking is more convenient in the sense that you don't have to install wiring to your Macs, you can move your Macs around inside the building, and an AirPort card enables you to take your portable Mac to various locations and get network and/or Internet access. So each has its advantages.

And there's one other consideration — if you have an Ethernet connection to your broadband modem, then you can't also use that same Ethernet port to connect to a local network. The solution is to either use Ethernet for your Mac's Internet access and AirPort for local networking, or you can add an Ethernet router to your network so that both local data and Internet data can exist on your network at the same time.

> **Tip**
>
> *Actually, if you have one Mac configured for an Ethernet-based Internet connection and it connects to other Macs via AirPort, then you can use the Internet Sharing feature to offer Internet access to those other Macs connected via AirPort, turning your Mac into a virtual base station. More on that later in the section "Internet access for your wireless network."*

Network terminology

As mentioned, Macs use TCP/IP to communicate with one another, and TCP/IP is the protocol that's used to access Internet data as well. So, while you're setting up your connection, you'll come across some basic terminology, most of which is related to TCP/IP. Here's a quick look at some of those terms:

✦ **IP Address.** The IP address is the unique address for a computer on a given network. When your Mac is connected to the Internet via a broadband modem, for example, it's given an IP address on the Internet so that you can access Internet data and, if desired, others can access your Mac. That IP address is a series of four numbers, as in 192.168.0.1 or 64.216.45.125. Each of those numbers in the series is always between 0 and 255.

✦ **Domain name.** A domain name is a name that's assigned to a particular IP address, in order to make the IP address easier to remember. While a given Web server's computer might have an IP address of 4.253.56.1, it might have a domain name of bigcorpswebsite.com, making it possible to reach that computer by typing an address such as `http://www.bigcorpswebsite.com` into a Web browser.

> **Note**
>
> *Domain Name Services (DNS) servers are computers that turn named Internet addresses (such as `www.yahoo.com`) into numbered addresses, such as 192.168.1.1.; they're usually servers that are provided by your ISP. Under certain circumstances, you may need to specify an IP address for a DNS server when you're configuring your Mac, so that when you type* ***http://www.macblog.com/*** *into a browser, your Mac knows what you're talking about.*

✦ **Subnet Mask.** The subnet mask is a number that determines the range of addresses that are part of the same network. It's usually in a form like 255.255.0.0 or 255.255.255.0, where the 255 is used to represent which portions of an IP address are part of the same network. This number is used for manually configuring an IP address, as you'll see later in this chapter.

✦ **Hub/Switch.** This is a device that helps you create an Ethernet-based network of computers; each computer connects to a port on the hub or switch using an Ethernet cable. A switch is "smarter" than a hub (and often faster), in that it can correctly route data from one computer to another, while a hub replicates data sent from one computer to all of its ports, and the non-recipient computers simply ignore it.

✦ **Base Station.** Apple's word for a wireless hub and router combination that connects AirPort-enabled Macs to one another and, often, provides Internet access to those Macs.

✦ **Router.** A router is a device that moves data from one network to another — for your purposes, that usually means moving data from the Internet to your LAN and back again. Routers have specific IP addresses on your LAN, and it can be important to know that address.

Configuring an Ethernet Network

If you put together an Ethernet-based LAN, you need a *hub* or *switch*. A hub is a device that enables you to connect four, eight, or more computers to one another using Ethernet *patch cables* (known as Category 5 or Cat 5) to connect each computer to the hub. A switch is a smarter hub that not only routes data efficiently, but also doesn't lose that efficiency as computers are added; whereas a hub can start to slow down when you connect more computers. (If you have a choice, I'd recommend buying a switch.)

Getting connected

Ethernet tends to be faster and a little more reliable than wireless networking, but you can't roam while connected like you can with a wireless connection. However, Ethernet ports are built in to all modern Mac portable computers (see figure 5.1), so connecting your portable either to an Ethernet hub or to a broadband modem is an option.

A hub or switch can also be built in combination with a router, which has the added advantage of being able to connect your LAN to the Internet. If you shop a computer superstore or electronics store, most likely you'll see a lot of different options in that last category — Ethernet router/hub combinations that enable you to connect four or more Macs so that you can run a small LAN and get Internet access to that LAN all at the same time. The router then connects through a WAN (Wide Area Network) or Uplink port to your broadband modem in order to complete the connection to the Internet. These days, this is probably the most common solution for home and small business networks.

When you connect an Ethernet cable to a modern Mac portable, it's automatically recognized by that Mac and activated in the Network pane of System Preferences as the Built-in Ethernet port (unless Ethernet has been turned off previously). You should be able to open the Network pane of System Preferences (choose System Preferences from the Apple menu and click the Network

5.1 Connecting an Ethernet patch cable to an iBook G4's Ethernet port.

icon) and see the Built-in Ethernet entry appear on the Network Status screen (see figure 5.2).

Configuring TCP/IP

Once you connect the cables between your Mac(s) and your Ethernet hub or router/hub combination device, you're ready to configure your Mac(s) to talk to one another using TCP/IP. How you do that depends, in part, on your needs and the hardware you have installed.

In order for a computer to join a TCP/IP network, it needs to have an IP address either self-assigned or assigned to it.

Letting your Mac self-assign an IP address

The easiest way to configure a network of Macs is *not* to configure them. In Mac OS X, Ethernet networks can be auto-configured when they're connected together; each Mac automatically selects an IP address that's designed to work with other Macs on that network.

To figure out if your Mac has self-assigned an IP address, open the Network pane of System Preferences and take a look at the Network Status screen. Find Built-in Ethernet and see if it reports that the cable is connected and has a self-assigned IP address (see figure 5.3).

5.2 When you connect an Ethernet cable to your Mac's Ethernet port and to a powered hub or broadband modem, it should be recognized, although it may report as not correctly configured.

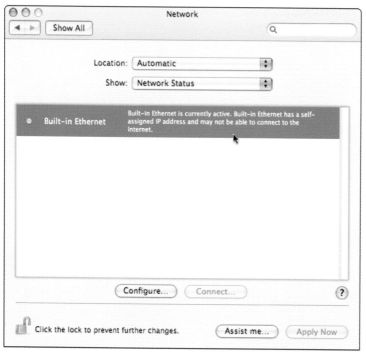

5.3 My iBook is connected to a hub and has assigned itself an IP address.

If your Mac doesn't self-assign an IP address, you can follow these steps to make sure that it does:

1. **In the Network pane of System Preferences, choose Show ⇨ Built-in Ethernet.** The Ethernet options appear.

2. **Select the TCP/IP tab.** You'll see the TCP/IP configuration options.

3. **Choose Using DHCP from the Configure menu.** A Mac that won't self-configure is usually set to Manually or None in this menu. Using DHCP will automatically assign an IP address if a true DHCP server can't be found. (Using a DHCP server is covered in the next section.)

4. **Click Apply Now.** When the Mac isn't able to find a DHCP server, it auto-configures an address.

A self-assigned IP address isn't ideal, because a network of Macs that have self-assigned IP addresses can't connect to the Internet — self-assigned addresses can only be used for local network applications. That said, you can do pretty much anything else that is discussed in this chapter, such as iChat, file sharing, and printer sharing.

Using a DHCP server for IP addresses

The most common way to configure Macs on a LAN is using a Dynamic Host Configuration Protocol (DHCP) server to automatically allocate IP addresses to your Macs (as well as

PCs and other devices connected to the LAN). DHCP is specifically designed for the job of allocating addresses to computers to join and leave the network; it works for Ethernet and wireless networks alike.

Of course, to take advantage of DHCP, you need a DHCP server. As you've seen already, when Macs can't find a DHCP server, they auto-assign their addresses, which is fine for a LAN where you don't need each Mac to have Internet access. But DHCP servers tend to be built in to Internet routers and router/ hub combinations. If you have such a device (or if your company or organizational LAN has a specialized server computer on it), you can connect your Mac to the DHCP server by following these steps:

1. **Launch the Network pane of System Preferences.**

2. **Choose the Built-in Ethernet device from the Show menu.**

3. **Click the TCP/IP tab if it isn't already selected.**

4. **Select the Using DHCP option from the Configure IPv4 menu.** This sets your Mac so that it will look for a DHCP server.

5. **Click Apply Now.** After a moment, you should see a new IP address appear in this tab, complete with Subnet Mask and Router entries (see figure 5.4).

If your Mac doesn't find a router, then it will once again self-assign an IP address, which you can see by returning to the Network Status window in the Network pane of System Preferences. You may need to make

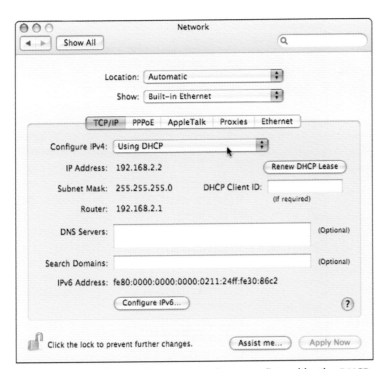

5.4 In this case, the IP addresses have been configured by the DHCP server that's built in to the router.

sure that the router is configured to act as a DHCP server, as discussed in the next section.

 Note *Routers aren't the only DHCP servers — if you happen to have a true server computer on your network, such as an Apple Xserve running Mac OS X Server, it can handle the DHCP serving responsibilities. Also, with such a server on your network, you may (in rare cases) use the BootP protocol for accessing the network, in which case you need to choose Using BootP in the Configure IPv4 menu instead of Using DHCP.*

Configuring a DHCP server

If you have a DHCP server built in to your hub or hub/router combination, you may need to configure it before it will act as a DHCP server to the computers on your network. To do that, you need to log on to the router's configuration by connecting your Mac to the hub/router through Ethernet and then signing in to the router's IP address using a Web browser. To figure out how to do this for your particular router, you'll need to consult its manual — most routers have a hardwired IP address that you can use to access a Web-style interface for configuring the router's features.

In order to connect to the router, you may need to manually configure your Mac's Ethernet TCP/IP temporarily so that you can access the router on the same subnet. Here's how:

1. **Connect an Ethernet cable from your Mac to a port on the router.** Use a regular port on the router, not one marked WAN or Uplink.

2. **Open the Network pane of System Preferences.**

3. **Select Built-in Ethernet from the Show menu.**

4. **Click the TCP/IP tab.** It may already be selected.

5. **Choose Manually from the Configure IPv4 menu.** This should cause the entry boxes next to the options in the window to light up, ready for input.

6. **For IP address, enter the same address as your router's address (as specified in its user manual) except with a ".2" at the end.** If the router's address is 192.168.0.1, then choose 192.168.0.2 for your Mac; if the router's address is 4.2.2.1, choose 4.2.2.2 and so on.

7. **Enter a subnet mask of 255.255.255.0.**

8. **Enter the router's address in the Router entry box.**

9. **Click Apply Now.**

With your Mac properly configured to be on the same network as the router, you can access the router's Web-based interface. To do so, open a Web browser window and type in the router's address in the address box, such as **http://192.168.0.1**, and then press Return to open up that page.

Once you connect to your router's configuration page, log on with the provided password (check your router user guide for the router) and locate the options and commands for turning on the DHCP server settings. For my Belkin router, that's on the LAN Settings page (see figure 5.5). There, I can turn on the DHCP Server and specify the range of addresses that it should hand out.

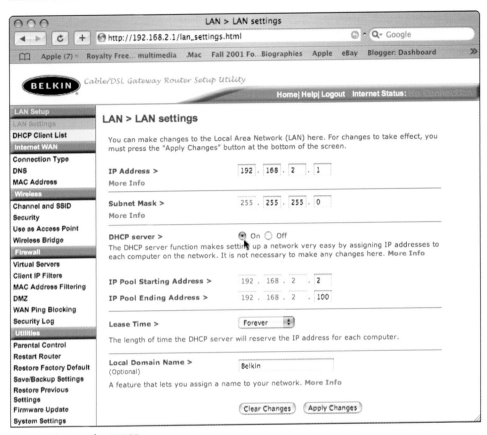

5.5 Turning on the DHCP server.

Once the router's DHCP server is on, you can return to your Mac(s), open the Network pane of System Preferences, and set the Mac back to Using DHCP on the TCP/IP tab for Built-in Ethernet. Now, your Mac will use the DHCP server to automatically receive an IP configuration.

Entering IP addresses manually

The third option for configuring your network is to manually enter IP addresses. This is the most difficult, but it has its advantages. With self-addressing and DHCP-based addresses, an individual Mac's IP address may change frequently. With manual addressing, you can give your Mac an IP address and stick to it. Some services don't really care whether an IP address changes much — File Sharing, Bonjour iChat, and others can find resources regardless of the local IP address. But others, such as Web serving and FTP serving, can benefit from a fixed IP address. For example, if you get to know that the machine in the family room is 192.168.0.4, then you can log on to it using an FTP program or even a remote access session from the Terminal application (if you happen to know a little about the Unix command line).

So, manual addressing isn't for everyone, but it is an option. What you need to do is choose an IP address that's compatible with the range of addresses used by your router (if you have one), then type an appropriate subnet mask, and then type the router's IP address (again, if you have one). You'll also need some DNS entries, if you plan to access the Internet via your LAN.

To configure a manual IP address, follow these steps:

1. **Launch the Network pane of System Preferences.**

2. **Choose the Built-in Ethernet device from the Show menu.**

3. **Click the TCP/IP tab if it isn't already selected.**

4. **Select the Manually option from the Configure IPv4 menu.** This sets your Mac so that you can enter an IP address and other items yourself.

Tip *You can press the Tab key to move from entry box to entry box.*

5. **Edit the entry boxes in the window as recommended:**

   • **IP Address.** There are some common schemes for private networks, the most common being to number your network starting with 192.168.x.x and filling in the x and x depending on how many computers you have and whether or not you have a router. If you have a router, then you should rely on it to help you make this decision — most likely the router is assigned an address such as 192.168.0.1. If so, then the rest of your Macs should be numbered something like 192.168.0.2, 192.168.0.3, and so on, with all the numbers the same except that last one. (The final number can go to 254, so unless you have more than

254 computers on your LAN, you're in good shape.) Note that in most cases if your router is 192.168.0.1 and you assign a Mac 192.168.1.4, then they won't be able to talk — those first three numbers need to be identical.

Note *Actually, computers with addresses 192.168.0.1 and 192.168.1.4 might be able to talk, depending on the subnet mask that's being used for the network. If the subnet mask is 255.255.0.0, then the last two numbers can be configured for different computers on the local network. Most LANs have a subnet mask of 255.255.255.0, meaning that it's only the last number of the IP address that can be configured to differentiate computers on that network.*

   • **Subnet Mask.** In practice, the subnet mask is very often 255.255.255.0, which means that the last numbers in IP addresses assigned for this Mac are considered part of the local subnet. (255.255.0.0 isn't totally uncommon, either.) If your subnet mask is 255.255.255.0, then computers with the addresses 192.168.1.1 and 192.168.1.2 see one another on the same subnet, while computers with the addresses 192.168.1.1 and 192.168.0.1 do not. If your subnet mask is 255.255.0.0, then those two addresses would be on the same subnet, as would be 192.168.5.9 and 192.168.254.4.

Tip *Don't be intimidated by the subnet mask concept. When you're choosing IP addresses for a manually configured network, simply choose addresses that increment up from the router's address, as in 192.168.0.2, 192.168.0.3 and so on. You'll be fine.*

- **Router.** If you have a router on your LAN, you need to type the address for it in this field. With a router address, you are able to access any networks to which that router is connected and aware of (in many cases, that's the Internet). Without a router address, you're stuck with just your local network. (And remember, your IP address needs to be in the same subnet as this router address.)

- **DNS Servers.** If you have an Internet connection through this LAN, you need to enter DNS server IP addresses here; consult your ISP to see if they offer DNS server addresses that you can use.

6. **Click Apply Now.** That will set your Mac to use the new configuration.

You can now check the Network Status screen (choose Network Status from the Show menu at the top of the Network pane) and/or test your settings by attempting to connect to another Mac. (See the sections on File Sharing and iChat later in this chapter for testing options.)

Activating and Configuring an AirPort Card

Aside from using Built-in Ethernet, you have the option of using AirPort technology to connect to a network wirelessly. Nearly all modern portable Macs offer AirPort support

as an option, and even the earliest PowerBooks that support Mac OS X but that don't offer an AirPort option can still accept a PC Card upgrade for wireless networking. Wireless is an interesting option for a home or small business office where you'd like some flexibility in terms of where you place your machines. Wireless tends to be slower than Ethernet and can be less reliable, but it's more flexible.

 See Appendix A for details on installing an AirPort card in your portable Mac.

Apple uses the name AirPort to refer to its wireless technology, but AirPort is the same as what's generally called *WiFi* in the Windows-compatible world, or, more specifically, IEEE 802.11, which is the official terminology.

Earlier Macs supported IEEE 802.11b, which was simply called AirPort; later Mac models support IEEE 802.11g, which Apple calls AirPort Extreme. The major difference is speed — 802.11b supports speeds up to 11 megabits per second, or about 1.5MB per second at best; 802.11g can reach speeds of 56 megabits per second, or about 7MB per second of data transfer. The specs are fully compatible with one another. An AirPort Extreme–enabled Mac can connect to a router that supports 802.11b or 802.11g, and an AirPort-based Mac can be similarly connected to any router — the speeds simply match up according to the capabilities of the card.

 Actually a network can be configured so that it is limited to 802.11g connections, which makes the network faster, but less compatible.

If your Mac has an AirPort card installed, then configuration of that card should be accessible in the Network pane. Open System Preferences and click the Network icon, then look for AirPort on the Network Status screen.

If the AirPort card says that it is not connected to a network, that should be okay until you're able to configure one. If it says the card is off, then you may have turned it off through the AirPort menu bar icon menu. Go back to the menu and turn AirPort on (see figure 5.6).

Once you confirm that an AirPort card is installed, you can use it to create and join a wireless network as discussed in the section "Using your Mac as a base station." If, however, your primary goal is to use your AirPort card to connect to public networks for Internet access, see Chapter 4.

Configuring wireless access

In order to connect your AirPort-enabled Mac to a wireless network, you also need to configure TCP/IP. However, if you have a wireless base station or hub, it's almost always configured as a DHCP server, so this configuration is straightforward. Here's how:

1. **Open the Network pane of System Preferences and double-click the AirPort entry on the Network Status screen.**

5.6 Turning AirPort on through the menu bar icon menu.

2. **Click the TCP/IP tab and make sure that Using DHCP is selected on the Configure IPv4 menu.**

3. **Click Apply Now.**

4. **Click the AirPort tab to select it.**

5. **On the By default, join menu, the Automatic setting will generally work (see figure 5.7).** If you have two wireless networks in the same general vicinity, you might want to choose Preferred Networks from the menu. In the entry box that appears, you can drag the networks that you do want your Mac to connect to in order to set each network's priority; you can also remove networks that you don't want your Mac to attempt to connect to (highlight a network and click the minus sign (–) icon).

6. **Make sure the option Show AirPort Status in Menu Bar is turned on at the bottom of the window.**

7. **Click Apply Now.** With those choices made, you can now rely on the AirPort Status menu bar item to manage connecting to networks.

8. **Pull down the AirPort Status menu bar item down and choose the name of the network that you want to use.** You can do this whenever you want to connect (see figure 5.8).

If the network you choose is protected by a password, you need to type it in the password dialog box that appears and click OK before you can gain access to the network.

You can also use this menu to create wireless networks and to shut off AirPort when you're not connected to a network (or when you're on battery power and want to conserve some energy).

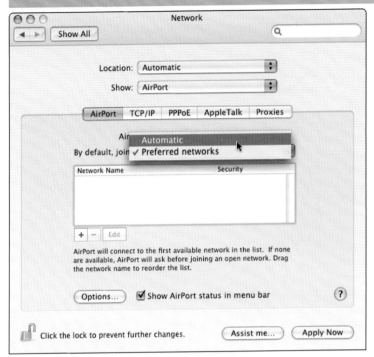

5.7 On the AirPort tab, you can determine if and how your Mac will attempt to automatically connect to the base stations it finds.

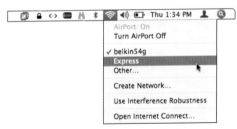

5.8 The AirPort Status menu bar item is handy for managing AirPort connections once the initial configuration is complete.

Tip

In the AirPort Status menu bar item menu you see an option to Use Interference Robustness if you have an AirPort Extreme card installed in your Mac. You can choose this option if you believe that something is interfering with your connection. Note that it slows the connection down to regular AirPort speeds.

Internet access for your wireless network

Along with serving as the hub of your LAN, wireless routers and AirPort base stations are often used for distributing Internet access to your connected computers. If you have a broadband connection, you may want to configure your wireless network to provide Internet access for your wireless Macs — even if you only have one Mac and you're using that wireless router or base station to give that Mac access.

Note

Actually, many of Apple's AirPort Base Station models offer a modem so that you can connect the base station to the Internet via modem and then share that connection to others on your wireless LAN. Most of the time, though, you'll want a broadband *connection, which can connect to the wireless router (or AirPort Base Station) and be used to offer Internet access to all your wireless Macs (and PCs, for that matter).*

If you have a third-party router, you'll find that setting up Internet access for wireless clients is pretty much the same as for wired computers.

If you have an AirPort base station or AirPort Express device, that setup is a little different; it's covered in Chapter 4.

Using Your Mac As a Base Station

So far you've learned about wireless networks that have wireless hubs and routers at their center. However, your Mac can create a computer-to-computer network, as well, that enables you to share files between Macs without requiring a hub — or any additional hardware, for that matter, assuming both (or all) of the Macs you want to connect have AirPort cards. This is great for when you're traveling or you meet others in an Internet café or similar and need to exchange files (or even play a network game). One of you can create a network that the others can join.

Creating a network

Here's how to create a network:

1. **Click the AirPort icon on the menu bar and choose Create Network.** A dialog box appears.

2. **In the dialog box, enter a name for your network in the Name entry box and choose a channel from the Channel menu.** If you're

in a public place, it's a good idea to choose a channel other than 11, as it's commonly used for wireless networks.

3. **If you'd like to create a secure network, click the Show Options button.** If you'd like to use a password for your network, click Enable Encryption, enter a password in the Password and Confirm box, and choose the type of WEP key that you'd like to use for the connection. You'll need to tell your other users the password.

4. **Click OK.** The AirPort menu bar icon on your Mac will change to show that your Mac is now a base station to which others can connect to — those others will now see your Mac in their AirPort menu bar icon menus.

Others can now connect to your Mac's network just as they would any other base station, so that they can share files with one another or share a printer connected to your Mac or any other Mac that's also connected to your network. However, note that your Mac needs to be active and awake in order for the others to share files; if you put your Mac to sleep or shut it down, the network goes away.

When you're done with the network, simply choose another AirPort connection from the base Mac's AirPort menu bar icon, or choose Disconnect from the Current Network.

Turning on Internet sharing

If you have an Ethernet connection to a broadband network, you can use your Mac's built-in Internet Sharing feature to share that broadband connection with others via your AirPort card. Here's how to do that:

1. **First, make sure you have an active Internet connection via Ethernet.** You can consult Chapter 4 for advice on configuring a broadband connection.

2. **Open System Preferences and choose the Sharing pane.**

3. **Click the Internet tab.** That reveals the Internet Sharing options.

4. **In the Share Your Connection From menu, choose Ethernet.**

5. **In the To Computers Using area, place a check next to AirPort.**

6. **Click the AirPort Options button.** That brings up the dialog sheet shown in figure 5.9.

7. **On the AirPort Options dialog sheet, give the network and name and, if desired, click the Enable encryption option.** If you opt to encrypt the data that's sent over this network, enter a password in the Password entry box, and then repeat it in the Confirm Password entry box. Then, choose the strength of encryption (40-bit or 128-bit) and click OK.

8. **Click Start.** That starts the Internet Sharing feature.

Now, other wireless Macs in your vicinity should be able to find in their AirPort menu bar icon menu the network you just created and connect to it in order to get Internet access.

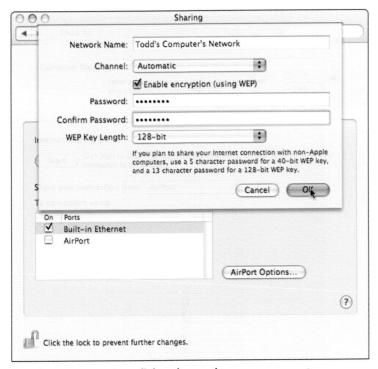

5.9 The AirPort Options dialog sheet, where you can create an AirPort network.

Tip *Windows-based PCs can connect to a Mac that has Internet Sharing active, too. Just make sure that if you use encryption, you choose a password that is PC-compatible. For 40-bit encryption, that means a password that is five characters long; for 128-bit encryption, the password must be 13 characters long. That way, the password will work when entered on a PC.*

Sharing Files and Printers

Generally the reason to create and activate a local network in your home or office is to share files; there may be other reasons, too, such as the ability to chat between machines or the occasional networked games. But for productivity purposes, file sharing usually wins the day. It is second only to sharing a printer in popularity.

Once your network connection is up and running (wired or wireless) and TCP/IP is configured, you can activate sharing services. Apple offers a few different ways that you can share files on a local network, as well as options for sharing printers depending on whether or not the printer itself is network capable.

Personal File Sharing

What Mac OS X calls File Sharing uses the Apple File Protocol (AFP) because it's designed primarily for making files available over a network to other Mac users. While it's possible for others to log on (Microsoft Windows computers can add third-party

software that adds client capabilities using AFP), this is primarily a Mac thing. If you've been around Macs for a while, you might know it as AFP over IP.

To turn on File Sharing, open the Sharing pane of System Preferences and select the Personal File Sharing option (see figure 5.10). When you do, you should see it start up and report to you that your Mac is now a server on your local network.

Once Personal File Sharing is selected, anyone on your network should be able to go to his or her Network icon in a Finder window Sidebar and locate your Mac as a server. That user can then connect to your Mac as a Guest or as a named user.

To log on as named users, they must have an account on your Mac, as defined by the Accounts pane of System Preferences. Guest users can access only the contents of the Public folder in your account's home folder, as well as the Public folders in any other accounts that are on that Mac. If the user signs into an account on your Mac, that user has access to his or her home folder and its contents; if the user is an administrator, then he or she also has access to the main level of the internal hard drive as well as any other mounted volumes.

You can return to the Sharing pane of System Preferences to turn Personal File Sharing off; simply deselect the option to remove the checkmark, or select Personal File Sharing and click Stop. When you do, if anyone else is connected to your Mac, a dialog box appears which allows you to choose how many minutes the other user has before file sharing shuts down. You can send a message to connected users to warn them.

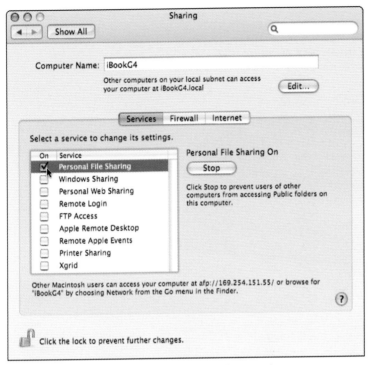

5.10 Turning on File Sharing is a single-click operation.

Creating User Accounts

To access a Mac for file sharing, you need an account on that Mac. Such an account is created in the Accounts pane of System Preferences. Here's how to add a user account to your own Mac for File Sharing (or for local log in — the same account is used for both):

1. **Open System Preferences and click the Accounts icon.** The Accounts pane opens.

2. **If it's closed, click the padlock icon at the bottom of the window.** The Authenticate dialog box appears.

3. **In the Authenticate dialog box, enter your username and password and click OK.**

4. **In the Accounts pane, click the + icon below the list of accounts.** A dialog sheet appears.

Continued

Continued

5. **In the dialog sheet, type a name for this user, then edit the user's short-name if desired.** Also, type a password twice — in the Password entry box and again in the Verify entry box. There's also a Password Hint entry box where you can type text that would help you recall the password in case you forget it.

6. **Click Allow User to Administer Computer if you want the user to have administrative access, and then click Create User.**

That's all it takes to create a user; now, someone can use that account to either log into the Mac while sitting at its keyboard or to use File Sharing (or other sharing tools, such as FTP) to access your Mac.

Connecting to a file-sharing Mac

To connect to a Mac on your network that has Personal File Sharing turned on, follow these steps:

1. **Switch to the Finder and choose File ➪ New Finder Window.** You can also press ⌘+N. A new Finder window appears.

2. **In the Sidebar of the Finder window, click the Network icon.** That opens the Network folder.

3. **Locate the server in your Network folder, and then double-click its icon.** The Connect to Server dialog box appears (see figure 5.11).

4. **Select the Guest or Registered User option.**

5. **If you choose Registered User, log on with a valid name and password for an account that's been created on that server Mac.** Once you log on, a window appears that enables you to choose from the available volumes (or shared folders) on that Mac, depending on whether you connect as a Guest or a registered user.

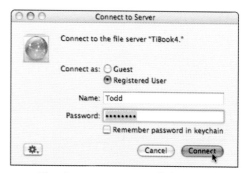

5.11 The Connect to Server dialog box is used to log on to remote Macs using File Sharing.

6. **Select a volume and click OK.** That volume or folder appears on your desktop and in the Finder window Sidebar, where you can access it in order to share files.

When you're done working with the volume or folder, click the small Eject icon next to its listing in the Finder window Sidebar or select the volume on your desktop (if it appears there) and choose File ➪ Eject.

iChat

Aside from the log-on, log-off style of file sharing, iChat AV has become a popular way to share files with users who are at their computers, thanks to the iChat Bonjour feature. (Bonjour was called Rendezvous in Mac OS X 10.3, but the name was changed for Mac OS X 10.4 and later.) When you first launch iChat, you're asked if you want to use the Bonjour feature to locate other Macs on your network and alert you to the fact that another user on your network has iChat active. You can then chat with them, by double-clicking the user's name and starting a chat session.

> **Note** *If you have already configured iChat and Bonjour isn't active, you can activate it by choosing iChat ⇨ Preferences, and then clicking Accounts and selecting the Use Bonjour Instant Messaging option. You can then log on and off Bonjour by choosing iChat ⇨ Log in to Bonjour and iChat ⇨ Log out of Bonjour, respectively.*

There's more that you can do, however. While in a chat session, you can click and drag a file from the Finder to the text field and drop it there. An icon appears for that file, which you can send to the other user by pressing Return. When the remote user clicks on that file's icon, it's downloaded to his or her Mac.

Likewise, you can send a file with iChat without first chatting with your recipient. Simply click and drag a file from the Finder to the person's name in the Bonjour window and then drop the file icon on that person.

When you do, a dialog box appears asking if you want to send a file to that person; click Send (see figure 5.12). When the recipient clicks Save File, the file is downloaded to his or her Mac.

Sharing a printer

Mac OS X also offers an easy built-in ability to share a printer that's connected to your Mac through USB with other Macs on your network. First, make sure your printer is properly connected and configured in the Printer Setup Utility, which can be found in the Utilities folder of System Preferences. If you previously installed your printer, it should already be set up.

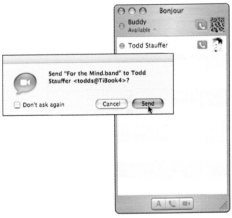

5.12 You can use iChat to share files between users.

Network Capabilities

If you have the option of adding network capabilities to your printer — such as through an add-on printer server component — it's usually a good idea. Sharing a printer is fine for low-volume printing, but in a workgroup situation, it's best to have a stand-alone printer that includes its own Ethernet or even wireless connection capabilities. That generally means that the print server has its own RAM and its own processor, and it won't slow down your computer the way that printer sharing will. It also means that the printer is available even when your Mac is shut down.

Printing to USB printers is covered in Chapter 6.

Now, to share the printer, open the Sharing pane of System Preferences and select the Printer Sharing option. That's all you have to do — any printers that are connected to your Mac can now be accessed by others on your LAN when they open the Print dialog box in any of their Mac OS X applications. As long as your Mac is up and running, they can print to those printers through your Mac, which serves as a printer server, spooling jobs and managing them as they are sent to the printer.

Internet Access for Your Network

If you want Internet access for your local network, you have two choices. You can connect one Mac to the Internet and then use Internet Sharing to distribute that access to other Macs; that's a handy stop-gap solution, but it may not work for day-to-day access, because it would require keeping that one Mac turned on and connected at all times.

What's more efficient is to get a special Internet router, which can be configured to connect to the Internet on its own and then distribute that access to all of the Macs (or other computers) that are connected to your Mac. That's what an AirPort base station does. For example — it routers its own Internet connection to wireless computers in the vicinity. Many third-party routers can do the same thing both for wired and wireless networks.

Routers cost just a few bucks in the computing superstores these days, so they're easy to add to networks where you want to

configure multiple computers to gain access to a broadband connection. In fact, many routers include four- or eight-port hubs/switches along with the router so that you can connect your entire network using one basic device.

You've already seen how to connect your computers to a hub or switch (wired or wireless) and how to use a DHCP server within a router to serve IP addresses to those machines. Serving Internet access to your LAN really isn't much different — you essentially just set up your router to connect to the Internet instead of one of your individual Macs. As long as your Macs are set up for DHCP services or configured manually with the correct Router address on the TCP/IP tab, the router can be accessed by your Macs to retrieve and send Internet data.

The first step, then, is to run an Ethernet cable from your router to the Internet connection provided by your ISP. If you have a broadband modem device of some sort, then you'll connect an Ethernet cable from the router's Uplink or WAN port to that modem (this is the port designed to connect your router to an outside network, as opposed to the hub or switch ports to which you can connect your Mac). If you have a direct cable connection for Internet service, plug that Ethernet cable directly into the Uplink or WAN port on your router.

 Most of the routers that you buy in the computer store are combination routers and hubs or switches. If the router you're working with doesn't have an integrated hub, then you'll want to connect another Ethernet cable from the router to the Uplink port on your switch or hub.

The next step is configuring that router to make the Internet connection. If your router is a third-party (non-Apple) model, then you'll likely configure it using a Web browser interface. Each router is different, so you'll need to consult your manual for the router, particularly to find out what the IP address is for the router and any passwords that are needed to get into the administrative screens.

Here are the basic steps:

1. **Make sure an Ethernet cable is connecting your Mac to the router.** You can restart your Mac, if you like, as that may cause it to retrieve an address from the DHCP server built into the router.

    Note *Restarting your Mac is the easier way to "reset" your Mac's Ethernet settings, but you can also do it another way: Open the Network pane of System Preferences, view your Built-in Ethernet settings and, on the TCP/IP tab, choose None from the Configure IPv4 menu. Click Apply Now and close the window. Then reopen the TCP/IP tab for Built-in Ethernet, choose Using DHCP from the Configure IPv4 menu, and then click Apply Now again.*

2. **Open a Web browser window and attempt to connect to the router by entering its IP address in the address bar and pressing Return.** If your Mac was set to Using DHCP and the router was, too, you might have automatically gotten a connection.

3. **Open the System Preferences application and click the Network icon.**

4. **In the Show menu, choose Built-in Ethernet, and then make sure the TCP/IP tab is selected.**

5. **Choose Manually from the Configure IPv4 menu.**

6. **In the IP Address entry box, type the address of the router but put a different final number, such as .2, at the end of the address instead of the router's last number.** If the router is 192.168.0.1, then set the IP Address to 192.168.0.2.

    Tip *You can press the Tab key to move from entry box to entry box.*

7. **For the Subnet Mask, type (or leave it set to) 255.255.255.0.**

8. **In the Router entry box, type the router's IP address, as given by its documentation.**

9. **Click Apply now.**

10. **Open a Web browser window and attempt to connect to the router's IP address.**

If you're successful, you'll probably be asked for a username and password — again, those are found in the router's documentation. Once you've entered those, you should see the interface that enables you to configure your router. You need to locate a section that governs the Internet connection — often it's listed as the WAN settings (for Wide Area Network). With my router, the next step is to choose the type of Internet connection that I have, as shown in figure 5.13.

If you have a cable modem or a direct Ethernet connection to your router from your ISP, then, at the point where you're selecting WAN or Internet Connection settings, you'll need to find an option that enables you to choose the address Dynamically or Using DHCP, so that the router can be assigned an IP address by your ISP.

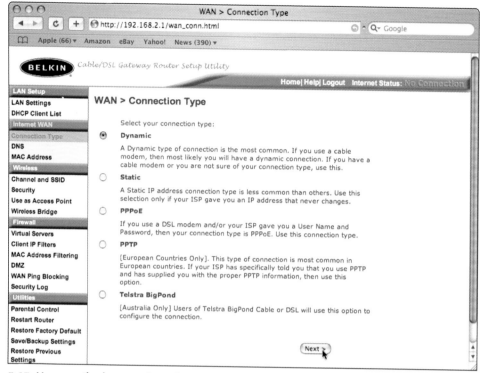

5.13 Here are the browser-based configuration options I have for my router's Internet connection.

If your Internet connection uses a fixed IP address (so that, for example, you can access your LAN from elsewhere over the Internet), then you many need to configure your settings Manually (or choose an option such as Static, depending on what your router calls it) to type those numbers yourself.

If you have a Digital Subscriber Line (DSL) modem or certain cable modems, you may need to configure your router so that it knows how to initiate a connection via PPPoE access. For PPPoE, you'll likely need to type a username and password for your access account (see figure 5.14).

Cross-Reference *Chapter 4 has more detail on setting up a PPPoE connection for your Mac; some of that same information can be used to set up your router for an Internet connection.*

Now, with the router configured to get Internet access, you may need to restart it. Once the router is restarted, if your Macs are configured to receive DHCP information from the router or to access it manually, then you can probably just begin surfing the Internet from your Mac — any connections that the router needs to make should happen automatically.

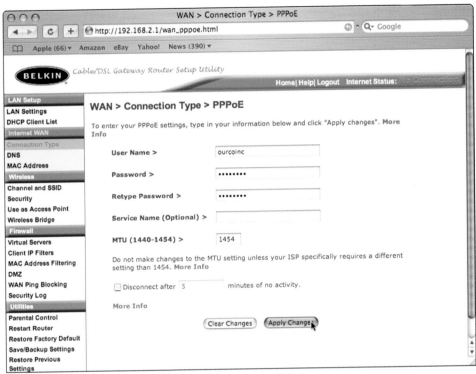

5.14 Typing PPPoE information so the router can connect to the Internet via DSL.

Use Multihoming to Your Advantage

Mac OS X includes support for a very handy networking feature called *multihoming*, which is the ability your Mac has to switch between network connection types automatically when needed. As useful as this capability is for the general Mac user, iBook and PowerBook users really find it handy because they tend to move their Macs around a lot.

Imagine a situation: There you are, hooked up to an Ethernet connection in your home office, but you decide that it's just too nice a day to sit inside and that you want to surf the Web out on the patio. So you disconnect the Ethernet cable and relocate to a chaise

lounge, open your portable, and load a page in your Web browser. OS X automatically detects that there is no Ethernet connection and opens an AirPort connection to let you continue working — all without any reconfiguration on your part (and if there's no AirPort connection, your laptop checks to see whether a modem connection can be made, and so on).

When you define a networking *location*), including the Automatic location provided by OS X, as part of that location definition, you can specify the Network Ports and their *priority* — meaning the order in which OS X checks for their availability. Taking maximum advantage of multihoming is simple: Make your most frequently used connection method the primary one, your next-most frequently used the secondary one, and so on, and disable any methods you don't employ so that your Mac doesn't waste time attempting to find a connection where none is available.

Cross-Reference *For more information about creating a network location, see Chapter 4.*

To specify the ports to be accessed and their priority, proceed as follows:

1. **Choose Location ⇨ Network Preferences from the Apple menu.** The Network pane appears.

2. **Choose your Location from the Location pop-up menu.** By default the location is set to Automatic, but if you created

others in Chapter 4, you'll see them here.

3. **Choose Network Port Configurations from the Show pop-up menu.** The Network Preferences pane redraws as shown in figure 5.15.

4. **Select the Port Configurations you want OS X to check, and deselect the checkboxes for the connection types you don't want checked.**

5. **Click and drag the Port Configuration entries up or down in the list to place them in the order you want.** Your first choice should be at the top of the list, last at the bottom.

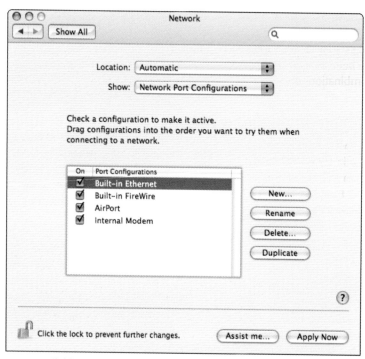

5.15 Available ports and their initial priorities appear when you choose Network Port Configurations from the Show pop-up menu.

A Bit More about Ports

If you don't want a particular port to be in the list, you can select it and click Delete. I tend to just turn the port off by deselecting its checkbox instead of actually deleting it. After all, I might be at a friend's or client's location and have need of that particular port type, and it's easier to turn it back on than have to add it back into the list. Ports are added automatically when they're recognized by your Mac; if you have a port that you've previously deleted and need to re-create, click the Add button and, in the New Port dialog sheet that appears, type a name for the port and choose the port that you're restoring from the Port menu.

Managing Your Firewall and Network Security

When you chose to purchase a portable computer running Mac OS X, avoiding the hassles such as spyware and the multiplicity of viruses and other malicious code that you hear about being a part of a Windows user's everyday life might have been a factor in your decision. There's a combination of factors that keep Mac OS X more secure from such attacks. In addition to the fact that there are just many more Windows machines out there, Mac OS X is built on a foundation of FreeBSD and many Unix-style technologies, and the Unix community (along with Apple's staff developers) tends to be comprised of security-conscious developers who

constantly test that underlying code vigorously. Also, Mac OS X has a built-in firewall that's designed to thwart many of the attacks that could come over an Internet connection.

 Note *While the Mac OS X internal firewall is nice for day-to-day surfing, it's no substitute for a hardware-based firewall that might be included with your Internet router. You should dig into that device's documentation and settings to learn how to take advantage of any special features that help keep you protected when you connect in your home or office.*

As shipped, your Mac OS X-equipped Mac is protected against attacks over both private and public networks. All the sharing services, such as Windows File Sharing, Personal File Sharing, remote login, FTP, Web sharing,

Internet Ports

When I talk about ports in this sense, I don't mean the physical ports on your Mac, but something called a "port" that is part of the Internet addressing scheme. For example, if your Mac's IP address is 192.168.0.5, then certain services that your Mac offers, such as Web serving, would be specified by a particular port address, such as port 80 (which is the common one for HTTP Web servers). So, your full address in that case might be http://192.168.0.5:80/ — Web browsers and servers know this automatically. So, for additional security, your Mac makes sure it opens only the ports it needs for accepted data from outside computers, while closing any ports that aren't active.

You can use these advanced firewall settings to further refine the security of your computer.

☐ Block UDP Traffic

Prevents UDP communications from accessing resources on your computer.

☐ Enable Firewall Logging

Provides information about firewall activity, such as blocked sources, blocked destinations, and blocked attempts.

(Open Log...)

☐ Enable Stealth Mode

Ensures that any uninvited traffic receives no response — not even an acknowledgement that your computer exists.

(?)   (Cancel)   (OK)

5.16 Become virtually undetectable in stealth mode.

and Printer Sharing are initially turned off — but they're easy to turn on if you want them on. The OS X firewall monitors all incoming network traffic, allowing only those connection types that you authorize to pass data to applications on your Mac, and only on the network ports that you've authorized.

In Mac OS X 10.4, a new feature enables your Mac's firewall to operate in *stealth mode*, not even acknowledging that your Mac exists if the connection attempt is outside the permitted set, as shown in figure 5.16.

Turning on services

Your control center for network security is located in the Sharing pane of System Preferences. That's where you specify which services you want to allow (via the Services tab), what traffic you want the Firewall to allow through (via the Firewall tab), and whether you want to share your Internet connection with other Macs on your network (Internet tab). I focus on those first two tabs, shown in figure 5.17.

Note

Making your Mac accessible from other computers can open it to attack, particularly if your Mac has a direct connection to the Internet at the same time that you have services such as Personal File Sharing activated. Because this is a system-wide security issue, Administrator access is required to turn Services on or off and to manage the OS X Firewall. Throughout the following discussions, remember that you have to unlock the padlock icon at the bottom of the Sharing pane to make the changes.

As with most things in this high-tech world of ours, there are tradeoffs between functionality and security when you enable network services. The cost of enabling a service can be relatively innocuous; for example, if you activate Personal Web Sharing on your Mac and others find you on the Internet, your own surfing and other tasks may be slightly impaired, particularly if the Web pages that are served from your Mac become popular.

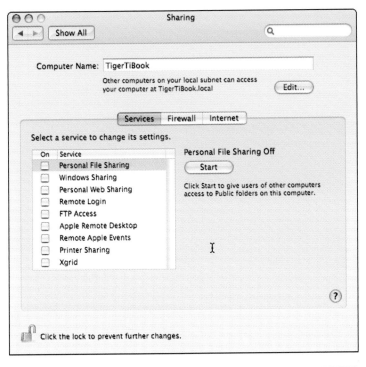

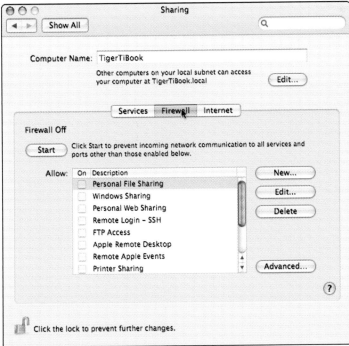

5.17 The Services (top) and Firewall (bottom) tabs combine to let you control your network security level.

That tradeoff could also be more significant to your day-to-day computing. For example, enabling File Sharing or Remote Login could allow others to use both your Mac's hard drive and CPU for their own purposes, impacting both your computer's perform-ance and the amount of disk space available to you for your own activities. And that's assuming that your users are authorized users on your LAN.

To activate a network service, proceed as follows:

1. **Launch System Preferences (by clicking its Dock icon, double-clicking its Finder icon, or any of the multitude of other methods OS X provides).** The System Preferences window appears.

2. **Click the Sharing icon.** The Sharing pane appears.

3. **Click the Services tab (see figure 5.17) if it isn't selected.**

4. **Click the On checkbox next to a service you want to start.** You can also start a service by selecting its name in the list and clicking Start.

To disable a network service, deselect its On checkbox or select it and click Stop.

Tip   *If you need to enable the more expensive (in terms of CPU, disk, and network bandwidth) services, such as Apple Remote Desktop, FTP Access, Remote Login, and Xgrid, you should disable them when their avail-ability is not necessary. In other words, don't just leave them on all the time unless you're in a closed network environment (no outside access) with only trusted users.*

Managing ports with the firewall

Restricting access to individual ports is the job of a firewall. Traditionally, firewalls have been either a stand-alone piece of hardware or built into a router. Mac OS X's software firewall, then, might seem superfluous if you already have firewall capabilities built in to your router or other connection hard-ware. But the truth is that life with a Mac portable is more complicated than that. When you're behind your router's firewall, you should be relatively safe. When you connect to the Internet through a direct con-nection to your broadband modem, then you introduce another level of security risk; sign on to the Internet at your local café, and you really open yourself up. That's when it's great to have a built-in firewall. And, it is also important to remember to turn off net-working services that you're not using.

Here's how to turn on the firewall.

1. **Launch System Preferences.** The System Preferences window appears.

2. **Click the Sharing icon.** The Sharing pane appears.

3. **Click the Firewall tab.** The firewall options appear (see figure 5.18).

4. **Click Start.** If you see a Stop but-ton, it means that the firewall is already running.

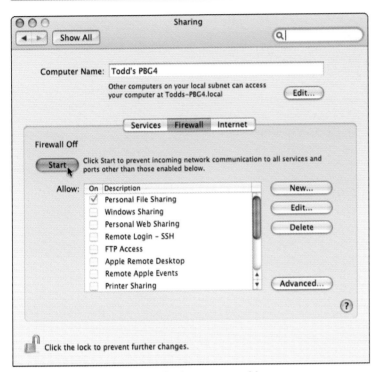

5.18 The Firewall tab in the Sharing pane enables you to manage your firewall.

When you activate the OS X Firewall, only communication using authorized ports is allowed to get past the firewall; all other incoming data is blocked. For example, Personal File Sharing uses ports 427 and 548 by default, so if you enable Personal File Sharing, communication on those two ports passes through. If Personal File Sharing is turned off and the firewall is turned on, then communication on those two ports is blocked. Similarly, Personal Web Sharing uses ports 80, 427, and 443. When you turn off Web Sharing, those ports are closed by the firewall.

Tip

It's worth saying that turning off a service, thanks to the firewall, is the best way to secure against unauthorized entry to your Mac, especially from an exposed connection like a wireless Internet drop in a coffee shop or a hotel. When you hit the road, make a point of turning off File Sharing, Web Sharing, and other services that you're very unlikely to make good use of outside a home or office environment. That just buttons your Mac up a little better from a security point of view.

Some ports, however, aren't managed automatically, and these can be turned on and off manually on the Firewall tab of the Sharing pane. They include ports like iChat Bonjour, iTunes Music Sharing, and others. If they are checked in the list of ports on the Firewall tab, that means those ports are open and will accept traffic; if you don't like that idea, make sure to deselect their checkboxes. If you do close any ports, however, remember that you've done so — if you fire up iChat or iTunes and get a dialog box complaining about the blocked ports, you'll know why.

If you install a new application that needs to have its own port entries in the firewall, you can add a new item; just click the New button. When you do, a dialog sheet appears (see figure 5.19), enabling you to choose the type of service that you're configuring

the firewall to manage and the port numbers that need to be opened up when using this service.

Finally, if you click the Firewall pane's Advanced button, the sheet shown in figure 5.20 appears. As you'll see when you visit the dialog sheet, the options are fairly well explained but are definitely worth understanding if you'd like to use the firewall to the greatest extent possible for online security.

✦ **Block UDP Traffic.** This prevents UDP communications such as network-wide broadcasts from making it through to your Mac. If you have trouble with Internet gaming, Webcasts, or streaming audio, check this setting to make sure it's not active.

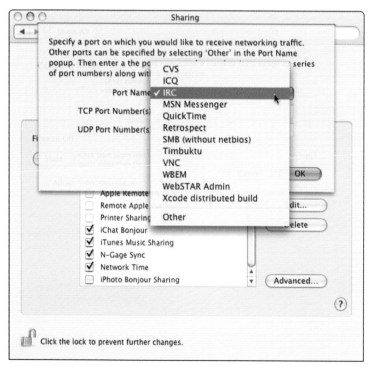

5.19 Specify additional services and, if necessary, different TCP and UDP port numbers on this sheet (consult the application you're installing for details).

UDP

UDP (User Datagram Protocol) is, like the TCP we're familiar with, a communications protocol sitting atop IP. Unlike TCP, though, UDP doesn't require a connection or perform error recovery — things that TCP does in order to ensure that data meant to arrive over the Internet does arrive. Because of this, UDP is much faster, but it is unsuitable for applications requiring data integrity, such as Web browsing (you want the text to be accurate). UDP is often used for network broadcasting and streaming audio and video applications where speed is more important than precision.

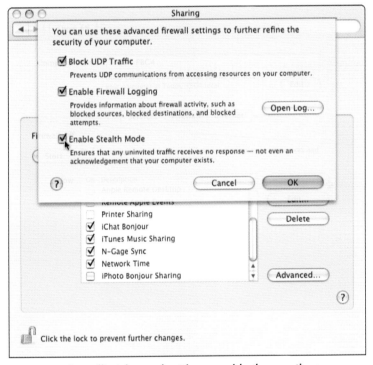

5.20 Your Firewall's Advanced settings provide three options.

✦ **Enable Firewall Logging.** This is primarily a diagnostic tool that allows you (or a network guru) to investigate what attempts were made to breach your firewall's barriers. Click Open Log to see what's been recorded if you've selected this option.

✦ **Enable Stealth Mode.** This is a new feature in Mac OS X 10.4 that guarantees no acknowledgment is bounced back to any computer trying to incorrectly access your computer. If you are pinged or port scanned by a computer that reaches a port that isn't turned on, then the lack of a response will usually suggest to the scanner that there's no computer here, meaning further investigation won't be prompted. (Port scans are sometimes used to find open service ports, which might then be exploited by a hacker or in an automated way by malicious code.

Note

*Aside from the Enable Firewall Logging option, the built-in firewall in Mac OS X doesn't really offer a lot of feedback. If you want to take a more active role in your own Internet security, you might look into a firewall application such as Firewalk X2 (*www.pliris-soft.com*) or the commercial offerings by Symantec, Intego, and others. With those, you can set them up to alert you when nefarious activity is detected, and they tend to be able to monitor outgoing traffic and generally snoop around your network connections.*

Tips and Techniques for a Better Portable Mac Experience

You're using a portable Macintosh for a reason. That reason isn't price — laptops cost a little more than equivalent desktop Macs. It isn't power, either — the iBook and PowerBook both have slower processors than the top-end Mac desktop models. What iBooks and PowerBooks offer are convenience, flexibility, and portability in a package that happens to also offer a mix of price and performance making that portability rather attractive.

Consider the difficulties involved in hauling even as small a desktop unit such as the Mac mini into a conference room or onto a plane to work while flying. Where do you plug it in? How do you juggle the separate keyboard, mouse, and monitor, as well as all the cables connecting them? Of course, it's an impractical idea to say the least.

Apple's designers and engineers have won many awards and other accolades for their laptop designs and implementations. In this chapter, I clue you in on ways to really leverage the power of that key advantage — portability — while digging deeper into portable features and add-ons that you'll want to integrate into daily life with your iBook or PowerBook.

Using Your Portable Mac As an Assistant

Apple provides a number of very capable applications with every copy of OS X, designed to make your Mac the center of your digital life, such as iCal and Address Book. These two little digital gems not only maintain and present your schedule, to-do lists, and contact information, but they talk to each other and to other programs on your Mac (in particular, Mail). As discussed later, you can also synchronize them to your iPod, a .Mac account, a PDA, or (for the Address Book) a cell phone. You can say goodbye to your day planner and rolodex and move into the twenty first century of time and contact management.

iCal: Appointments and reminders

Appointment calendars and to-do lists are two byproducts of a busy life (or a bad memory), and they're two items that iCal can make into truly helpful and minimally intrusive aids for your busy life. For many folks, iCal is almost shocking in both its simplicity and power.

Figure 6.1 illustrates the window you see the first time you open iCal. The pane in the upper left lists your calendars (iCal starts you off with two: Home and Work). The lower-left pane presents a quick glimpse of the current month (called the *mini-month*), along with navigational buttons that allow you to step back and forth by a month at a time, so that you can select the time period you want to view or edit. (You can also choose View ⇨ Go To Date to go to a specific date in the past or future.) The bulk of the window contains a week of calendar data, but you can switch that to be one day or one month by clicking the Day, Week, or Month button below the calendar presentation. The drawer displays information about the currently selected calendar event and can be hidden by clicking the rightmost button at the bottom of the window (the one with the little *i* in a blue circle).

6.1 Welcome to iCal.

Note *You can hide or show the mini-month by clicking the center button of the left-hand group of three buttons that are below the mini-month calendar. You can also drag the bar above the mini-month upward to reveal more months at once. Alternatively, you can display a Notifications pane in its place by clicking the Hide/Show Notifications button, which looks a little like an arrow and an "in box" that would sit on your desk.*

If you have tasks to perform that don't have a scheduled time, you can create a to-do list to track them. Just click the list button that is third from the left at the bottom of the iCal window. When you do so, the calendar area compresses a bit to make room for the To Do list pane, as shown in figure 6.2.

Double-click in the To Do list's white area and a new item appears, as shown in figure 6.3, or choose File ⇨ New To Do (⌘+K). Type

a name for the new item and press Enter/Return. The Info drawer (see figure 6.4) displays the information for a selected To Do item, including a completed checkbox; a priority pop-up menu; a due date checkbox that, when selected, has an editable date to its right; an alarm pop-up menu from which you can choose an action to be performed; a calendar pop-up menu from which you can choose a calendar with which the To Do item should be associated; a URL field in which you can type the URL for an associated Web page or e-mail address; and a Notes field in which you can add descriptive information.

Note *There's a very faint button at the right of each To Do item that, when clicked, displays a pop-up menu from which you can choose a priority if you don't have the Info drawer open. You can also click the completed checkbox without opening the Info drawer.*

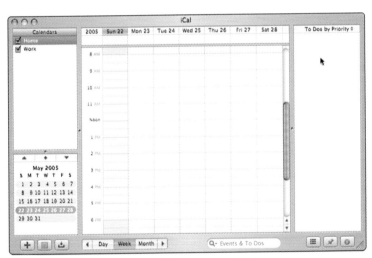

6.2 Keep a To Do list along with your scheduled events.

6.3 Double-clicking in the white space creates a new To Do item.

Scheduled activities have defined start and end times or defined durations in terms of days and are called *events* by iCal. An example of the former would be a doctor's appointment and an example of the latter would be a holiday, such as Memorial Day (last Monday in May in the United States).

To create an event is simplicity itself. Just select the calendar to which you want the event to belong, click the day on which you want it to occur in the mini-month display, and choose File ➪ New Event (⌘+N). Then in the Info drawer, supply the information defining the event, including:

✦ **Name:** whatever you want to call the event.

✦ **Location:** denotes the venue.

✦ **all-day:** a checkbox indicating that the event runs throughout the day.

✦ **from** and **to:** starting and ending dates and times of the event. (An event could be all-day for multiple days, for example.)

✦ **repeat:** a pop-up menu that allows you to define an event as recurring, in which case iCal places it on the schedule for all the dates specified.

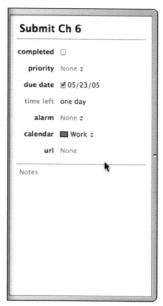

6.4 To Do items have various associated fields.

✦ **attendees:** a list of other participants.

✦ **calendar:** a pop-up menu where you indicate the calendar in which the event should be recorded.

✦ **alarm:** a pop-up menu where you can specify what sort of a reminder should be used (and when), such as an e-mail, a beep, or a notification alert.

Tip *The alarm can also launch AppleScripts or open files, and alarms can go off whether or not iCal is running, which makes iCal (among other things) a very effective automatic scheduling application. For instance, you could set iCal to run a backup application or a script that automatically logs your Mac onto a central computer and downloads important data. In other words, iCal can be about much more than appointments and ToDo lists.*

✦ **url:** a text field in which you can specify a URL related to the event.

✦ **Notes:** a text field in which you can place descriptive information, such as an agenda.

Caution *When you specify attendees, iCal interfaces with your Address Book. This integration provides the basis for iCal to send invitations through the Mail application to your attendee list (see the Send button at the bottom of figure 6.5). How-ever, if an attendee is not in your Address Book or is in the Address Book but lacks an e-mail address, you must specify an e-mail address as part of the entry or the name disappears from the attendee list when you exit the field.*

When you specify a noncustom, repeating event, you must indicate when you want the repetition to stop. Never is one of the choices, or you can specify a termination date or number of occurrences. A custom repeating event, on the other hand, presents the palette shown in figure 6.6, where you can specify the frequency of recurrence: for example, every third month on the second Thursday of the month.

For many people, the Home and Work calendars may be all they'll need. But you may have many other topic headings under which your obligations fall, such as kids' after-school events, sporting events, and so on. To meet this need, iCal provides the capability to add as many calendars as you need or think you need. You can either click the plus (+) button at the bottom left of the iCal window or choose File ⇨ New Calendar (Option+⌘+N). Give the calendar a meaningful name and associate a color with it — when you run out of the predefined colors, you can choose Other and select any color you desire from the standard Color Picker.

And, if your own calendars prove inadequate to satiate your calendar-related cravings or you want to give others access to your schedule, iCal lets you publish your calendar or subscribe to the calendars published by others.

Tip *In addition to published personal or business-related calendars, you can find a broad variety of calendars in such genres as holidays, sports schedules, TV or movie schedules, concert series, and so forth. Two really good places to start your search are* www.icalshare.com *and* www.apple.com/ical/library.

Status Conference
iChat

all-day ☐
from 05/26/05 at 9:00 AM
to 05/26/05 at 10:00 AM

repeat None ⧨

attendees Dennis R. Cohen
Todd Stauffer
Michael Roney

calendar ▧ Work ⧨

alarm None ⧨

url None

Notes

To send invitations, click Send (Send)

6.5 Invite your attendees to the event by clicking Send.

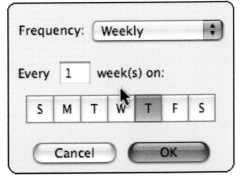

6.6 Use this palette to define custom event repetitions.

To publish a calendar, you must have access to a WebDAV Internet server. A .Mac account fills that requirement. There are others, however, even such free servers as iCal Exchange (www.icalx.com), but you still must create an account at those sites. With an active Internet connection, simply select the calendar and choose Calendar ➪ Publish.

| Note | WebDAV is a special type of Web server that allows the Web documents to be edited directly using certain applications, as opposed to requiring you to log into an FTP server and upload documents on the "back end" of the Web server computer. |

In the sheet that appears, you can choose .Mac or a Private Server from the Publish on

pop-up menu, as shown in figure 6.7. Here's what each does:

✦ **.Mac.** If you choose .Mac, then you can give the calendar a name (if you'd like it to be something other than the default) and make some choices about what items are published and whether changes are published automatically. (.Mac knows where to publish your calendar based on your entry in the .Mac pane of System Preferences. If you have a .Mac account, the username and password for that account should be stored in the .Mac pane.)

✦ **a Private Server.** If you plan to publish your calendar to a private server instead of the .Mac service,

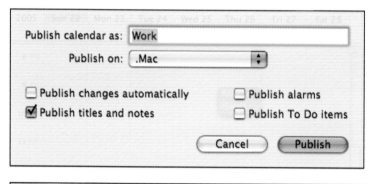

6.7 Choosing to publish on .Mac displays the top sheet and choosing a non-.Mac WebDAV server expands the sheet as seen at the bottom.

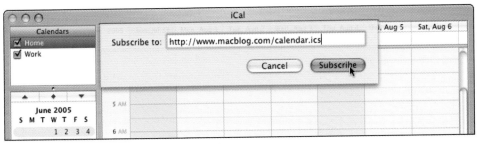

6.8 Tell iCal where to find the calendar you want.

then you'll need to enter the Base URL for the location where you'd like the calendar to be published on your WebDAV server (something like `http://www.macblog.com/calendars/`) and the Login (username) and Password for an account that can access that WebDAV server. You can then make the same choices about what to publish and whether to publish changes automatically.

Click Publish and iCal uploads your calendar to the location you've specified in the Publish on field.

Subscribing to a calendar is even easier than publishing one, assuming you know where the calendar is located. Proceed as follows:

1. **Choose Calendar ➪ Subscribe (Option+⌘+S).** The sheet shown in figure 6.8 appears.

2. **Type the URL of the calendar to which you want to subscribe.** iCal connects to the site and a new sheet, shown in figure 6.9, appears.

3. **Give the calendar a title (or keep the suggestion), and specify the options you desire for this calendar.**

6.9 Tell iCal whether and how frequently you want the calendar refreshed, and whether to keep or discard alarms and To Do items.

4. **Click OK.** The calendar appears in your Calendars list with a small curving arrow to the far right, as shown in figure 6.10, indicating that this is a subscription rather than a local calendar.

6.10 Subscribed calendars are indicated by a curving arrow on the right.

The ability to compartmentalize or consolidate your calendars at will and the connectivity available due to publication and subscription are big pluses in making your electronic calendar, iCal, a lot more useful than paper calendars. But the best is yet to come. Being electronic makes searching for information easy and instantaneous. OS X's ubiquitous Search box is present at the bottom of your iCal window, and it packs a lot of power. Click on the magnifying glass pop-up menu at the left of the Search box to restrict your search to any of the categories offered, as shown in figure 6.11.

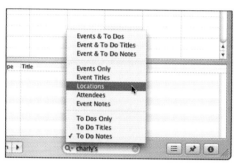

6.11 Restrict your searches to any of these categories.

Just start typing in the Search box and iCal begins displaying everything that matches what you type. Continue typing and the results list continues to refine, as shown in figure 6.12. When you see the item you seek in the results list, double-click it and iCal displays the date in question with the event selected.

As time passes and you continue to use iCal, its database grows. By default, iCal retains all data not explicitly deleted. Preserving the data provides a handy audit trail when your boss or significant other asks, "Just when did you meet with Joe Blow?" Some people, possibly including you, will find the audit trail unnecessary and the burgeoning size of your iCal data-base annoying. iCal includes two handy options in its Advanced Preferences (iCal ➪ Preferences), shown in figure 6.13: Delete events ____ days after they have passed and Delete To Do items ____ days after they are completed. Select the options and type the amount of time you want data retained. Henceforth, iCal trims your database of old entries.

You'll see a few other interesting options on the Advanced tab of iCal Preferences, including options that enable you to selectively hide To Do items when they are outside the displayed calendar's timeframe, and you can choose when and how To Do items are hidden once they've been completed.

Also on the Advanced tab of Preferences is the option Turn on Time Zone support, which adds a new menu to the iCal window, in the top right, where you can choose your current time zone. If you travel a lot, this can be a great option, because it allows you to instantly see your calendar in terms of the current time zone. (This does mean, however, that you need to schedule meetings in different time zones according to your current time zone; if you have a 7 a.m. Tuesday meeting in Los Angeles and you're setting your schedule while you're still at home in Chicago when you enter it into iCal, you need to set it for 9 a.m. Tuesday. Then, when you get to L.A., switch iCal to US/Pacific time and your appointments will automatically move themselves back two hours to reflect local time.

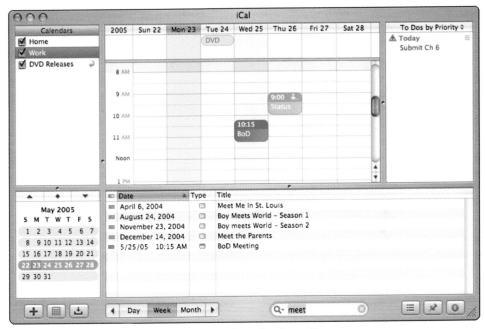

6.12 This shows all event titles containing the string "meet."

Even though your laptop is convenient and portable, there are occasions when paper is more useful. iCal provides a plethora of printing options, as illustrated by the Print dialog box shown in figure 6.14. To print all sorts of calendars from iCal, all you have to do is choose

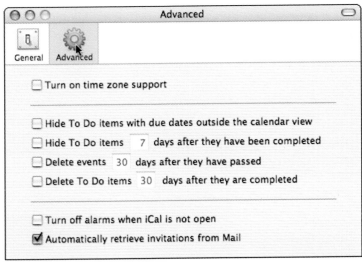

6.13 iCal's Advanced Preferences allow you to set two automatic pruning options.

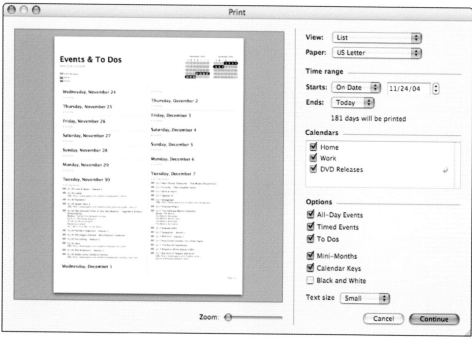

6.14 iCal sports a flexible and convenient Print dialog box.

File➪Print. With its handy, built-in preview pane, you can fine-tune your printing options and parameters located on the right side of the dialog box. You can even zoom in on the preview to check details. Unfortunately, you can only see the first page of the preview.

You'll need to experiment with the Print dialog box to get the full power of it, but you can start with the View menu, which lets you set how much detail you want to see per page (Day, Week, Month) and then choose a paper size from the Paper menu. Then use the Time Range to determine how many pages of calendars you want, and use the Calendars section to choose which calendar topics you want to print. Finally, in the Options section, you can determine what will appear on your calendar page — and what won't. (Click to place or remove checkmarks to determine which items will appear on the page.)

When you've made all your choices, click Continue and you'll then see the standard Print dialog box that enables you to send those calendar pages to your printer.

Address Book and vCards

Address Book is the central nexus for all contact and contact-related information on your Mac. Phone numbers, street addresses, e-mail addresses, iChat contact information, birthdays, FAX numbers, URLs, and more repose in an Address Book record and can be accessed by you or appropriate software applications. For example, iChat uses Address Book to find instant messaging addresses, and Mail retrieves e-mail addresses.

Contact information is entered and presented via a card metaphor. But the cards are of varying size and can even include a photo or other image. Figure 6.15 shows a typical Address Book card (for a fictional individual).

As you can see in figure 6.15, the default presentation includes three columns, as follows:

✦ **Group:** This column lists groups of cards. There are two default groups: All, which includes all the cards, and Directories, which provides access to any network (LDAP) directories to which you have access.

✦ **Name:** This column lists the names of the contacts in the group selected in the first column.

✦ The third, unnamed column displays the card for the individual selected in the Name column. If more than one name is selected, the first name (alphabetically) has its card on display.

Tip   *You can toggle whether the Group and Name columns are displayed by choosing View ⇨ Card Only (⌘+2) and View ⇨ Card and Columns (⌘+1).*

Initially, your Address Book will consist of only two cards, one for you that is created when your account is created and one for Apple Computer.

An Address Book would be almost useless if there were no way to add contacts to it. You can create a new card by choosing File ⇨ New Card (⌘+N) or by clicking the plus (+) button at the bottom of the Name column. In either case, you are presented with a new card primed for data entry, as shown in figure 6.16.

For each field in which you want to enter data, either press Tab to move to it or click in it and type the information. Fields are

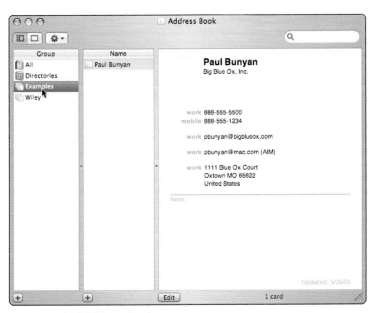

6.15 A typical Address Book entry.

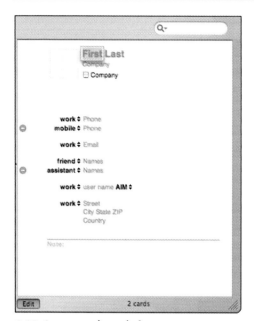

6.16 A new card, ready for you to enter data.

grouped by type. Name and company information appear at the top. Proceeding down you find phone numbers; e-mail addresses; names of friends, family, and associates; instant messaging IDs; and then postal addresses. A free-form Notes field appears at the bottom of the card. If there's a second (or greater) instance of a field you don't want included, click the red minus (–) sign in the left margin to remove it from the data entry form. Each of the bold field labels is a pop-up menu, as indicated by the arrowhead pair that follows the label, so you can change work to home, or vice versa, without having to add subsequent instances of a field type (when the last field of a given type is populated with data, a green plus (+) sign will appear in the left margin so that you might create additional instances of that field type). If there is a field, such as Birthday, that you want to add to a card, you can choose Card ⇨ Add Field.

Note *The fields that appear in your default card are defined in your Address Book Preferences on the Template pane. You can choose Card ⇨ Add Field ⇨ Edit Template or choose Address Book ⇨ Preferences (⌘+,) and click the Template icon to edit the template. Add or delete instances or additional field types using the + and – buttons and the Add Field pop-up menu.*

Tip *There are times when you will want to have a company entry that is not related to any individual in your Address Book. The Apple Computer card is an example of such an entry. In that case, select the Company option, type a company name, and leave the First and Last name fields empty. You can also toggle whether a card should sort by the company name or the individual's name by selecting the card and choosing Card ⇨ This is a Company (⌘+\).*

Deleting a card is simple. If you want to remove a card from your Address Book, select it and choose Edit ⇨ Delete Card.

As with almost every other core Tiger application, Address Book leverages the power of Spotlight. Just type any identifying sequence of characters into the Search box at the upper right of the Address Book window and Address Book will winnow the matches, on the fly, as you continue typing and refining your search string.

Having a set list of recipients for your e-mail is common. For example, you might serve on your homeowner association's board of directors and need to send information to the other members of the board on a regular basis. You could, obviously, manually add these recipients to each e-mail you send to the group, but this would be a wasteful expenditure of both time and effort, and be subject to error. Address Book lets you create *groups*, which are collections of cards that bear some defined relation to each other, even if it is only obvious to you (such as the previous example). Now, you can tell Mail (or your other Address Book-aware mail application) to send the mail to the group and it creates the list of individual recipients. To create a new group, click the plus (+) button at the bottom of the Group column or choose File⇨New Group (Shift+⌘+N). Then drag the names from the Names list to the new group's entry in the Group column.

In keeping with Finder Smart Folders, iTunes Smart Playlists, and iPhoto Smart Albums, Address Book offers Smart Groups. Smart Groups are groups that dynamically define membership based upon criteria you select. To define a new Smart Group, choose File⇨New Smart Group (Option+⌘+N) or press the plus (+) button at the bottom of the Group column while pressing Option (the + changes to a cog icon). A sheet appears, as shown in figure 6.17, in which you name the group and specify the criteria defining group membership.

Another Address Book feature is something that most of us take for granted—printing. Address Book doesn't just print pages of text lists, it also prints labels, envelopes, and pocket address books. Figures 6.18, 6.19, 6.20, and 6.21 show the Address Book Print dialog box with the Style menu set to Envelopes, Mailing Labels, Lists, and Pocket

Address Book, respectively. You can specify which attributes (fields) to include in the printout for Lists and Pocket Address Books.

Address Book comes programmed with a wide variety of envelope sizes and styles—International, North American, and Japanese. Additionally, you can define and save your own custom layouts.

When it comes to mailing labels, Address Book comes with a database of Avery Standard (U.S.) and Avery A4 as well as DYMO label sheet layouts. You can also define and save Custom layouts in addition to those provided.

Two-column lists suitable for inclusion in a loose-leaf notebook are also available.

You can print either an indexed or compact-format pocket address book, fitting up to six pages on a single 8½-x-11-inch sheet of paper. Choose Indexed from the Flip Style pop-up menu to produce pages of varying widths as indicated by the image in the Print dialog box's Preview pane.

.Mac and syncing

While not a universal truth, it is a fairly common state of affairs for a laptop warrior to also own and use one or more desktop systems (or even have more than one laptop). A .Mac account and Tiger's .Mac syncing feature make keeping your contact list, calendars, Safari bookmarks, Mail accounts, rules,

6.17 Define a Smart Group's criteria in this sheet.

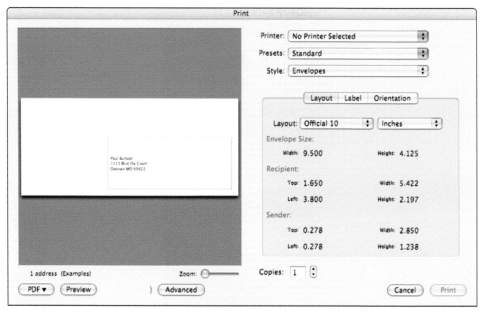

6.18 You can use Address Book to print envelopes.

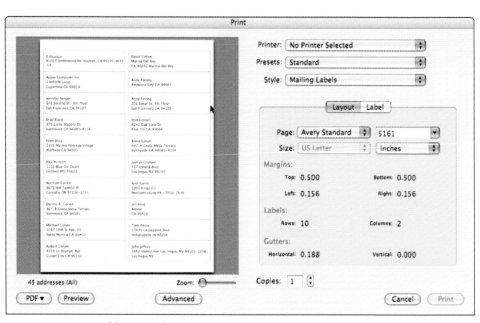

6.19 You can use Address Book to print Avery, DYMO, and Custom labels.

6.20 You can set up Address Book to print basic lists.

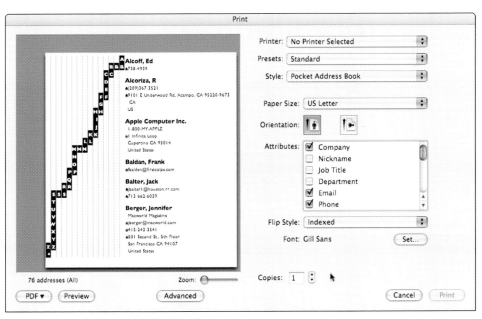

6.21 You can also use Address Book to print pocket address books.

signatures, and Smart Mailboxes, and even your passwords in synchronization regardless of which Mac you're currently using.

The .Mac System Preferences pane's Sync tab, shown in figure 6.22, provides centralized access to synchronizing these disparate but convenient settings and information repositories.

You can tell your System Preferences to synchronize in several ways. Choose from these options in the Synchronize with .Mac menu:

✦ **Automatically.** This causes an update whenever you connect to the Internet, and data changes in an application you set up for synchronization.

Note *If you choose to sync automatically, a synchronization action takes place hourly so long as you have an Internet connection. This allows your Mac to acquire updated information from the .Mac repository that might have been placed there by another Mac.*

✦ **Every Hour**, **Every Day**, or **Every Week.** This invokes a synchronization on the schedule specified. If

you aren't connected at a scheduled time, .Mac will skip synchronization and wait for the next scheduled time.

✦ **Manually.** This leaves synchronization activities under your direct control.

 Tip *Select the Show status in menu bar option to create a Sync menu on the right side of your menu bar. This will save you a trip to System Preferences when you want to synchronize information.*

iSync and PDAs or phones

If you've got a PDA, mobile phone, or similar device that you carry around with you for notes, contacts, and appointments, then there's probably an excellent chance that you want to be able to use that device with iCal and Address Book. That's exactly what iSync is designed to do — it enables you to create and manage connections from your Mac to your other information devices. Once that connection is in place, you can reconnect and synchronize data between iCal and Address Book on your Mac and anything that you add or change on your external Personal Information Management (PIM) device, as long as it's compatible with your Mac.

Determining compatibility

Compatibility is the first thing you need to consider when you want to synchronize your Mac and a PDA or a mobile phone. Most Palm OS-based devices can be synchronized with your Mac if you have the correct USB-style cabling, but it can take some special setup to make a Palm OS PDA work, including some setup from within the Palm Desktop software.

6.22 Synchronize your data and settings with a .Mac account.

Note The instructions for configuring iSync and Palm OS devices to synchronize data can be a little involved. The best way to track them down is to launch iSync (found in the main Applications folder) and choose Help ⇨ iSync Help. In the Help Viewer's search box, type **Palm OS Sync** and press Return. You should see a help article that will walk you through the process of setting up your Palm OS device to sync with iCal and Address Book using iSync.

6.23 PocketMac, once installed, enables you to use iSync with your PocketPC device.

Another popular type of PDA is a Windows-based PocketPC PDA (in actuality most of these run a version of Windows called Windows Mobile). These can't be simply connected to a Mac and synchronized — instead, you need a third-party application to do a little translating. Two popular options that work in conjunction with iSync are The Missing Sync for PocketPC by MarkSpace (www.markspace.com) or PocketMac (www.pocketmac.net) shown in figure 6.23. Both offer the ability to synchronize appointments and contacts between your Mac and iSync, meaning you can use iCal and Address Book on your Mac and still update the PocketPC address book and calendar applications. Likewise, these third-party offerings tend to go above and beyond iCal and Address Book, offer synchronization for e-mail, Microsoft Office applications (such as Entourage and/or Word and Excel), and have the ability to work with photos and multimedia files on each platform.

Other devices that require third-party applications for synchronizing include popular platforms such as Blackberry wireless devices and the T-Mobile Sidekick (also called the HipTop). In the case of the Sidekick, you actually end up synchronizing your data not directly over a cable, but rather using the online service that's included with

your Sidekick — the software uses the over-the-air update features of the Sidekick to receive your addresses and appointments.

As for mobile phones, Apple lists a number of compatible phones and phone manufacturers on its Web site (www.apple.com/isync) that are directly compatible with iSync. Generally speaking, many Motorola and Nokia phones are compatible with iSync, as are many Sony Ericsson phones. Apple lists fewer Panasonic and LG model phones, although some of them may work with third-party software.

Getting connected

Once a PDA or phone is either deemed compatible with iSync or made compatible with iSync via a third-party solution, you're ready to connect to iSync and synchronize your data. How you go about doing that depends on the technology you use to connect.

If your device connects to your Mac with a USB cable that's included with the device (or that's designed specifically for it, even if you had to buy the cable separately), then getting connected may just be a case of attaching the cable to the device and then attaching that cable to your Mac. If your device is recognized, you may see a message in the Finder telling you that a new USB peripheral has been connected.

The real key, though, is in the iSync application. Launch it from the Applications folder on your Mac, and see if your device is recognized at the top of the window; if you see it there, iSync should be ready to work with the device that you plugged in. If you don't see the device, then you may need to choose Device ➪ Add Device and then see if iSync is able to locate the device. If it can't locate the device, you check your connections and cables and make sure that the device has power.

If you have a device that connects with Bluetooth wireless, then you may have to take some extra steps.

1. **Turn on the device and ensure that it has Bluetooth turned on so that it's ready to be paired with your Mac (see figure 6.24).**

2. **Choose System Preferences from the Apple menu.**

3. **Open the Bluetooth pane.** On the Devices tab you see devices that are already paired with your Mac.

4. **If you're trying to set up a device that isn't yet paired, choose Set Up New Device.** That launches the Bluetooth Setup Assistant.

5. **Walk through the steps of the Assistant in order to pair your device.**

6. **Once your device is paired with your Mac, return to iSync and choose File ➪ Add Device.** If the device is compatible with iSync, you should be able to see the device and add it to iSync. It then appears at the top of the iSync window.

6.24 In this example, a Bluetooth-enabled Blackberry is paired with the Mac.

If the device isn't compatible with iSync, you may see it in the window but not be able to add it. (That's what happens with the Blackberry that's shown in figure 6.25; without third-party software installed, the device can't be added to iSync even though it's paired with the Mac.) If that happens, the device either won't work with iSync at all or you need to get third-party software to act as a go-between for iSync and the device.

Configuring and synchronizing

Once your device appears at the top of the iSync window you should be able to select the device and see the options that you have for synchronizing it. For hardware that's recognized internally by iSync, those options are generally along the lines of enabling you to synchronize your contacts and appointments (see figure 6.25).

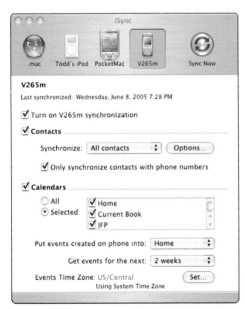

6.25 This Motorola mobile phone (the V265) can synchronize with Address Book and iCal.

For each item that iSync can synchronize, you should see some additional options. For example, when I synchronize with my mobile phone, I can choose whether or not I want to synchronize contact information in both directions, or in one direction only. (If I'm adept enough at using my mobile phone's keypad to enter phone numbers and information about the people I meet, then I might want those entries added to Address Book on my Mac.) Often those options are dimmed until you turn on synchronization for a particular application; once you do, you can set the relevant preferences as well.

With third-party utilities, things may be a little different. For example, when using PocketMac to connect to a PocketPC-based PDA, the actual iSync interface is secondary to the application itself, which pops up when you click the big icon in the iSync window. Then, of course, via the PocketMac window, you've got tons of control over what gets synchronized — PocketMac Pro offers lots of settings for e-mail, contacts, appointments, and so on (see figure 6.26).

Finally, once you set up iSync's options as they relate to your device or your third-party software, you're ready to synchronize your data. That's the easy part. With your device turned on and attached or paired to your Mac, open iSync and click the Sync Devices button. That should put iSync into motion.

 Note
Your option is to synchronize all of your devices at once or none at all; if there's a particular device that is connected but that you don't want to sync, you should open it in iSync and turn off the synchronization function. If the device isn't attached, then iSync should skip it.

In most cases, the window animates such that the bottom draws up into the top of the window and the Sync Devices button spins.

6.26 When you use PocketMac, the iSync window is more of a jumping-off point for accessing the PocketMac software.

You'll then see a progress bar move across the bottom of the window to show how far into the synchronization process iSync has moved (see figure 6.27).

While iSync is synchronizing data, you may be asked some questions in dialog boxes that appear; iSync generally checks with you when there are a large number of changes to be made to make sure that important data isn't being overwritten or that you aren't somehow synchronizing an item or a device in a way that you don't intend. Whenever more than 5 percent of your data is changed or overwritten, warnings such as the one in figure 6.28 appear.

6.28 When more than 5 percent of data items are going to be changed on your target device, iSync checks with you to make sure it's what you want to do.

Aside from that, the synchronization experience should be straightforward. iSync reports its progress and lets you know if it has problems. Once everything is synchronized, iSync reports that the process was successful.

Synching with your iPod

If you're among the millions of iPod owners, you know what a great device it is for listening to your music (or audio books). What

6.27 The progress bar indicates how much of the synchronization process has completed.

you might not fully realize is that the iPod is also a handy repository for contact and calendar information. Using iTunes 4.8 or later, you can synchronize your Address Book contact information, as shown in figure 6.29, and your iCal calendars, as shown in figure 6.30.

 Note If you're still running a version of iTunes older than 4.8, you can add your iPod as an iSync device as described in the iSync coverage in this chapter and use iSync to manage the Address Book and iCal information.

If you choose to download your Address Book information to the iPod, you can opt to synchronize either all contacts or just those in specified groups.

Note You'll find the contact information on your iPod in the Contacts folder as iSync.vcf. You can import them into your Address Book by mounting the iPod as a hard drive and double-clicking the iSync.vcf file. That launches Address Book and starts importing the records.

You can opt to synchronize all calendars or just selected calendars in the Calendars tab.

Note Each calendar is stored as a separate ICS file in the iPod's Calendars folder. Each has the calendar name with iSync- prepended as its name. You can then import those calendars into iCal on any Mac to which you attach the iPod.

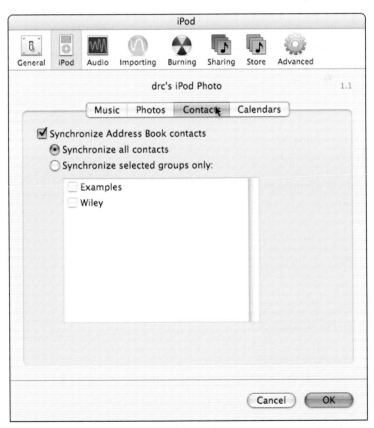

6.29 The iTunes Preferences' iPod pane's Contacts tab synchronizes your Address Book and iPod contact information.

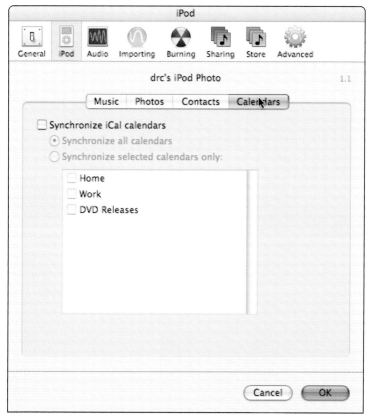

6.30 Use the Calendars tab to download your calendars.

Working from the Road

Ah, the open road — just you, a portable Mac, and blue skies forever. Or something like that.

The truth is that computing on the road can sometimes be a pain, because being away from your desk can sometimes toss challenges at you. I look at some of those possible challenges here and propose some creative solutions that can keep you working (and, ideally, prevent trips to electronics

stores every few hours to pick up something you forgot) at times when you're away from the comfy confines of your home or office and may need access to some important resources.

Using your iPod for backup and file exchange

Your iPod is a hard drive, albeit with a lot of extra circuitry and software. But, the basic fact is that it is a hard drive that can be used as removable storage through either FireWire or a USB 2.0 connection. (Kind of clever of

Steve Jobs to convince millions of people to carry a hard drive around in their pockets, eh? Probably wouldn't have worked if he'd just come out and said it.)

At the time of this writing, the largest-capacity iPods have 60GB hard drives. Depending upon how much music, photo, contact, and calendar information you placed on your iPod, you could well have sufficient space to transport files or even back up a significant portion of your Mac's hard drive.

I think this fact is critical for portable Mac users who are working from the road, as an iPod can be used not just for music, but as a portable backup solution as well. Before setting out on a trip, for example, you can back up important files — your presentation, spreadsheets, databases, contacts, and critical e-mail — to your iPod. If something happens to your portable Mac, you can pull out your iPod and carry on using someone else's computer. (In fact, that's a good reason to take the USB cable with you when traveling, even if you tend to use FireWire with your Mac; you never know when you might want to connect your iPod to a Windows-based PC, and they don't all have FireWire ports.

By default, however, even though your iPod is a hard drive, it doesn't pop up in the Finder. Instead, you need to first open iTunes, and then connect your iPod if it isn't already connected. The iPod appears in your Source list, and, when selected, a small iPod button appears at the bottom of the iTunes window. Click that icon or choose iTunes ⇨ Preferences and select the iPod tab. In either case, you see the iPod preferences shown in figure 6.31.

On that screen is the option Enable Disk Use. Select that option and close the preferences dialog box; now, you should be able to switch to the Finder and see the iPod in the Finder window Sidebar. The iPod works exactly as would any external hard drive with one difference — when you access the drive, you can't directly access any of the music files that may be stored on the iPod through iTunes. You can, however, directly access some of the folders that your iPod uses for other purposes, such as the Contacts and iCal folders. If you like, you can add items to those folders (.vcard and .ics files, respectively) and they are accessible from your iPod. Otherwise, you can create folders and store files directly on the iPod to the extent that its capacity allows you to.

 I would suggest that if you use your iPod for important backup items — particularly financial records, business stuff, or anything that you don't want available for public consumption — that you store those items on an encrypted disk image. See Chapter 3 for details on creating such disk images.

When you finish working with your iPod, you can eject it from the Finder; simply drag it from your Desktop to the Trash, or click the small Eject icon that appears next to the iPod icon in the Finder window Sidebar. That ejects the drive from the Finder and simultaneously from iTunes, making it safe for you to disconnect the iPod from your Mac and take it with you.

 Remember that when your iPod is connected by FireWire or USB 2.0, it can draw a lot of power from your Mac, which may be an issue if your Mac is running on a battery. The iPod is designed to recharge over a FireWire or USB 2.0 cable, so whenever it's connected, it will use your Mac's battery to recharge it's own.

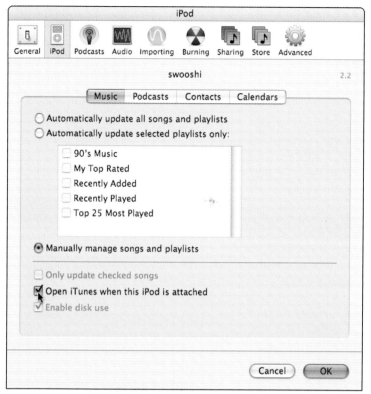

6.31 Use the iPod preferences in iTunes to change how your iPod behaves in the Finder.

Dealing with e-mail on the road

Before you do much traveling, spend a little time considering your e-mail situation. If you're like me and use a portable Mac as your desktop Mac, you like to be able to take all of your e-mail with you and you like to use a desktop application for managing that e-mail. (I'm partial to Mail, which is included with Mac OS X and happens to be available in a nicely improved version in Mac OS X 10.4.)

When you move around with your e-mail program, however, you're probably going to run into a problem. While you can likely download or access your e-mail from any-where — a modem connection, a WiFi hotspot in a coffee house, the high-speed Internet access provided by your hotel — what you can't always do is successfully send e-mail, at least not in the way that your e-mail application is configured for your home or office Internet connection. That's because most outgoing e-mail servers (usu-ally SMTP servers, for *Simple Mail Transport Protocol*) won't allow you to connect to the server if you're not on the same network as that server. In other words, if your e-mail program is set to send your e-mail out from the SMTP server provided by your cable company ISP at home, then you probably won't be able to send e-mail out via that SMTP server from a hotel room in, say, Las Vegas.

Note *Actually, that may be a good thing. If you're in Las Vegas, maybe you don't need to be surfing the Internet — maybe you need to be out having a good time. (And my apologies to you if you live in Las Vegas — allow me to tempt you with some equally enticing exotic location such as Knoxville, Tennessee. Hey, it's actually pretty nice there.)*

In some cases you can use an SMTP server that's hosted by a different company from your current ISP — usually this works if your home ISP offers an SMTP server that you can *authenticate* with a username and password.

Many SMTP servers don't require a username and password, which is why they tend not to accept outside traffic. If your SMTP server can accept a username and password, however, it may also allow you to access it from a network other than the one you use at home. Ask your ISP's tech support people if something like that is possible. Then, to set up authentication, you need to dig into the options in your e-mail applications — in Apple's Mail, for example, you choose Mail ➪ Preferences, click the Accounts tab, and then at the bottom of the screen, click Server Settings. There you can type SMTP authentication information if your SMTP server supports it (see figure 6.32).

If you can't get your e-mail to go out over your home-office SMTP server and you don't

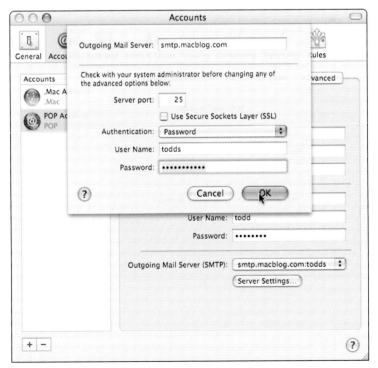

6.32 On the Accounts tab of Mail preferences you can set up authentication for an outgoing server.

have the option of authenticating, then you're going to need another plan. If you connect to the Internet over a modem dial-up ISP that you only use for traveling, for example, then that can be your Plan B — you configure your e-mail application so that it can access that ISP's SMTP server.

If you connect through a WiFi hotspot or a connection provided by your hotel or a similar arrangement, then things may be tougher. If possible, ask around and see if the local network drop also offers an SMTP server that can be used by the clientele; your hotel may very well offer one, while the coffee shop is probably a little less likely, but might still make it happen. If you come up with an SMTP server that works, then you can enter it for this account in your e-mail program. In some applications, you need to replace the current SMTP server setting with the new one. (Remember that original setting, however, for when you get home.)

In Mail, you can have more than one SMTP server available to your accounts, so if you need to add another one, you can, without overwriting the your home connection's information.

1. **In Mail, choose Mail ⇨ Mail Preferences.** That opens the Mail Preferences window.

2. **Click the Accounts tab of Mail Preferences and choose Add Server from the Outgoing Mail Server (SMTP) menu (see figure 6.33).** That opens a dialog sheet that's very similar to the one shown in figure 6.32, except that you add the SMTP server address, not just change the authentication settings.

3. **Add the new server address and any authentication information that you may need.** In a coffee

6.33 Choose to add a new SMTP server if you have access to a different one while you travel.

shop or hotel, that probably isn't necessary, although it might be important if you're adding a server so that you can send e-mail from your satellite office or from a client's business.

Okay, so what if neither of those works for you? One thing I often do is switch to using my .Mac account exclusively when I'm on the road; even when a message comes in from another account, when I'm replying, I have the option of switching to .Mac for the reply, which you can do from a simple menu in the Reply (composition) window when you have multiple accounts configured. Because .Mac accounts use an authenticated SMTP server for outgoing mail, it's always easy to send e-mail from pretty much anywhere.

If you need to use a particular e-mail account but you don't have access to an authenticated SMTP server, you might consider using a Webmail application instead of your Mac's built-in Mail or a third-party e-mail application. These days many ISPs provide a Webmail interface that makes it possible for you to access your e-mail from a Web browser window instead of downloading it to an e-mail application. The advantage with using the Web browser is that you don't have to worry about incoming or outgoing server issues; because you're accessing that e-mail

Change Your SMTP

In some cases, you may be able to change your SMTP port and get around your ISP's limitations (or limitations of the ISP that you're using from a hotel room or coffee shop). In Mail Preferences, choose the Accounts icon; on the Account Information tab for the account that you're using to send mail, click the Server Settings button. There, you can update the server to use the port 587. That may enable you to get mail out through that server. (The default, port 25, is often blocked.)

directly on the mail server, replies or new messages can be sent easily from the interface (see figure 6.34).

Of course, the downside to using a Webmail interface is that the mail isn't stored locally on your Mac, so you need to have Internet access at the time that you're wanting to read and respond to your e-mail. (In Mail, for example, you can work offline and messages can be read and replies can wait in the Out box until you connect again to the Internet.) And, while you can get back home or to the office and download the incoming messages

that you leave on the server (even if you've already read them), Sent mail isn't stored in your e-mail program, because the sent mail was sent through the Web interface.

Tip If you've got a .Mac account, you can always access and manage your .Mac e-mail from a Webmail interface at webmail.mac.com. That can be convenient not just for accessing your e-mail from a strange Internet connection but also when you're using another person's computer.

6.34 Here's the Webmail interface that one of my ISPs makes available for accessing that e-mail account on the road.

Not interested in Webmail? Well, there's one other option, although it's a bit more advanced. Mac OS X has a built-in e-mail server that you can use for sending e-mail (remember, it's built on top of a Unix-like OS that has all that sort of stuff buried), with the added advantage that it doesn't require you to have an SMTP server — ever. Instead, you use PostFix Enabler (www.cutedgesystems.com/software/PostfixEnabler/, $10), which turns on that local SMTP server. With the application installed and active, you simply set your SMTP server to the address localhost, and PostFix does the rest, enabling you to send e-mail from your Mac without regard for the SMTP server that's provided or not provided by the local ISP — you are your local ISP, at least insofar as sending e-mail is concerned.

Note PostFix can also be used to receive e-mail as an incoming e-mail server, but that's a bit harder to configure; also note that you'll sometimes have trouble using PostFix for outgoing e-mail if the ISP you're using blocks other servers from being used on their networks. If that's the case, consult the Cutting Edge Systems Web site for details and hints. (One hint: change the SMTP port from 25 to port 587, as discussed earlier.)

Printing with strangers

Need to print? Your Mac has the built-in ability to recognize a number of different types and brands of printers, so you'll often find that you can simply hook up and go. Not all the time, but most of the time.

Probably the best tool in your arsenal for connecting to other people's printers is a 4-pin-to-6-pin USB cable, which is the standard cable used for most inkjets and USB-based personal laser printers. The reason I

recommend bringing such a cable is because many PC users still use a PC-style parallel cable to connect to printers that support both USB and parallel. So, they may not have a USB cable for you to use even if they're willing to loan you the printer.

For a similar reason it's a good idea to travel with an Ethernet cable and an Ethernet crossover cable, which may sometimes be necessary for connecting to an Ethernet-based printer directly (and it can come in handy for connecting to certain cable modems and other devices, too, depending on your Mac model). If your PowerBook supports Gigabit Ethernet then you may be able to skip the crossover cable, although I think it's a welcome addition to any laptop travel bag. Of course, you don't have to connect directly to an Ethernet-capable printer; if you connect your Mac to the same hub or switch that the printer is connected to — or if the printer is connected to a wireless network router — then you should be able to detect the printer once you're set up to access that network.

Note Of course, Bluetooth is another option for connecting to a Bluetooth-enabled printer, if you happen to have Bluetooth support for your Mac. If you suspect that you should be able to connect to a printer via Bluetooth, open System Preferences, go to the Bluetooth pane, and click Set Up a New Device to walk through the assistant and pair your Mac to the printer.

Once you connect to a printer, you find that there are essentially two types of printers that you encounter, based on the printer *language* that is used for sending commands. Printers that use the PCL (printer control language) protocol historically tend to be PC-compatible printers; however, these days, the Mac OS is perfectly capable of speaking to PCL printers. (I use multiple such printers, both laser and inkjet, in my office.) Hewlett-Packard originally developed PCL, and the company is still a strong proponent of the language. Other printer manufacturers use their own proprietary languages, or PostScript emulation or PDF printing, which is becoming more popular.

With your Mac, non-Postscript printers require slightly more individualized drivers than do PostScript printers, which are the other type. PostScript printers generally use the same driver, which is built into the Mac OS, but with PostScript Printer Description (PPD) files that are used to differentiate the models and their features.

Of course, if you don't know the type of printer that you'll be connecting to before you connect, then you'll need to hope that it's a model that Apple supports with bundled driver software. To find out, follow these steps:

1. **Connect the printer to your Mac.**

2. **Open the Printer Setup Utility found in the Utilities folder inside your Applications folder.**

3. **In the Printer Setup Utility, click Add or choose Printers ⇨ Add Printers.** The Printer Browser appears (see figure 6.35). If you successfully select a printer and it's turned on, then it should appear in the Printer Browser.

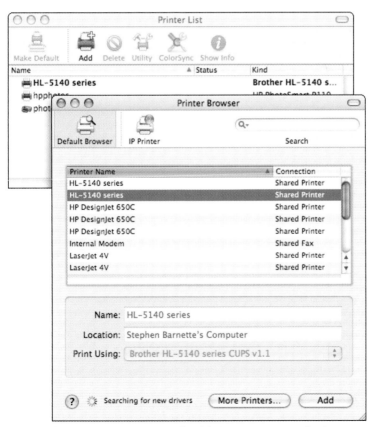

6.35 In the Printer Browser you should see any connected printers.

Activate Apple Talk

If you are trying to connect to an AppleTalk laser printer over a network connection, don't forget that you need to have AppleTalk turned on for the port (Built-in Ethernet or AirPort) that's being used to access the network on which that printer is located. Open the port in question in the Network pane of System Preferences, and then click the AppleTalk tab. Select the Make AppleTalk Active option, and then click Apply Now. You should now be able to access an AppleTalk printer over that network port's connection, if the connection and printer are both correctly configured.

4. **Select the printer in the list and see if you can locate a manufacturer and driver that match the printer through the Print Using menu at the bottom of the window.**

If you don't see the printer, it likely isn't connected or turned on, or it may have a bad cable. If you see the printer but it doesn't seem to be properly recognized, that's a good indication that you need to install a driver for that printer. If possible, access the Web site for that printer's manufacturer and download a Mac-specific driver, which you can then install and retest. If you don't have Internet access, you might not have much luck printing; your best bet in that case is going to be to attempt to get the file that you want to print to another person's computer (you could burn a CD or use a local network connection) and have that person print it for you.

Bringing a printer with you

Another solution to hunting around for a printer that works with your Mac is to bring your own printer. Unless you're driving on your trip and have the room available, that probably means you'll be looking into a portable printer. Fortunately, a few such beasts are available and they aren't terribly expensive. Here's a quick look:

✦ **Canon IP90 (**www.canon.com**).** Canon's current portable USB model offers up to 16 pages per minute (ppm) in black printing and 13 ppm in color. It can print photos and weighs only 4 pounds. It also offers a number of options, including a battery kit, a Bluetooth adapter, and a car charger.

✦ **HP Deskjet 450 series (**www.hp.com**).** These DeskJets are designed to be compact and easy to configure, offering a variety of extras including Bluetooth and optional six-ink photo printing. It can print nine pages per minute in black and white, and eight pages per minute in color, weighs 4.2 pounds, and can be outfitted with a battery for printing when you're not near an electrical outlet.

✦ **Pentax Pocketjet printers (**www.pentaxtech.com**).** A little pricier than the others, but sleeker and much lighter at only slightly over a pound. Capabilities range from battery-powered printing to Bluetooth, but the printer is slower and offers less quality than the others, thanks to its thermal printing approach. It also requires special paper. Still, it's amazingly light and easy to pack if you need to be able to print in a pinch.

Save as a PDF

Mac OS X has built in to it the ability to save files as PDFs instead of printing them. This can be handy for a file that you need to have printed by someone else, particularly if that person doesn't have the same application that you used to create the document. For example, if you use Apple's Pages to create a document and you need to send it to a PC user for printing, simply choose File ⇨ Print, and in the Print dialog box, choose Save as PDF from the PDF menu. In the Save dialog box, give the document a name. The resulting document is a PDF file, which can be transmitted to PC users and viewed in (and printed from) Adobe Reader.

Faxing to and from your Mac

Because your Mac portable ships with a modem (at least, all of them that I'm aware of do), then you'll be happy to know that you have a fax machine built right in. If you have a document that you can print, then that document can be faxed using the Print dialog box in any Mac OS X application.

Setting up fax receiving

To set up your Mac so that you can receive faxes, follow these steps:

1. **Open the Print & Fax pane of System Preferences.**

2. **Click the Faxing tab (see figure 6.36).**

3. **Select the Receive faxes on this computer option.** This causes your Mac to begin checking for incoming calls on the line attached to its modem. (This works out particularly well if you have a dedicated line for your Mac, although the fact that you can turn it on and off easily can work for a hotel room or similar situation, too.)

For the other settings, you can type your local fax number (it's sent with your faxes as the return fax number) and you can choose various behaviors for how your Mac responds when it receives an incoming fax, such as where the incoming faxes should be saved and whether you want them e-mailed or printed automatically.

Because your Mac's modem is built in, it should be recognized and configured by the Mac OS without any additional steps. If you have an external modem or otherwise feel that you need to tweak settings for some reason, you can do that by clicking Set Up Fax Modem. That launches the Printer Setup Utility, which is used for locating and configuring connected modems as well.

Finally, note the Show fax status in menu bar option. Select that option if you want quick access to the Faxing tab and you want to see status messages whenever a fax is being received or sent.

Sending faxes

Assuming your modem has been set up and configured to dial correctly and it is connected to a phone line, faxing is simple. Begin by creating and setting up your document the way you want it to be. Next, choose File ⇨ Print and in the Print dialog box, choose PDF, Fax PDF. When you do, you see the Print dialog box rework itself into the Fax interface (see figure 6.37).

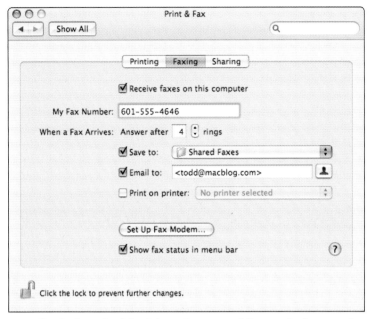

6.36 The Faxing tab of the Print & Fax pane of System Preferences is used to set up fax receiving.

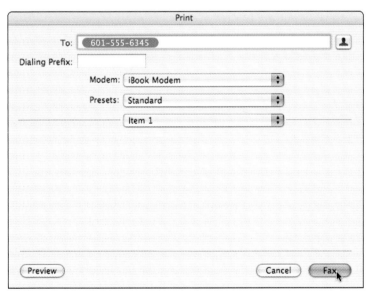

6.37 You can fax directly from any application that supports printing.

In the To field, type the phone number to which you're sending the fax; you can also type a name or click the small Person icon to open an interface to your Address Book so that you can select a recipient that way.

From the Modem menu you can choose the modem that you want to use for the faxing (on the off chance that you have more than one), or you can choose to open the Print & Fax Preferences pane from this menu (which were discussed earlier).

The Fax interface also includes an unlabeled menu that you can use to set a variety of options; with Fax Cover Page selected, for example, you can turn on the option Cover Page and then type the text for that cover page in the text field area.

Another interesting option from that menu is the Scheduler option, which can be used to specify that this fax is to be sent later; if you're disciplined about connecting your Mac to the phone line and leaving it awake (or setting it to wake up) for late-night faxing, for example, you can set this option so that all your faxes go out at a certain time.

 Tip *In the Energy Saver pane, you can set your Mac to turn itself on and off (or wake from sleep) at certain times of the day. On the Sleep tab, just click the Schedule button.*

With those choices made, simply click Fax when you're ready to send your fax. That prints the document to a PDF and hands it off to the modem for faxing; you should see your modem's icon appear in the Dock and a status message via the Fax Status item in the menu bar. To see the progress, click the modem icon on your Dock and visit your modem's fax queue, as shown in figure 6.38.

6.38 Your modem's fax queue, which is similar to a print queue, manages outgoing faxes.

With a fax in the queue, you can select it and click Hold to stop it for a moment; highlight it and click Resume to continue with the faxing. To stop the fax modem temporarily from doing any faxing, click Stop Jobs. Once stopped, you can click Start Jobs to start them again. Notice also that you can click the Completed tab to see faxes that have been sent from your Mac.

Tip

If you're ever in a pinch where you need to get documents into your Mac electronically but don't have a scanner handy, you might try faxing the documents to yourself, perhaps from the hotel front desk or business center. You won't have the highest quality, but it may be enough to attach to an e-mail and send to a colleague or customer if necessary.

Another Faxing Option: eFax

The fact that Mac OS X offers a built-in fax option is nice, particularly if you have a dedicated phone line and you can set your Mac to receive faxes as needed. I admit, however, that I rarely use my Mac for receiving faxes, and more and more, I use it only infrequently for sending faxes. That's because I've discovered the wonder of getting faxes in my e-mail and sending faxes via the Internet, thanks to eFax.

eFax is a subscription service (www.efax.com) although basic service is free if you're willing to accept any telephone area code that you're given and you only need to accept a small volume of faxes per month. If you'd like to specify an area code (so that your number is a local call for people in your area) or if you'd like to offer a toll-free fax number to anyone who wants to send you a fax, you'll need to pay the monthly service fee.

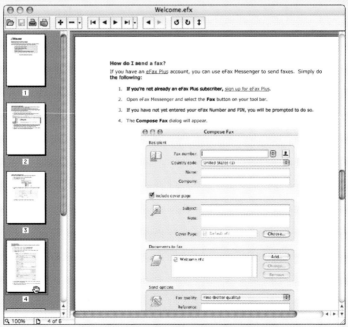

eFax can be used to display and manage incoming faxes.

For receiving faxes, though, nothing could be better. As long as you have access to your e-mail, you can get faxes — you don't have to be plugged into a landline or near your fax machine. Instead, faxes sent to your personal number — from a regular fax machine or from a computer — are received by eFax and then converted to an image and forwarded to your e-mail account as an attachment, either in the special eFax format or as a standard image or PDF file. Faxes in the eFax format have to be displayed by the eFax software, as shown here.

Obviously, one fun advantage to electronic faxes is the fact that you can forward them to others — in fact, when received, eFax can send the faxes to more than one person at once. You can then file your faxes away in your e-mail program or save them to a folder on your Mac and store them for later access; you can even rename them if you're diligent enough to do so; that way you can quickly get back into a fax you've archived and have a sense of what it's about.

With the right service agreement, eFax also enables you to fax out via the service. To do that, follow these steps:

1. **Save a document that you want to fax as a PDF.** You can choose File ⇨ Print and then click PDF in the Print dialog box to print the document as a PDF.

2. **In eFax Messenger, choose File ⇨ Fax.** That brings up a fax interface.

3. **Type the recipient information, cover sheet details, and specify the file that you want to fax.** When you send it, it won't use your modem to send the fax; it connects to the eFax service through the Internet and eFax faxes it to its final destination.

ASPs: Exploring Web-based applications

I've already mentioned how handy it can be to use the Internet for Webmail access, and in the previous sidebar I mentioned using the Web for faxing. The truth is, there are many application service provider (ASP) options on the Web that you can use for all sorts of reasons, from sales contact management to accounting and project management. ASPs continue to be a popular alternative to certain types of business and professional software, particularly when aimed at small and medium-sized businesses. Any small business can probably appreciate the option of spending $30 per user for a networked, shared application that's not only pretty sophisticated, but that also doesn't require

you to have any special server hardware or infrastructure. Instead, the ASP provides access to the software through a simple Web browser.

 Note *Because you can get at your data through any Web browser, a hosted solution is often good at sharing data among multiple users. But it also means that you need to trust the company that's storing your data for everything from privacy and data security to trusting them to stay in business and make regular backups.*

Of course, that Web interface can offer some drawbacks as well. Take, for example, a popular ASP solution — customer relationship management (CRM) software. Hosted

CRM solutions are fairly easy to find from a number of different companies and even in different countries and languages. In most cases, the CRM application is designed to make it relatively easy for a salesperson to track his or her clients, sales opportunities, and use some sort of step-by-step plan to remind him or her when to call back for follow-up, when to send more materials, and when a meeting or phone conference appointment has been set (see figure 6.39).

If there's an obvious drawback to using an ASP for something like customer relationship management, it's that you need to have an active Internet connection in order to access the application and update it. By contrast, a non-ASP CRM application — in other words, a regular sales/contact management program designed to run directly

on the Mac the same way that Microsoft Word or iCal does — is active even when you don't have access to the Internet.

One plus in the ASP column (vs. a traditional Mac application) is that ASP solutions don't have to be written specifically for the Macintosh the way that Mac applications do. And, because they're Internet-based, it's often easier to use them in groupware or networked environments, particularly in small businesses, because you don't have to create your own network to run the server version of the software. In other words, by using an ASP, when you do have Internet access you might find yourself updating a record in your group contact application or project management software that other coworkers or colleagues can see, thus adding to your productivity even when you're sitting in an Internet café.

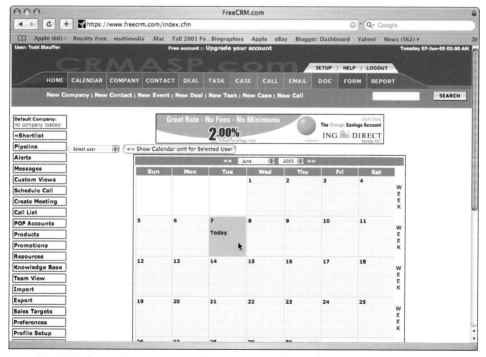

6.39 FreeCRM (www.freecrm.com) is a customer relationship manager you can log on to and use over the Internet.

Note

In a sense, Apple's .Mac service offers a series of ASPs that, to one degree or another, are written specifically (or at least primarily) for the Macintosh. The Homepage tool, .Mac e-mail, and iDisk can all be seen as ASP applications.

So, what can ASPs do? Well, there's probably an ASP for pretty much anything you can think of. In my experience, though, there are some key solutions that you might consider for a variety of purposes including the needs of small-to-medium-sized business or organizational needs. Some options include:

✦ **Customer relations.** CRM software can do anything from manage a sales pipeline (from first contact to managing the client after a sale) to taking sales orders and managing inventory to queuing customer support questions or managing a call center. Some popular CRM applications include SalesForce.net, FreeCRM.com, Salesboom.com, StudioCRM.com, and many others.

✦ **Accounting.** NetSuite (www. netsuite.com) is well known for its full-blown accounting packages that can be used for a small or medium-sized business. NetSuite Small Business, for example, can be used for online accounting, inventory management, an online store, and customer relationship management all in one package.

✦ **Project management.** One of the coolest sites I've seen in a while is BaseCamp (www.basecamphq. com), an ASP designed to help you manage projects. The software tracks milestones for projects, To-Dos, and allows for collaboration and contact among the people involved in the project. It even integrates with iCal and allows you to share calendars and such. Other such tools include WorkSmart.net, TeamSoft.com, CopperProject.com, and ProjectForum.com.

✦ **Database applications.** QuickBase (www.quickbase.com) from Intuit isn't cheap (it's aimed more at corporate accounts than small business), but it offers some very unique capabilities that enable you to build all sorts of applications including CRM, project management, document management, and others.

✦ **Personal information management.** The same folks who make BaseCamp make BackPack (www. backpackit.com), another great tool for individuals and small business people who simply want a Web solution that enables you to jot down ideas, notes, or create collaborative pages that can be used for a variety of reasons (see figure 6.40). With BackPack, the idea isn't completely unlike a *wiki*, which refers to certain types of Web sites that can't be edited while you're viewing them. With BackPack, a Web page becomes easy to edit and it can be shared with others or kept private, making it both a collaborative tool and a fairly easy way to design and maintain public Web pages. Many wiki-style sites are available for information management and collaboration such as JotSpot.com, XWiki.com, and ProjectLocker.com.

And there are many other options from which you can choose, from document management ASPs to those focused specifically on managing contacts to those designed for online content management or e-commerce.

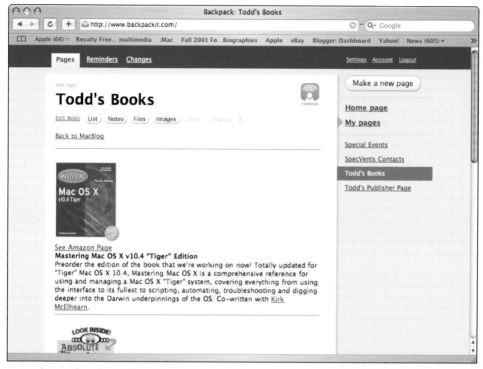

6.40 The BackPack service gives you an online application where you can collect text, ToDos, images, and other items for managing your personal information.

And there are specialized ASPs, too, like ASPs designed to track travel expenses or time-and-billing information. And, of course, you probably take advantage of service providers without thinking about the fact that you're accessing an online application, from online tax forms to news aggregators to portals of all kinds.

The trick is to determine when it is more helpful to run the application on the Web instead of on your Mac, and then find an application you like and trust to handle your data and collaboration. From there, it's just a matter of whether you can afford the application — and how often you spend time on a high-speed Internet connection.

Using Voice over IP

The people who know me well know that I've been saying for years that the days of our spending extra money on long-distance phone calls are numbered. That doesn't make me a seer — it makes me someone who has seen the power of an application like iChat AV, discussed in the next section. What iChat AV proves is how easy it is for the typical Mac user to start up an audio conference over the Internet, thus incurring no additional charges for long distance.

In recent memory, other companies have begun to see that potential and come up with products that take advantage of the broadband connections that have continued to become more pervasive. The result is a boom in Voice over IP (VoIP) technology and providers — companies that let you talk over an Internet connection.

With VoIP, you can often chat with an individual who is using a multimedia computer and the same VoIP service at no cost at all. But the real trick is using a VoIP service to connect to a regular phone line, a mobile phone, or some other telephone solution that is not a part of the provider's network and doesn't use a computer on the other end. In that case, we're finding that providers are often willing to offer flat-fee or very low-cost connection fees regardless of the distances involved.

If you want to use your Mac for a VoIP connection, you're going to need software, VoIP service, and you'll probably want a headset of some kind so that you can carry on a conversation without being forced to speak loudly to your iBook or PowerBook. In a pinch, you can actually use the microphone and speakers in your Mac portable for VoIP, but a headset is certainly a more elegant solution. (Look for a USB or Bluetooth model that includes a headset speaker and microphone combination and that is specifically compatible with the Mac. Also, realize that only the latest PowerBook models are powerful enough to support a Bluetooth headset for VoIP conversation.)

Companies that support the Mac for software-based VoIP connections include Vonage (www.vonage.com) and Terracall (www.terracall.com). With service from one of the these providers, you can launch an application such as X-Pro Softphone and dial not only other users with the Softphone software (see figure 6.41) but use the VoIP service to make calls to landline and mobile telephones.

6.41 The Softphone software can be used to dial out from your Mac and connect to others for inexpensive long-distance conversations — a good idea for business trips.

The Skype service (www.skype.com) offers similar VoIP services and the option to dial out to regular landlines or receive calls to typical telephone numbers. It has the distinction of offering its own software that's available for a number of different computer platforms, including Mac OS X.

When you're at home or in the office, you can still use your VoIP service, but when you're near a stationary network connection, you can switch from using a softphone on your Mac to using a network adapter, which enables you to plug the adapter into your Ethernet hub and a regular telephone into the adapter. That way you can make calls just as if you were picking up the phone on a regular landline and making a call, except that the call is routed over the Internet and takes advantage of your VoIP service.

AIM

Aside from a Mac, a number of devices these days are built with onboard AIM (AOL Instant Messaging) compatibility; the AIM service and iChat are intertwined such that you can use your .Mac account seamlessly with AIM. I've grown partial to the Sidekick II (www.hiptop.com) recently as a PDA and phone replacement, using my .Mac account with the AIM tool for Web chat even when I'm sitting in a meeting or otherwise away from my desk. Many popular cell phones, smartphones, PDAs, and Blackberry devices support AIM, too.

Note *A few companies, such as ZyXEL (www.zyxel.com) are making WiFi-based VoIP phones that can be used to place a VoIP call from a WiFi or AirPort network without any additional adapters or cables — all you need is a VoIP provider and, conceivably, you can head down to the local coffee shop, connect to its wireless network, and start making calls.*

iChat AV and audio conferencing

Computer chatting, instant messaging, and the like aren't just kids's toys, as diverting as they may be from time to time — iChat AV is very effective for professional collaboration and communication. I've used it to work and share files with the people in my office on my local network, and, at the same time, I've used it to collaborate with colleagues in another part of the country — even one coauthor who lives in another part of the world.

Just as an example, for this book Dennis Cohen and I used iChatAV to communicate and coordinate our efforts; Dennis, who is in California, has been able to chat with me in Mississippi, share files, swap outlines, and so on. We both also use iChat AV to communicate with our editors and other coauthors on other projects. If you're running Tiger and

your laptop has enough muscle, you can have up to a ten-way audio conference — a virtual conference room with no travel involved for any participant and minimal expense (just the ISP charges you're already incurring for e-mail and Web browsing).

The muscle referenced here however, limits both what iChat AV connections you can initiate and in what iChat AV conversations you can participate. Initiation (also known as *hosting*) requires more computer and connection resources than participation. The chart listing what you need for each iChat AV activity type is on Apple's Web site at www.apple.com/macosx/features/ichat. No Apple laptops current at the time of writing are adequately endowed to initiate a four-person videoconference, but 1GHz or faster G4 PowerBooks and G4 iBooks can participate in those videoconferences. Because you can't (yet) initiate multiperson videoconferences on your laptops — and only 1GHz and faster laptops with broadband connections can participate — this discussion is focused on audio conferencing.

Getting started with iChat

If your laptop is a G4 running at 1GHz or better, you can host up to ten-way audio conferences, and any iBook or PowerBook running Tiger can participate in one, even if your Internet connection is through the built-in modem. The first time you launch iChat AV, you see the window shown in figure 6.42. Click Continue and the screen shown in figure 6.43 appears. If you already have a .Mac account or an AOL Instant Messenger screen name, fill in the blanks accordingly. If not, click Get an iChat Account and register for a free iChat account via Mac.com.

6.42 When you launch iChat you first see an introductory screen.

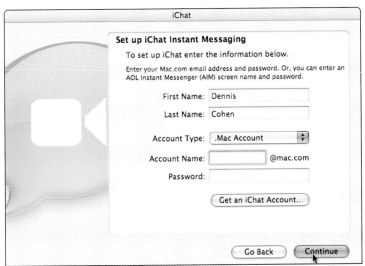

6.43 Move a little farther and you are guided by the assistant to configure iChat.

Note

The free iChat account includes a 60-day trial .Mac account. Even if you don't continue with the .Mac account after the 60 days, your iChat account remains active.

Proceed through the rest of the iChat setup screens. You'll be asked whether you have a Jabber account (the odds are that you don't unless your employer has a Jabber server set up for instant messaging). Then, you'll be asked whether you want to use Bonjour messaging. Bonjour is the new name for what used to be called Rendezvous, a protocol for communicating with other computers on your local network. Next will come a screen for setting up a camera, such as the iSight, for video and audio conferencing. Finally, you're told that you're all set up.

Note

Bonjour is different from Jabber and AIM, in the sense that the second two types require centralized computers. With Bonjour, Macs on your local network that are also using iChat are automatically recognized and placed in your Bonjour window. You can then have text, audio, and video chats or file sharing sessions without requiring some sort of central server computer on your network.

Initially, you're presented with windows containing lists for each type of messaging that you enabled (Jabber and/or Bonjour) as well as a Buddy List window for iChat AV. Initially, your Buddy List is empty, but you can add people to it by choosing Buddies ⇨ Add Buddy or clicking the plus (+) button at the bottom of the Buddy List window and

selecting entries from your Address Book (yes, iChat AV is yet another application that takes advantage of your OS X Address Book, just like Mail and iCal). If you want to add someone who isn't in your Address Book, click New Person. Only people with Instant Message addresses can be added, so you'll need to add that information to their entry. Adding a new person to your Buddy List also creates an Address Book card for him or her.

Note

You don't have to worry about synchronizing your Buddy List with your other Macs. Your Buddy List is stored on an Instant Message server and is available to you whenever you log on to your iChat account, regardless of the computer used.

Tip

If your buddy has multiple Instant Message addresses, you can add them all, separated by commas. Then, regardless of what screen name they use to log on, they appear in your Buddy List as online.

Text chatting

To begin an iChat session, all you need to do is double-click an entry in your Bonjour, Buddy List, or Jabber window. If that person's entry is active (that is, if it isn't grayed out) then it means the user is online and may be available for chat. You'll see a window appear (shown in figure 6.44). At the bottom of that window is a small entry box, where you can type the text that you want to send to the other person. Do so and then press Return to send it.

6.44 Double-click a buddy or other user and you get a small window that you can use to attempt to contact that person.

Once you send the text you also set a chat session into motion. The person on the other end of this conversation sees an alert appear on the computer that you are trying to reach him or her. If you do, and the other person responds, then you see that response appear in the window (see figure 6.45).

6.45 If the other user responds, you see that response on the screen.

To continue the conversation, just type in the box at the bottom and press Return. Note that you can type long entries if you like — just don't press Return until you're ready to send a block of text. (Most of the time it's best to send short snippets to keep the conversation going, but sometimes you get on a roll and type away at a single entry.) As you type, you notice that certain items, such as Web addresses and e-mail addresses, get turned into links. Also, you can type certain types of emoticons (also called smileys) that appear as small graphical items (see figure 6.46). You can also choose from a number of different emoticons from the small smiley-faced icon at the far right of the text entry box.

6.46 Links and smileys get changed automatically.

One of the most useful iChat features is the ability to transfer files directly to anyone on your Buddy List (or in your Bonjour window). Just drag the file icon from the Finder onto the user's entry in the Buddy List (or in the Bonjour window) and let go. iChat will ask your recipient whether he or she wishes to receive the file and if accepted, away it goes. No fuss, no muss, no messing with e-mail attachments or remote network connections.

Note *Bonjour chats tend to be quite a bit faster for file transfer than those through your Buddy or Jabber lists because Bonjour is using your local network.*

When you finish a conversation, click the Close button in the chat window. (You might want to type "Bye" first just to be polite.) That ends that chat session, although you'll still be online to receive instant messages from that user or any others that have you in their buddy lists or who are available via Bonjour chatting.

If you no longer with to receive instant messages, you can either change your availability to offline (from the small menu under your name in the Buddy List or Bonjour windows, choose Offline), change it to Away or similar (which means you can still receive IMs, but you're telling others not to expect an instant reply), or quit iChat.

 Note *Curious about receiving iChat requests? When someone attempts to start a conversation with you, an alert dialog box appears on your screen. You can click either Decline or Accept. (You can also type some text before clicking Accept if desired.) If the request comes from AIM, you can click the Block button to block this user from making requests in the future. From there, if you've Accepted, you can continue the conversation as described.*

Using audio and video chatting

iChat AV employs graphic buttons indicating in what sort of conferences your buddies can participate. A single telephone indicates that they can audio chat. A telephone stack button indicates that they can audio conference. A single camera button indicates

that they can video chat, while a camera stack button indicates that they can participate in videoconferences. The lack of any button indicates that there is no microphone or camera attached that can be used for audio or video chatting (or that their version of iChat or AIM chatting software doesn't support AV chats) and you're reduced to text messaging.

To start an audio or video chat, click the appropriate button for the remote user with whom you would like to chat. If you click audio chat, an alert window pops up on that person's screen to represent your request. If he accepts the chat then his chat window will reconfigure into the audio chat window, which shows your voice level as you talk to give you a sense of how well your Mac's microphone is picking you up (see figure 6.47).

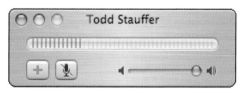

6.47 The audio chat window shows your voice level as heard by your Mac.

Talk as long as you want or as long as your connection holds out. Note the Mute button in the window, which can be used to mute the microphone while you're having a chat; you can also change the volume level from that window. When you're done chatting, you can say goodbye to the other person and click the Close button.

As for videoconferences — they work pretty much the same way; click the video icon next to the remote user in the Buddy List or other connection window; if the conference is accepted, that person appears on-screen.

Talk until you're all talked out, and then click the Close button to end the videoconference.

> **Tip** *iChat AV is a very rich application, with lots of ways to customize your Buddy List, your icon, your status message, and so forth. iChat Help covers this material quite well and there really aren't enough available pages to echo all the information that you already have available. Check out iChat Help (Help ✦ iChat Help) for more hints and tricks.*

More uses for .Mac

In addition to the .Mac synchronization described earlier in this chapter, a .Mac account provides a number of additional capabilities that you might find useful for working from the road. Among these benefits are:

✦ An e-mail address, accessible from anywhere via a Web browser and very easy to access via one or more instances of an application like Mail, thanks to the fact that it's IMAP-based and, thus, allows you to store on the server messages that you have read, as long as your allotment isn't filled.

✦ A total of 250MB of remote disk storage, part of which you allocate to your e-mail storage and the rest available as a WebDAV server for public Web pages, Web-based file sharing, and for your personal iDisk.

✦ Quick and easy Web authoring and hosting, including integration with iPhoto and iMovie to put real pizzazz into your Web pages.

✦ When synchronized, you can get browser-based access to your contacts, appointments, and bookmarks, even if you're not using your own Mac (or from your portable when you generally use a desktop Mac).

✦ Lots of free and discounted software or add-ons. For example, currently Apple offers its Backup utility, a variety of Dashboard widgets, 300 GarageBand loops, and online tutorials for most Apple-labeled applications are among the freebies at the time of this writing.

For working from the road, I recommend at least considering paying the subscription for .Mac, simply because a number of services both within the Mac OS itself and from within a Safari window work a little better with .Mac.

Of course, you can get similar services — Google.com offers Gmail, which allows you to manage all of your e-mail through its hosted service using a Web browser. Similar options are made available by Yahoo.com (which also supports storing your contacts and appointments through the site's premium services), and a number of other services, most of which rely on advertising for their revenue instead of a subscription fee. As long as you feel secure with your data stored at an online service, it's a great way to back up what you're doing on your portable and to make it easier to access important items like addresses and e-mail while you're traveling.

Adding a key drive to the mix

What's a key drive? Picture a small, fits-on-a-keychain-sized device with a connector that you can just plug into an available USB port and fill with data. Other names that such drives go by include keychain drive, flash drive, or pen drive — whatever you call them, they seem a little like science fiction, but can be very handy in reality. Available from a broad range of manufacturers in a myriad of capacities from 64MB to 4GB at the present time, you can find the smaller ones for as little as $10 for 64MB and $50 for some 1GB models, though the list prices are somewhat higher. Currently, those having more than 1GB capacity are exponentially more expensive, running into multiple hundreds of dollars. These prices reflect the cost for the contained flash memory that makes the units so useful and compact.

When you connect a key drive, your Mac treats it like a removable hard drive. If you have your Finder preferences set to display mounted volumes on the Desktop, an icon appears there, as shown in figure 6.48. Also shown in figure 6.48, you see that the drive appears as a volume in a Finder window Sidebar and in a Finder window set to Computer.

Some manufacturers make even more versatile models. Fuji, for example, offers a key drive known as the Fuji XD Reader and MP3 Player. This handy little device includes the firmware to use the drive as an MP3 player with separate, interchangeable XD flash memory cards. Just remove one XD card and insert another and you've got the key drive equivalent to a removable cartridge drive like the Zip. It comes with case, headphones, and a AAA battery for about $30 to $35.

 Note   *Although key drives are labeled as being USB 2.0 devices, you can also connect them to USB 1.1 ports – they'll just transfer data much more slowly. As an example, transferring 430MB to a 1GB key drive through a USB 2.0 connection takes well under 1 minute but drags on for almost 14 minutes on a USB 1.1 connection.*

Media readers and digital photography

Arguably the most significant, or at least the largest, computer-spawned industry of the last dozen years is digital photography. As the cameras get smaller and the resolution of the photos they take gets larger, increasingly greater demands are made on compact,

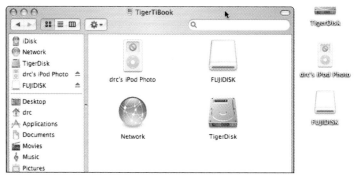

6.48 The Finder treats a key drive just like a removable hard drive.

high-capacity, high-speed data storage. This jumpstarted the flash memory industry, in which there are now four major competing formats: the original MemoryStick, Compact Flash, SD/MMC (Secure Digital/Multimedia Card), and xD.

Each format has significant corporate muscle behind it. Sony invented and champions the MemoryStick, Olympus pushes xD with a little assistance from Fuji, and almost everyone else has standardized on the more open Compact Flash (www.compact flash.org), and SD/MMC (www.sdcard. org) formats.

Because the cards are removable storage media for digital cameras and other devices, enterprising vendors quickly recognized a market for devices that are the flash memory equivalent of a floppy drive so that users don't have to use their cameras as transfer devices when loading the data into a computer. In fact, some USB floppy drives also have slots for one or more of the memory card formats.

When you insert a flash card into a media reader, the flash card mounts as if it were a removable hard drive. You can then access the files by copying them from the card to your hard drive. When you're done, eject the disk by dragging it to the Trash or by choosing File ➪ Eject in the Finder. Now you should be able to remove it from the card reader without creating any problems.

If you insert a card that contains image files, you may also find that iPhoto launches, just as if a camera were attached. (Actually, you may see a dialog box that asks you if you prefer to have iPhoto or another application launch to import those photos; iPhoto is a handy default for a variety of reasons, not the least of which is how easy iPhoto makes it to preview and manage your images.)

Tip *One advantage of mounting a camera's memory card through a media reader is that you can selectively import images into iPhoto by dragging and dropping rather than employing iPhoto's all-or-nothing import capability.*

Burning optical media

You burn music CDs in iTunes, and if you have a SuperDrive, you burn DVDs in iDVD. Additionally, you can use iPhoto to burn photo archive CDs and DVDs. OS X makes it easy for you to burn data CDs and DVDs as well, directly from the Finder. And, when you're on the road, burning data to disc may be even that much more important, because it may be your best option for swapping data with others when you don't have network capabilities in common.

Tip *Finder, iTunes, iDVD, and iPhoto are all perfectly adequate for burning special types of optical media; however, a dedicated and versatile burning program will offer you even more flexibility and power. Try Toast Titanium from Roxio (you can find it online for about $80).*

The control center for handling CDs and DVDs, not surprisingly, is System Preferences' CDs & DVDs pane, shown in figure 6.49. Mac OS X assigns iTunes, iPhoto, and DVD Player as defaults for existing recorded media, but you can change those settings if you wish. On the other hand, no assumptions are made as to what should be done when blank, recordable media are inserted. Figure 6.50 shows the prompting dialog box that appears, asking you what you want to do when a blank CD is inserted (the DVD prompt differs only in the wording, replacing CD with DVD).

6.49 Set your CD and DVD preferences here.

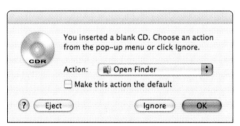

6.50 If you don't set a default action for blank optical media, this is the prompt you'll see.

Clicking Eject is self-explanatory — it causes your Mac to spit the disc back out. If you click Ignore, the disc remains in the drive and you continue working with no further action taken. Clicking OK accepts the setting chosen from the Action pop-up menu. Assuming you chose Open Finder, a CDR (or DVDR) icon appears on your Desktop and an Untitled CD burnable folder appears in your Finder Sidebar, as shown in figure 6.51.

Click and drag items you want burned onto the Desktop icon or into the burnable folder's window until you're ready to burn, and then click the Burn button. The status information at the bottom of the Finder window tells you how much of the disc's capacity you're currently using.

Tip

In Mac OS X 10.4 and higher you don't have to insert a disc first in order to create a burnable folder — instead, you can simply choose File ➪ New ➪ Burn Folder, and then select a location for the folder and give it a name.

Using disk images

Once upon a time, Mac software was distributed on floppy disks (which weren't very floppy as they had hard plastic shells around the medium). Floppies had very limited capacity, less than 1.44MB — the original Mac floppies only held a bit under 400KB. By the time Apple introduced the iMac, the floppy was useful only for the transport or backup of very small files and the floppy drive was eliminated as a component one could expect to find. Shortly thereafter, the floppy drive was eliminated from the entire Macintosh line as almost all software began to be distributed on CD-ROM. But this was also about the time the Internet kicked into high gear and people started ordering and downloading software electronically.

6.51 Finder places icons for the blank CD on your Desktop and a burnable folder in the Sidebar.

Disk images (virtual disks) predated this change in the way software is distributed, but burgeoning electronic distribution gave massive impetus to their use. One of the largest users of disk image files (you'll see them with a .dmg file extension) is Apple itself. Just go to www.apple.com/support and download any of the software updates and the odds are that you'll receive a disk image file for your effort. They're far from the only company to use disk images, though—you'll see them available from almost every developer of Macintosh software. Figure 6.52 shows the disk image file for StuffIt Standard Edition available from Allume Systems (www.allume.com).

StuffItStandard9.0.1.d
mg

6.52 StuffIt is one of many software products available for download as a disk image.

Open a disk image file by double-clicking or by selecting it and choosing File ➪ Open (⌘+O) and you'll see a removable disk icon appear on your Desktop and in the Finder Sidebar, as shown in figure 6.53. From that point on, you interact with the disk's content just as you would with any other removable disk.

Another place you encounter disk image files is when you remove a user account in OS X. One of the options is to archive the account's home directory—that archive is a disk image file. You can also create your own disk image files using Disk Utility (located in your Utilities folder). Open Disk Utility and you see New Image as the second icon in the Disk Utility window's toolbar (see figure 6.54). Proceed as follows:

1. **Click New Image.** The sheet shown in figure 6.55 appears.

2. **Type a name for your new image, set format to Read/Write, and set the size and encryption as desired.** If you'd like to password protect your data, you can turn on encryption; see Chapter 3 for details.

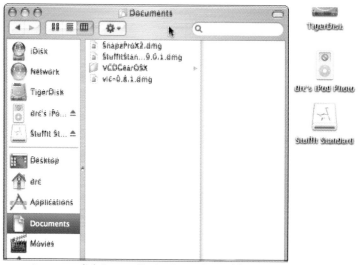

6.53 An open disk image file looks and acts like any other disk.

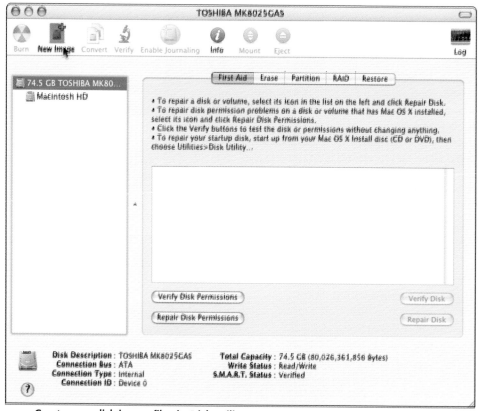

6.54 Create new disk image files in Disk Utility.

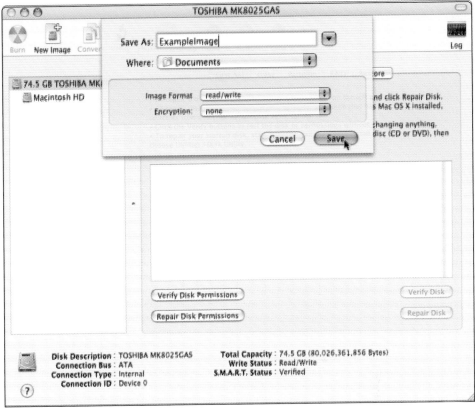

6.55 Define your new disk image here.

3. **Click Create.** A new disk image file appears in the list of volumes at the left of the window and on your Desktop.

4. **Click and drag the items you want in the virtual disk to the disk image volume.** If you want the virtual disk to remain read/write, you're done. If, however, you want it immutable, continue with Step 5.

5. **Select the DMG file in Disk Utility's list of volumes and click Convert Image in the Disk Utility toolbar.** The sheet shown in figure 6.56 appears.

6. **Choose the desired final image format from the Image Format pop-up menu.**

Simple, easy, and incredibly useful – disk images should be a regular part of your user arsenal. Encrypted read/write images, in particular, can come in very handy if you want to keep one particular set of data really private.

Cross-Reference See Chapter 3 for more discussion on using encrypted disk images – or turning your entire home folder into the equivalent of an encrypted disk image in order to keep your files secure.

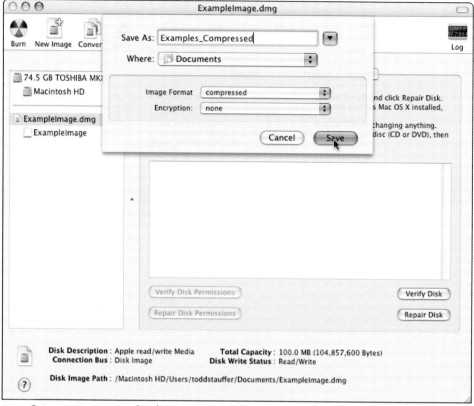

6.56 Set new parameters for the converted disk image.

Sharing Data Securely

On the road, you may sometimes find that you yearn for the ability to access the local network in the home office (or your office in your home, whatever the case may be). In some cases, that can make the difference between getting away at all. For example, at my day job in a newspaper office, the ability to access the server computer (or a server computer) to gain access to the files and documents I need to work on means being able to do a little editing from the road and still get the newspaper out on time.

Ideally, a connection to the home network should be secure, such that prying eyes can't easily get at the data that's being transferred between computers. The same, of course, is true when you surf the Web or access other Internet services – particularly when you spend time on unfamiliar wireless networks or hotel broadband. You may find that you prefer the security of tunneling (using special secure protocols to keep others from gaining access to your data) through the public network and using some form of secure connection or encryption to connect to various Internet services. This section touches on some of those possibilities.

Sharing files remotely

If your home network has a fixed IP address and a server that supports Apple Filing Protocol (AFP) is available at that IP address, then it's possible for you to connect to the network and share files from a remote location. All you have to do is switch to the Finder, choose Go ➪ Connect to Server, and then type the URL for the AFP server along with the AFP protocol, as shown in figure 6.57. Most of the time such a machine will be an Apple server (such as the XServe running Mac OS X server), although you can conceivably put one of your Macs in the DMZ of your LAN's firewall or reroute AFP requests to a particular Mac and you could log on to Personal File Sharing that way. Likewise, if you have a single Mac on the Internet and it has a fixed IP address and Apple File Sharing turned on, you can access it using this same approach.

Note *Enough acronyms for you? AFP is the protocol used for File Sharing on a Mac, so now we're talking about File Sharing over the Internet. The DMV is the "demilitarized zone," which is a corny way of saying that a particular computer on your network is set outside the protection of your router's firewall so that it can be accessed directly on the Internet.*

6.57 Connecting to a remote server for file sharing over the Internet.

Unfortunately, this approach isn't terribly secure by default. However, if your remote server supports a more secure connection, you may be able to make this file sharing session more secure. In the Connect to Server window that appears (where you type a username and password), click the small action menu icon that appears in the bottom-left corner, and then choose Options. On the Options dialog sheet that appears, deselect the Allow sending password in clear text option and select the Allow secure connections using SSH option (see figure 6.58). If the remote server is set up to serve an SSH-encrypted connection, you can connect in that way, which is better than no security at all.

Note *SSH stands for Secure Shell, and it's a method of logging into a remote computer securely, so that others can't access your data easily.*

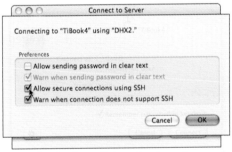

6.58 The Options dialog sheet can be used to change security preferences.

If the remote server can't accept the SSH connection, then it's up to you to decide whether you want to continue with the session; if you do, your data is more vulnerable to being intercepted on the Internet, because data travels between your networks without encryption.

Tip

If you're interested in being able to access and transfer files in a secure way, you might look into the secure FTP features that Mac OS X offers at the command line or through a graphical front end such as Fuga (`rsug.itd.umich.edu/software/fuga`*). Another option is iGet (*`www.fivespeed.com/iget/`*), which offers secure FTP connections as well.*

Browsing by proxy

Another issue that might come up when you surf on other people's networks is how much they know about you and the sites that you visit. While it's relatively unlikely that someone would snoop, the truth is that a typical router or firewall can be used to capture the outgoing URL requests made by computers on the network, which could allow a coffeehouse or hotel to build a history of the places you visit while you surf, including the IP addresses for your personal servers or corporate sites.

If you prefer to keep your browsing history to yourself, one solution is to use a proxy server. With a proxy server, all of your requests are sent to that server, usually through an encrypted connection, so that no one but you and the proxy know what it is that you've requested, thanks to the encryption, so that the entire transaction is secure. Then the proxy server makes the request for you, so that the sites you visit only see that proxy server, not your own Mac's IP addresses and other information that can generally be found out about you and your Mac relatively easily.

If this option sounds interesting, you'll want to shop the different services. Some popular options include ProxyWay.com, Anonymizer.com, FindNot.com, MetroPipe.net,

and many, many others. Some services offer blocking and proxy for a number of different Internet applications; others focus on your Web browser. When surfing, the basic proxy services simply enable you to access them through your Web browser; once you're logged on to the proxy server over a secure SSH connection, you can anonymously browse to whatever sites you need to get to, including your e-mail, banking, and so on — assuming, of course, you trust the proxy server!

In other cases, you may be given a proxy server address that you can add to your Internet connection setup by opening the Network pane of System Preferences, selecting the port that you use for this Internet connection (AirPort, Built-in Ethernet, etc.) from the Show menu, and then clicking the Proxies tab (see figure 6.59). On the Proxies tab, you can turn on the Web Proxy option by clicking to place a checkmark next to it; then enter the address for your Web proxy server in the entry box label Web Proxy Server.

Encryption and security for e-mail

Oddly, e-mail is one of the least secure Internet applications in use — and we all tend to include some sensitive, personal stuff in e-mail, everything from falling in love to dealing with our attorneys and making or breaking business deals. And yet, for all the fits we throw over the notion of sending a credit card number over an unsecure connection, we're willing to do all of this e-mail business in what is, essentially, plain text being sent over the Internet.

Two things can make e-mail more secure. First, you can lock down the connection from your Mac to the mail server that you're using for your mail so that the file packets that pass

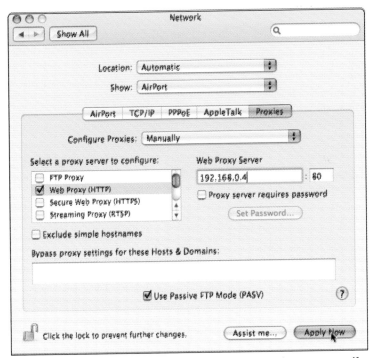

6.59 Use the Proxies tab when configuring a Network port to specify proxy servers to use for Web surfing and other Internet services.

from your e-mail server to your Mac are encrypted. That's a good thing if you're spending time on a public network or using someone else's Internet wireless or broadband, such as an Internet café, airport, or convention center, because you might not want their IT people (or the people who have hacked the public network) to gain access to your e-mail as it comes off the server.

Second, you can scramble the e-mail messages that you're sending to others in such a way that your recipient can read them but others can't.

Securing e-mail connections

The solution to the first issue — securing your actual e-mail connection — is to tell your ISP that you want a Secure Sockets Layer (SSL) connection to your mail server — this

is the same sort of connection that's used for secure Web transactions. If the ISP can make that happen, then you next need to set up Mail to use SSL when connecting to the server. Here's how:

1. **Launch Mail and choose Mail, Preferences.**

2. **In the Mail Preferences window, click the Accounts icon.**

3. **Select the account that you want to use for an SSL connection, and then click the Advanced tab for that account.**

4. **At the bottom of the Advanced tab screen, select the Use SSL option and choose the type of password that your ISP wants you to use from the Authentication menu.**

You might also want to secure your connection to your outgoing (SMTP) mail server. Here's how:

1. **In Mail Preferences, click the Account icon, and then select the account that you want to configure.** The Account Information tab should be selected automatically.

2. **At the bottom of the Account Information screen, click the Server Settings button.** A dialog sheet appears.

3. **Select the Use Secure Socket Layers option.**

4. **Type a method of authentication, a username, and password.**

Note   *This encryption is only between you and your mail server, so that anyone who intercepted data between your Mac and the server would be hard pressed to read it. But what about the security of the e-mail once it leaves your ISP's server computers? That's what the next section focuses on.*

Encrypting e-mail

The other part of the solution is to make sure that e-mail messages that you send to others — particularly messages of a sensitive nature — are encrypted before they're sent, so that only the intended recipient can read the message.

Most e-mail encryption is accomplished using something called a *public key* system. The way it works is that someone publishes his or her public key on special key servers, so that anyone who wants to can encrypt a message using that public key. Now, you send a message to that person. When it's received, that person uses his or her *private*

key to decrypt it; otherwise, if he or she doesn't have the private key, then it can't be read. Because a hacker or accidental recipient wouldn't have that private key — and the recipient should — then only the recipient is able to read the message.

Getting set up with encryption keys is a little outside the scope of this book, but you may be interested to know that both Mail and Keychain Access can get in on the action. In the Keychain Access application, you can choose Keychain Access ➪ Certificate Assistant to walk through the process of creating a certificate, which can be used to establish your identity with trusted server companies and also to create your public and private key combination.

Once you have a certificate in place, you can use a tool such as PGP Desktop (www.pgp.com) to encrypt your e-mail messages, through either a Mail plug-in or by copying your messages to a special utility and encrypting them, then copying them back.

Secure chat

Another Internet service that isn't as secure as it could be is iChat, where it can be tempting to say all sorts of things in an AIM chat over the Internet — after all, it certainly feels secure. Unfortunately, it's not.

For the most part, it's probably okay if your chats go across the Internet without encryption. But every so often there might be something you want to send — a credit card number or bank account or hotel confirmation code or similar — and you'd like it to be encrypted. A fun tool called Secret Service (www.mizog.com/productinfo/service/index.html) is designed to do just that, enabling you to easily encrypt small snippets of text using the Services menu in the application in which you're working. For iChat, for example, you simply highlight the text you want to encrypt and choose iChat ⇨ Services and choose the Secret Service menu, followed by the type of encryption you want to use (see figure 6.60).

The real solution for secure chatting is to use a tool other than AIM; if you can access a Jabber server, for example — preferably an iChat Server that you set up on your Mac OS X Tiger Server back at the office — then you can use it for secure chatting between coworkers.

Tip *Another option is PGP9 (www. pgp.com) that can encrypt a number of types of data and communications included in e-mail, AIM, and iChat conversations. You can also use it to encrypt your data files and to "shred" sensitive documents so that they cannot be recovered with undelete utilities.*

Going Cross-Platform

One reality for the portable Mac user is likely the need to maintain some level of compatibility with Windows users. If you're traveling for work, you'll likely encounter Windows-based networks in your remote offices or when visiting clients; you may find it helpful to have a sense of how to access those networks. It's also worth knowing that you can share files from your Mac, making them available to Windows users connected to the same LAN.

Want more? Sometimes there's an application that only runs in Microsoft Windows; it might be a vertical business application (one designed specifically for a particular industry) or an application that you're otherwise required to use. If your computing needs require Windows, you can run it — in

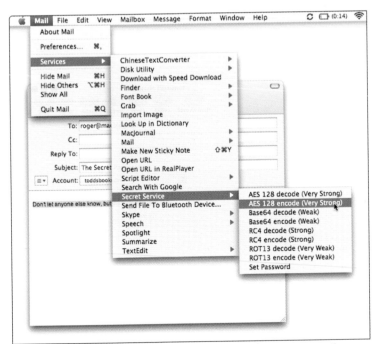

6.60 The Secret Service menu can be used to choose a type of encryption for chat, e-mail, or any other snippet of text you want secured behind a password.

fact, Microsoft is happy to sell us Mac users a copy in the form of VirtualPC, an application that emulates an Intel-based PC, enabling you to install and make use of applications that are written specifically for Microsoft Windows.

Accessing Windows networks

The first step in connecting to a Windows-based network is the same as connecting to or creating your own Mac-based network — you need to plug in to the network's hub or get configured to access the network wirelessly, if that's an option. If you opt for Ethernet, that means connecting an Ethernet cable from your Mac's Ethernet port to an available port on the hub or switch for the network (or, if your building or office is wired for Ethernet, you might be connecting to a wall socket which, in turn, connects to the network's switch).

If you're connecting wirelessly, the drill is similar to connecting to a Mac-based AirPort network, except that you're likely making that connection with a third-party wireless router. Follow these steps:

1. **Turn on AirPort in the AirPort menu bar icon, and then choose the appropriate wireless network that appears in that menu.** With the connection made, your next step is the protocol. You'll need to configure TCP/IP for the port that you've chosen.

2. **Open the Network pane of System Preferences.**

3. **Choose the port you want to use for networking from the Show menu and select the TCP/IP tab for that port.** More than likely you'll set up TCP/IP by choosing Using DHCP from the Configure IPv4 menu; if you need a manual configuration or otherwise do some tweaking, you'll probably get that information from the system administrator for that Windows-based network.

With the connection configured, you're closer to connecting to the Windows machine. To make that happen, you need to know a few things about the Windows computer that you want to connect to including the Workgroup or Domain name to which the Windows computer belongs and a valid username and password on that Windows machine.

If the Windows computer is in the same subnet as your Mac, you should be able to access it by selecting the Network icon in the Sidebar of a Finder window. First, you see the name of the Workgroup or Domain; open that Workgroup or Domain (double-click if you're viewing the Finder window in List or Icon view, or single click in Columns view). Now you should see the name of the Windows computer to which you want to connect. Double-click (or single-click in Columns view) that icon (see figure 6.61).

Using a Windows-based server is pretty much the same as using a Mac-based server, at least as far as file sharing goes. If there's a difference, it's that you may find that your user account is limited to certain folders on the PC. In Windows, you can set up file sharing so that particular folders are offered as shared points, and that's what a remote user is given access to.

6.61 When you locate a Windows-based server, you can double-click to log on just as you would a Mac-based server.

Logging off the Windows-based server is the same as with Mac file sharing; simply select the file server's icon in the Finder and choose File ➪ Eject, or click and drag the icon from the Desktop to the Trash. In a Finder window sidebar, you see a small eject icon next to the shared volume's icon — that works, too.

Sharing files with a Windows machine

So what about the reverse situation — you want to offer users on Windows computers the opportunity to share files on your Mac? It's even easier. You need to:

1. **Connect the PC to your network using TCP/IP as your protocol.** If you have a router with a DHCP server, you can tell the Windows machine to retrieve a DHCP connection.

2. **Open the Sharing pane of System Preferences.**

3. **Select the Windows Sharing option.** After you turn on Windows Sharing you see a new button called Accounts.

4. **Click the Accounts button.**

5. **Choose the user or users who will be authorized for Windows Sharing.**

6. **Note your Mac's IP address and close the Sharing pane.** The IP address will be needed on the Windows PC in order to access your Mac.

Now, you should be able to log on from the Windows machine to your Mac using one of the accounts that you enabled. (Your Mac should appear by default in a workgroup called Workgroup.) Here's how to access your Mac from the Windows PC:

1. **Choose Start ➪ My Network Places.**

2. **Choose Add a Network Place.** The Add Network Place Wizard appears.

3. **Click Next at the intro screen, and then select Choose Another Network Location and click Next again.** The What Is the Address Of This Network Place screen appears.

4. **In the Internet or Network Address entry box, type the IP address for the Mac machine *and* the shortname of the account that you're going to log into, following the form in this example:**
`\\192.168.0.8\todds;`
Click Next. A password dialog box should appear if your address and username are valid.

 Caution *Note the use of backslashes (\) when you're entering these addresses in Windows; If you use the forward slashes that you may be more used to for Web browsing and so on, then you won't be able to complete the connection.*

5. **In the password dialog box, type your username and password on that remote Mac and click OK.** If the remote Mac accepts your login, then you'll see an entry box in the wizard where you can give this new PC-to-Mac network connection a name.

6. **Type a name for this connection, click Next, and then click Finish.**

As a result of the wizard, you'll have a new entry in your My Network Places folder. Whenever you need to access that Mac's files, simply open up My Network Places and double-click the connection's icon.

 Caution *In order for a Mac to allow a Windows user to connect, it has to juggle some password technology. The reason you have to enable accounts, for example, is so that your Mac can store those passwords less securely so that they work with Windows; Apple recommends that you un-enable those accounts when you're done sharing and before you turn off Windows Sharing.*

 Note *If you just can't seem to get your Mac to accept the password as typed from Windows, it's possible that you have odd characters or capitalizations in the password that aren't translating cross-platform. Open the Accounts pane of System Preferences and change the password for that account.*

To turn off Windows Sharing, first disable any of the accounts you enabled with the Accounts button on the Sharing tab. Click the Windows Sharing option or select Windows Sharing option again to deselect them, and then click the Stop button.

Printing to a Windows shared printer

If you're on the road a lot, there's a decent chance that you'll be in a situation where you want to access a printer that's being shared by a Windows-based PC. In most cases, this is a printer that's connected directly to that PC — by USB or perhaps even a parallel cable — that's being shared through Windows printer sharing. Fortunately, the Mac can pick right up on that type of sharing and — assuming the printer is Mac-compatible — you should be able to print to it. Here's how that works:

1. **Connect to the network.** Plug in your Ethernet cable or connect to the wireless network that includes the Windows machine and its connected printer.

2. **Configure the printer connec-tion.** You can do this by launching the Print Setup Utility in the Utilities folder inside your Applications folder, or you can launch the Print command within an application and then choose Add Printer from the Printer menu. The upshot is the same — you look at the Printer Browser in the Printer Setup Utility. If a shared Windows printer is found, it'll be in the Printer Browser.

3. **Select it in the list and then choose an appropriate manufac-turer and driver for the printer.** If you don't have a good match, consider downloading a printer driver from the printer manufac-turer's Web site. There's nothing like a good printer driver to improve the printing experience.

Once you connect and select a driver, then printing should be about as easy as printing to a local printer or one connected through more conventional means. The only difference is

VPN: Access a LAN Remotely

So what do you do if you want to access a remote network over the Internet, but you want to keep things secure? With a Mac network, you can connect to a Mac OS X Server computer using SSL and encrypt the connection. In the Windows and Unix world, something along those lines is called a virtual private network (VPN) and it's a special deal. Fortunately, it's something that your Mac can use, too.

In order to work with a VPN you need to have one established — more than likely this is something that's been done at the organization level with the company or organi-zation for which you work. You then attempt to connect to it from your Mac; a VPN can use one of two major protocols, L2TP over IPsec or PPTP. Both are a mouthful, but all you really need to worry about is which option is required by your IT depart-ment. (PPTP is popular with corporations while L2TP over IPSec is a common choice for ISP-based private tunnel networks.)

When you're ready to create the VPN, you open Internet Connect by double-clicking its icon in the Applications folder and then selecting VPN from the toolbar. (If you don't see VPN on the toolbar, choose File Í New VPN Connection. With that selection made, a dialog sheet is likely to appear asking which sort of VPN you want to create, as shown here.

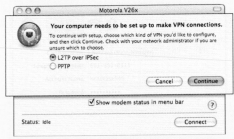

Choose your protocols for a virtual private network.

Choose the protocol that you need to use and you're returned to the Internet Connect window. Now you need to specify the server's address, your account name, and your password on the remote system. Click Connect, and if all goes well, you connect to the VPN and are ready to take advantage of its file sharing or other services.

that you need the Windows computer to be up and running in order for you to successfully send the print job.

Running Windows applications

Every once in a while you're going to come across an application that doesn't have a native Mac OS X version; in my business, there are newspaper and magazine applications — particularly for sales management — that are designed only to run on PC. (There happen also to be some good Mac packages, based partly on the strength of FileMaker Pro as a cross-platform solution.) If you come across a vertical application that doesn't work with the Mac or a particular Windows application that you simply think does the job better (or that your company requires you to use, perhaps for sales quotes or similar access while on the road), you should know that there is a solution — VirtualPC. VirtualPC is an application package that is now owned by Microsoft (purchased from a company called Connectix). What VirtualPC does is literally emulate, in software, all of the hardware that is generally associated with a Windows PC. As a result, with VirtualPC running, you can launch the Windows operating system (you can buy it when you buy Virtual PC), and then you can launch Windows applications.

VirtualPC isn't ideal under every circumstance — it's slower than a PC would be if it were the same speed as your Mac, and it isn't optimized for high-end applications that require a lot of processing power or graphical processing, including, for the most part, games. Instead, you'll want to use it with business applications, database tools, and other types of applications that won't run as native Mac OS applications but that don't require extraordinarily powerful PCs to run.

Tip *Microsoft also offers a program called Microsoft Remote Desktop Connection Client for Mac, which enables you to access a PC that is running Windows XP Pro as its operating system. You can then control the PC and run applications on it from your Mac, while viewing the results on your Mac's screen. If you happen to have access to a powerful PC over a network, this is an excellent way to make use of it from your Mac.*

Giving a Better Presentation

In this section, I focus a little bit on giving a presentation, if only because that's one of those things that you're a little more likely to do with a portable than you are with a desktop. The purposes for giving presentations have become considerably more democratized in recent years, too, as they've moved from the exclusive domain of the boardroom or sales office to classrooms, churches, and nonprofit group and fundraising meetings. So, let's look quickly at some of the key software that you can use for presentation on your iBook and PowerBook and then at some tips and devices that can help make the experience more enjoyable — or at least more high tech, and hopefully more successful.

Presentation applications

The Mac offers an array of options when it comes to presentation applications, ranging from the relatively simple to use — and, for iBook users, *free* — AppleWorks to Apple's own Keynote software, which is designed to give slick, impressive presentations.

Note *I'm not going to specifically discuss PowerPoint, which is Microsoft's venerable presentation software that's part of the Microsoft Office suite. PowerPoint is an industry standard, and PowerPoint for Mac offers compatibility with the Windows versions, as well. If you have the full version of Microsoft Office for Mac, you've got PowerPoint, and it's worth exploring — it's great software with many powerful, professional-level features.*

Using AppleWorks

AppleWorks is Apple's included office suite of applications, offering a number of different tools including a basic word processor, basic spreadsheet module, basic database, and so on. It's actually a wonderful application that people have been using for years. Recently, Apple has been somewhat slow to update it, focusing instead on Pages and Keynote, its two newer office applications that float somewhere between the basic capabilities of AppleWorks and higher-end office software such as Microsoft Word and PowerPoint.

If you have an iBook, then AppleWorks is already on your Mac — Apple ships AppleWorks with all its consumer models. Launch AppleWorks by double-clicking its icon in the AppleWorks folder that's inside the Applications folder. After it starts up, you see the Starting Points window appear, as shown

in figure 6.62; to begin a presentation, click the Presentation icon.

When you start the Presentation module, a blank screen appears with a few different floating windows. The key window for the Presentation module is the Controls window, where you control the slides for your presentation. The Controls window opens to the Slide tab (see figure 6.63), where you can add slides to your presentation and select the transitions between them.

Where you want to start, however, is on the Master tab, which is where you design the look of your *master slide* or slides. By creating a master slide, you can design the overall appearance that will be used when you create new slides — they will all be based on your master design. So, click the Master tab (the one that looks like a star) in the Controls window and then double-click the master slide's icon. Now, in the document window, you can use AppleWorks's drawing tool to create the look for your master slide.

If you do not want to design your own master slide, AppleWorks offers some other options. Prior to opening the Presentation tool through the Starting Points window, click the Templates tab. There you see a few different presentation types — Elegant Presentation, Geometric Presentation, and so on — that you can use as a jumping-off point to get started.

6.62 AppleWorks offers a number of different modules for getting work done, including a special Presentation module.

6.63 The Controls window is how you manage your presentation.

With your master slide or slides (you might want different types of slides) created, you can switch back to the Slides tab and begin to create slides. Click the plus (+) icon to create a new slide, and then double-click that slide in the Controls window to bring it up for editing. Make your edits and additions and then move on to the next one. This is how you build your presentation.

Also on the Slides tab, you see a menu. That menu enables you to select the transition effect that is used to open a slide. Select a slide in the Controls window, and then choose from that menu — Box, Radial, Zigzag — and when you're playing back the presentation, that effect is used when this slide is brought onto the screen.

At the bottom of the tab you see a few icons; these options enable you to choose whether to make the slide printable or whether it should be viewable. This can be handy when you want to leave slides in your presentation but you don't want to use them; click the closed-eye icon (see figure 6.64) and that slide won't appear in the presentation.

6.64 You can determine whether slides print and/or whether they appear in the presentation.

As you edit slides in AppleWorks, note that you can do something interesting with the AppleWorks tools. On the left-hand side of the AppleWorks interface (by default) is the main AppleWorks palette, with icons at the top for changing to various drawing modes and shapes; you also see icons that let you move from a word processing mode to a spreadsheet mode, and so on. AppleWorks, overall, operates on the theory that you can add different *objects* to most AppleWorks documents, using the tools from one module in an object within a document you're creating in a different module. In other words, if you want to create a table of data in a presentation you're creating, you can do that by clicking the spreadsheet tool, drawing a box, and then using the full power of the spreadsheet module to build that chart or table that you want to include in your presentation.

> **Tip**
>
> *You can name your slides just as you name a folder in the Finder; click the name and wait a second; when it becomes highlighted you can start typing. Naming slides is important for later organization.*

Once you have a number of slides in your presentation, they may become more difficult to manage on the Slides tab, simply because you can only see a few slides at once, depending on how large you've made the window. If that's the case, switch to the Groups tab (it looks like a small folder) where you can rearrange slides by clicking and dragging them. You can also create folders in this view (click the plus icon) for grouping slides together into, for example, outline sections or topic areas. This can make it easier to rearrange entire portions of your presentation at once.

Finally, to display your presentation, click the Show tab. On that tab (see figure 6.65), you see a number of options:

✦ **Auto-advanced every ___ seconds.** Turn on this option and set the number of seconds that Appleworks should wait for each slide to display before it automatically moves to the next one.

✦ **Show cursor.** Turn on this option if you'd like to have the cursor on the screen; you can use it for pointing and emphasis, if desired.

✦ **Show controls.** Turn this on if you'd like to see controls for QuickTime movies and other multimedia that you've embedded in the slides.

✦ **Play automatically.** Turn this option on if you want QuickTime and other multimedia to play automatically when the slide is displayed; the secondary options can be used to set how those items are played, and whether AppleWorks should wait until the multimedia has finished before allowing you to advance the slide.

Note

The fact that AppleWorks slides can incorporate QuickTime video and audio is very interesting, as it makes it possible to narrate presentations automatically, for example, or to show video portions for making a presentation more interesting. To add multimedia elements while editing a particular slide, choose File⇨Insert to locate a QuickTime-compatible movie or audio file.

6.65 The Show tab is where you make final decisions about your presentation.

Once you make your choices, click the Play button. Your Mac's display changes to 640 × 480 resolution (as that's the resolution of the slides that you create) and the presentation begins. As the presentation plays, use the space bar, right arrow, or down arrow (or click) to advance the slide; use the left arrow or up arrow to return to the previous slide; or press End or Home to jump to the end or beginning of the show, respectively. To stop the presentation in the middle, press Esc and you return to regular screen resolution and the AppleWorks interface.

Using Keynote

AppleWorks's presentations are somewhat basic, although incorporating transitions and QuickTime support make it possible to offer some fairly detailed presentations, particularly if you already have AppleWorks and aren't particularly interested in paying more for presentation software.

Apple's Keynote, however, is certainly the next step up. Designed exclusively as presentation software, Keynote begins by offering you a palette of professional slide designs that enable you to instantly jump into an attractive set of slides. When you first open Keynote, a dialog sheet appears that enables you to select the design theme you want to use for your slides. Do so and then click Choose (see figure 6.66).

With the theme chosen, you'll now be in the Keynote interface. There's more going on here than with AppleWorks. To create a new slide, click the New button in the toolbar and a slide is added to the list; with that slide highlighted, pull down the Masters button menu and you can choose a different master slide to use for this slide (see figure 6.67). With the slides in place, follow the on-screen instructions and double-click text to edit it.

While you edit the existing text on the slide, you can add items to the slide by clicking the Text, Shapes, Table, or Chart icons in the toolbar. When you do, each adds its own style of object to the slide, which you can then drag around to position. Note that with text, you can select it on-screen and then use the Format menu to change the font's look, color, and so on.

Note *Adding a table or chart is a little more complex than adding text or shapes, so when you click those options, small windows appear to help you manage those features. For a table, for example, you choose the number of rows and columns and set the borders. When you're done with that formatting, close the Table or Chart Data Editor by clicking the close button.*

6.66 Choose a theme for your slides.

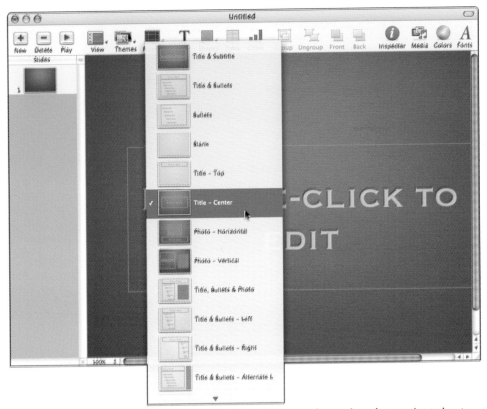

6.67 Choosing the most effective master slide within your theme for what you're trying to communicate.

Down the side of the Keynote window you see the slides as they're added — you can click and drag those slides around to rearrange them or select a slide and choose Slide⇨Skip Slide if you want to leave a slide in the presentation document but not have it appear as part of the show. You can also change the view in Keynote so that the slide icons are outline items instead or so that they don't appear at all; click the View button on the Keynote toolbar to make those choices.

Tip The Show Notes feature in the View menu enables you to see notes that you can attach to any (or all) slides in your presentation. You can later print these notes to use when you're giving your presentation.

As with AppleWorks, Keynote is very friendly to multimedia files; click the Media button in the toolbar and a small window appears that enables you to browse the media you have on your hard drive, including the movies, audio, and photos that you've stored in your home folder. To add an item, simply click and drag it from the media browser to your slide.

Caution *Adding a lot of multimedia to your presentation can add significantly to the size of your Keynote file; for ultimate portability of your Keynote document, keep the movies and sounds to a minimum.*

When you've arranged your slides and formatted and filled them with interesting text, you may want to dig a little deeper and add transitions and effects. To do that, select the slide and open the Inspector by clicking its button on the toolbar. In the Inspector, choose the slide icon to see the Slide Inspector shown in figure 6.68.

6.68 The Slide Inspector gives you control over transitions.

Setting an effect for the out-transition for this slide is easy; simply choose a transition from the Effect menu and set a duration in the Duration field. If the effect offers a direction, you can choose that in the Direction menu. The Start Transition menu is actually a bit deceiving — this command is used to determine whether or not your slide show is automated. Set whether or not this slide will change to the next Automatically or On Click, which really means whenever you advance the slide by clicking, pressing the space bar, and so on. If you choose Automatically, you need to set a Delay, as well, so that Keynote knows how long to wait before changing the slide.

With your slides edited and transitions set, you're ready to play back that presentation. To start, select the slide where you want the presentation to begin and click the Play button in the toolbar or choose View⇨Play Slideshow. Press the space bar (or right arrow or down arrow) to advance slides, and the left arrow or up arrow to go back. Press Esc to return to the Keynote interface.

Remember to save your work as you edit, and explore the Print settings, which enable you to print notes along with your slides so you can have a printed copy while you're presenting.

Tips for a better presentation

I may not be a world-class presentation pitchman, but there are a few suggestions I have for making your entire presentation experience go a little better, regardless of the software that you use. Here they are in no particular order:

Presenter Display

Keynote has a wonderful feature for use with PowerBooks that supports dual monitors, called Presenter Display. With this option, what you see on your PowerBook's display is different from the signal sent to your external video port and, hence, to an overhead projector, television, or whatever output you use for your presentation. On your display, instead of simply seeing the slide, you see the current slide, the next slide, a timer, the current time, and even notes for the current slide. This is a great way to keep a presentation going smoothly and helping you to casually transition from slide to slide. To set up Presenter Display, choose Keynote⇨Preferences and click Presenter Display.

✦ **Back up your presentation file.** If you have a .Mac account and/or can carry your presentation backup with you on disc do it. This can be a lifesaver if you're in a different city and have trouble with your Mac, as you can hopefully still give the presentation using another computer.

✦ **Test your presentation.** Before giving your presentation, test it to make sure that all of the transitions work, all of the slides appear as you expect them to, no stray text or elements pop up accidentally, and that all linked files — QuickTime movies or objects pasted from other applications — appear in the presentation as expected.

✦ **Check your tech.** Make sure your video out port works correctly before you travel, and once you arrive at your presentation site, check your portable to make sure it works well, that it's connected to battery power, and the screen savers and Energy Saver settings are configured so that your Mac doesn't turn itself off, blank the screen, or go to sleep during the presentation.

Tip

I like to give my presentations from a different user account on my Mac. That account is one that doesn't have anything else going on it — no iCal entries, no e-mail applications, no special background chat identifiers, no additional Dashboard items — so that nothing pops up or interrupts the presentation. If I need to switch back to the Desktop for some reason, there's only a clean space and not a bunch of clutter that defines my typical Mac workspace.

✦ **Take adapters.** Most of the projectors I encounter offer a VGA connector that can be connected to your Mac; with today's PowerBooks and iBooks, you often need an adapter so that you can hook up to such a projector. Also, if you do a lot of traveling to give your presentation, you might consider getting additional multimedia adapters for your Mac's output so that you can connect directly to televisions or other monitors and not just to a computer-style projector.

✦ **Keep it simple, part one.** Just because your presentation software is capable of whiz-bang transitions doesn't mean you should allow it to do them. In my opinion, it's okay to go from one slide to the next without a transition, or even to use a fade-out transition or something similar only to end a topic area or a portion of the talk, as a visual cue to your participants that it's about time to get up and stretch their legs. If you do transition between each slide, it's probably best to use the same transition between each, unless you're giving a presentation that's specifically about all of the cool transitions that come with the software.

Tip
Keynote was named in part because of the success that Steve Jobs has giving media-event keynotes to Apple's product rollouts throughout the year. One of Steve's tricks is additive transitions, in which a slide displays a portion of the slide first, and then the rest of the slide at a dramatic moment (as in..."Quarterly Results" at the top of the slide and then "$15 trillion profit!" as an addition to that slide at the right moment.

✦ **Keep it simple, part two.** For your presentation itself, I recommend keeping your slides relatively simple — the text that you put on a slide should be the key statistic or the particular fact that means the most to your audience. That visual aid will help drive home the point that you're trying to make with the words that you toss at them verbally.

✦ **Hand out your slides.** Presentation applications can do a nice job of printing the slides or printing an outline from the slides' main points that you can hand out to the people who are attending your talk. Unless the copying costs are prohibitive or there's supposed to be a big quiz at the end of your discussion, I think that you get much better attention from people to what you have to say if they don't feel they have to jot down every word. You also have a better sense of what the most important parts are than they do, so your slide printouts or outline serves as a solid basis for the notes that they do take.

✦ **Get a remote.** A few manufacturers make remote controllers that will work with your iBook or PowerBook to advance slides and run your presentation leaving you free to move around. Most of these remotes have both a receiver and a transmitter; you hold the transmitter and point it in the general vicinity of the receiver to get things done. Remotes are available from companies such as Griffin Technology (www.griffintechnology.com) and Macally (www.macally.com). Figure 6.69 shows an example.

6.69 A remote control gives you the freedom to move around the stage area during presentations.

Troubleshooting and Maintaining Your Portable Mac

7

In This Chapter

Maintaining your
portable Mac

Addressing common
problems

◆   ◆   ◆   ◆

Any piece of electronic or mechanical hardware
requires maintenance to minimize malfunctions, and
no piece of complex software is completely bug-free. But,
regardless of how much maintenance you perform, sometimes things still go wrong: A circuit fails, a piece of hardware
wears out, or there is an obscure software anomaly. Your
iBook or PowerBook is a Mac, which makes it computer hardware that is subject to the immutable Laws of Murphy.

As a portable, it is more susceptible to these laws than the
typical desktop machine. Unlike a desktop, your portable
needs to switch from battery to AC power, is carried from
place to place and banged around, is moved from horizontal
to vertical, and needs to function while bouncing on a lap or
tray table on a train, car, or airplane.

In this chapter, I discuss the most important preventive and
restorative measures you can take to avoid troubles and to
recover from them when prevention isn't enough.

Maintaining Your Portable Mac

Most of the software and some of the hardware troubleshooting discussed in the following pages is not specific to portables, but it can help you keep ahead of a number of maintenance and troubleshooting issues that you're likely to encounter with your Mac. Later in the section, I look at some of the items that you should take along with you when you travel with your portable, including some items that can help with recovery or troubleshooting.

Fixing permissions and disk directories

As previously mentioned (more than once), Mac OS X is a Unix (BSD variant) operating system. One consequence of this underlying structure is that every file on your hard drive has a set of associated *permissions* telling which users or groups are authorized to read, write, or execute a file or directory. Most software that is installed using Apple's Software Update technology or other installer packages requires an Administrator username and password before the installation can take place. The reason for that is simple — the installer has to obtain the permissions necessary to make system-level commands in order to perform the installation (such as getting write access to the Applications directory or to the Contents folder within an application package when performing an update). That requires a password because you only want authorized applications and installers to have such privileges.

Occasionally, a software installer will alter the ownership or permissions on a file or folder for a sequence of modifications and not change the ownership and permissions

back to their original state when finished. This is considerably more common for third-party software applications that have their own installers. The result might be benign, but it might also render the software or certain of its components inaccessible.

Apple's Installer application includes a *bill of materials* (BOM) file for every package it installs (PLG or MPLG file) and saves that information to the /Library/Receipts folder. The BOM file includes a list of the correct owner and permissions for every component installed. Apple's Disk Utility (located in /Applications/Utilities) includes functionality to verify and repair permissions — and it uses the BOM files as its knowledge base. You can see the Disk Utility window showing the Verify Disk Permissions and Repair Disk Permissions buttons in figure 7.1 on the bottom left of the First Aid tab.

 Note *Repairing permissions is chicken soup for Mac OS X. It won't hurt anything and it might help to cure problems, particularly if you're experiencing slowdowns with a particular application or trouble getting a certain program to launch or work correctly.*

While repairing permissions shouldn't be considered a periodic task, it is recommended that you repair permissions after each software installation or upgrade.

 Note *You can only repair permissions on a hard drive that has Mac OS X installed.*

Clicking Repair Disk Permissions will both verify and, if necessary, repair permissions in one pass. Just sit back and let it do its thing. The only reason to click Verify Disk Permissions that I can think of is that you only want to know what's wrong, but want to either bypass the repair process or delay it until a later time.

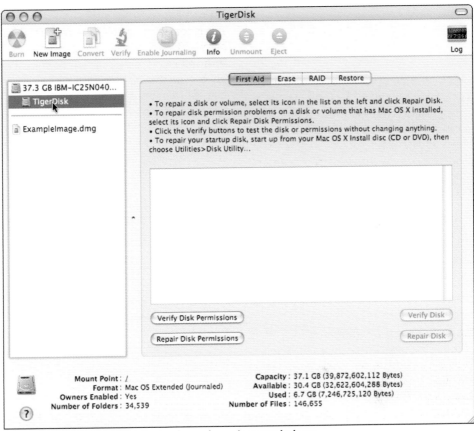

7.1 Disk Utility's First Aid tab checks and repairs permissions.

Note

For more information – possibly more than you really want to know – about permissions, reference the Apple Knowledge Base article Troubleshooting permissions issues in Mac OS X (http://docs.info.apple.com/article.html?artnum=106712).

Also on Disk Utility's First Aid tab are a pair of buttons to verify and repair a hard drive volume.

Note

To repair your startup disk, you must start up from a different volume, such as your Mac OS X Install CD or DVD and run Disk Utility from it.

As with Verify Disk Permissions, Verify Disk is a check of status, and Repair Disk will both verify disk directory integrity and, if necessary, make repairs to the disk's directory structure. There is no user interaction in this process and the repair process is not as versatile as that available in some third-party tools, such as Alsoft DiskWarrior (www.alsoft.com) or Micromat TechTool Pro (www.micromat.com), described later in this chapter. The "first" in First Aid is accurate – Disk Utility's First Aid function should be your first line of defense when directory problems are suspected (I run DiskWarrior if First Aid encounters more problems than it can handle).

Note

First Aid, when combined with File System Journaling (introduced with Panther and the default with a new Tiger installation) is far more robust than in the past when First Aid was considered a very high-level utility. You may find you don't need to run many other disk doctor utilities, unless you encounter a critical situation that requires file recovery.

Disk defragmentation

Apple refers to defragmenting a disk as *optimizing* the disk. Optimization is a process where the physical locations of files on a disk volume are rearranged in order to improve access time. Over time, as you modify files and the disk becomes filled, newly saved individual files on that disk become scattered *(fragmented)* across it. Collecting these fragments and rewriting the file contiguously is a major component of disk optimization — it makes disk access faster and makes file corruption a bit less likely.

The other component in disk optimization is the placement of files needed for system startup into what is referred to as the hot band, so that these files used to start your Mac are accessed as quickly as possible.

Unless your hard drive is almost full **and** (not *or*) you frequently create or modify very large files — such as the DV Stream video files created when importing video from a digital camcorder in iMovie — you might not notice a performance improvement as a result of defragmentation. To perform an in-place defragmentation, you need a third-party utility. Two well-regarded OS X-compatible defragmentation utilities are Disk Defrag (Intech, www.speedtools.com, a component of the $90 SpeedTools Utilities package) and Defrag (Coriolis Systems, www.coriolis-systems.com/iDefrag.php, $30).

The other way to perform a defragmentation is to back up all of your files, reformat your hard drive, install the Mac OS, and then copy those files back to your Mac. This process is considerably more time consuming, but cheaper, and with the extra step of making a full backup of your files, it's a good opportunity to archive files and perhaps even do a bit of spring cleaning. If you have an external hard disk, you can shortcut this process a bit by cloning your internal drive, which copies the entire drive to another drive for backup or transfer purposes. See the sidebar "Back It Up or Clone It" later in this chapter.

Mac OS X 10.3 and higher do a better job of self-optimizing, so you may find that in most cases you don't need a third-party tool. The exception to that is someone who works with a lot of different files that get copied to, changed, and then deleted on your Mac (magazine production, video editing, Web serving, and so on), at least much more so than a typical office or consumer Mac would be used. If that's the case for you, you might consider a tool that offers specific compatibility with your version of Mac OS X 10.3 or higher.

Optical drive cleaning

One of the most fragile and failure-prone components of any computer system is the optical drive. Just as CD and DVD players in your home entertainment center occasionally encounter difficulty recognizing or reading the media you insert, the CD/DVD drive in your laptop will experience all the same problems and more — after all, it gets bounced around and not only reads, but also writes, increasing the number of things that can go wrong.

Other than the common-sense precautions of minimizing the amount of jostling your drive experiences (especially while in use) and not inserting foreign objects into the drive, there really aren't too many precautions you can take against misalignment of the laser or other internal breakage.

All recent Mac laptops use slot-loading drives. This means that you insert the disc into a slot until your Mac pulls it in. Some earlier models, such as the G3 (Pismo) PowerBook and many first- and early second-generation iBooks, used tray-loading drives. Tray-loading drives are more versatile, allowing different media sizes (mini-CD/DVDs and business card CDs/DVDs in addition to the standard CD-R/DVD-R sizes), but require more vertical space, which makes for thicker computers. They also add parts that are more subject to breakage—the jokes about people using CD trays as coffee-cup holders may not be as true these days, but that tray sticking off the side of your seat and into the aisle is prone to breakage.

Cleaning an optical drive consists primarily of cleaning the lens; any reputable commercial CD or DVD head-cleaning disc will do the job if you follow directions. Do not insert foreign objects, such as swabs, into your optical drive slot. Similarly, do not blow compressed air into the drive—compressed air introduces significant temperature changes and condensation. Additionally, the blast pressure can easily damage fragile components in the drive mechanism.

The portable Mac's first aid kit

When you use your laptop at home or in the office, you have all your computer resources pretty much right at hand—your OS X install CD or DVD for emergency restarts, your collection of cables, your backup disks, and software tools like DiskWarrior or TechTool Pro are a little too much to haul around, but provide you with security when you're not on the road.

That said, you should consider at least some of these items to be part of your portable Mac first aid kit, if only because there's no better feeling than being prepared when you're on the road and trouble hits. So, here's a quick look at some of the items that you should consider taking with you when you back your portable Mac into its bag for travel:

✦ **Cables and cords.** I recommend the following as a practical set of cables to keep at hand while traveling with your portable Mac:

   • **Phone cord.** This comes in handy for sending or receiving faxes or, if no network connection is available, for sending and receiving e-mail. E-mail requires a dial-up account of some sort.

   • **Two Ethernet cables.** I suggest taking a regular Category 5 patch cable and a special *crossover* cable for situations where you need to create an instant network with another computer that isn't already networked. Although modern Mac laptops can autosense the cable type and you won't need a crossover cable to connect to another modern Mac, most Windows and Linux/Unix computers don't have that autosensing circuitry, nor do older Mac models.

- **FireWire (IEEE-1394) cable.** Having this kind of cable is invaluable if you encounter problems and need to restart in FireWire Target mode so that another Mac can be used to help you troubleshoot your disk difficulties. You can find retractable FireWire cables, such as IOGear's ReelQuick, that take up only about 1 square inch when not in use (www.iogear.com) — remember that you want a 6-pin to 6-pin cable for connecting two Macs.

- **USB cables.** Always useful for connecting peripheral devices, these cables are particularly handy when you need to con-nect to a PC user's small laser or inkjet. Many PC users have USB-compatible printers, but may use a Mac-unfriendly parallel cable for their printer connection.

✦ **AC adapter and spare battery.** If your experience using your laptop while traveling is typical, your battery will run low at very inconvenient times — usually when no AC outlet is available for you to plug in and start recharging. This is why a spare, fully charged battery is a critical com-ponent of your emergency kit. Similarly, you want that AC adapter available so that you can operate on AC power, and thus recharge your battery, whenever those elusive AC outlets are available.

If you're traveling internationally, you may want to have the appro-priate adapters on hand for local power plugs. In fact, Apple makes a kit for current model iBooks and PowerBooks, available from the Apple Store online or from Apple retailers. Also, if you'll be taking a car or plane, you may want a power adapter that works in a car's lighter port or in the airplane's power connector. You can find some designed specifically for portable Macs.

✦ **Emergency boot disk.** This could be a copy of your PowerBook or iBook's installation CD or DVD (or a copy of a newer version of Mac OS X's installer, if you've upgraded), but a basic installation of OS X on a portable FireWire drive is more flexible. An iPod (which is an external FireWire drive, after all) or one of the pocket drives like SmartDisk's FireLite line (www.smartdisk.com) allows you to combine an emergency boot disk and a working backup into one small, light, and portable package.

You should have a copy of your emergency utilities like DiskWarrior and/or TechTool Pro installed on the emergency boot disk.

✦ **Backup media.** This applies to both the files you need to work with away from home base and the files you create while traveling — backups are even more critical when on the road than at home because, in addition to the increased jarring and impact, lap-tops (particularly a really nice Mac laptop) are like magnets to thieves and other miscreants.

While CD-Rs or DVD-Rs can fill the bill nicely, you should also consider the convenience of a *keydrive* for this role. Unless you're backing up large media files (video or large quantities of photos), much of a CD's (or DVD's) capacity is wasted.

Additionally, if you back up to optical media, you either need one disc per backup session or you need to go to the extra effort of doing the write without finalizing the disc — and then, each backup session still mounts as a separate volume for you to traipse through seeking the file(s) you want. A keydrive is a much more convenient and dynamic solution if you have lots of small files.

As previously noted, this list is an all-other-things-being-equal set of tradeoffs. Personally, both Dennis and I tote an iPod, a USB cable, a FireWire cable (Dennis's is an IOGear ReelQuick 6-pin to 6-pin), a Cat 5 cable, and a phone cord in our laptops's carry bags. Dennis also takes a 1GB keydrive, as well as a few blank CD-Rs and DVD-Rs, but the latter are for transferring data and other files to clients, friends, and family rather than for backup purposes (the job better suited to the keydrive and iPod). I take a car/airplane adapter because I seem always to be running out of power, but I skip the extra battery because I'm a cheapskate. I tend to back up my most important files (presentations, documents I need to edit while traveling) on my iDisk, and I sync my contacts to .Mac so that I can recover them from another computer if need be.

You need to make the decisions based on your particular situation, including the size of your computer bag and how much you generally intend to carry, but the list is a good starting point.

Must-have troubleshooting software

What discs and applications should you have with you at all times while on the road with your portable Mac? The list here is fairly short, but some of these can be critical for an important file recovery situation.

Mac OS X's Disk Utility is the first line of defense, and you'll find it in every OS X installation (in the Utilities folder inside the main Applications folder) and available on your OS X Install CD/DVD. Realize that you can't rely totally on the Disk Utility in your Utilities folder, because you may need to boot from that CD (or from an external FireWire volume) in order to run certain Disk Utilities tools on your startup disk.

I am also a very big fan of Alsoft's DiskWarrior package (www.alsoft.com). When recovering from disk directory damage, I have never found anything even nearly as good. This is particularly true if you ever lose a disk on startup, whereby it becomes unbootable or unresponsive. DiskWarrior (see figure 7.2) works by recataloging your hard drive and rebuilding those directory databases, which will sometimes bring a disk magically back to life. Note that DiskWarrior should be used for startup recovery before Norton or a similar tool, as those other utilities hamper DiskWarrior's effectiveness.

 Tip *You can run DiskWarrior when you aren't having a critical problem, too, if you'd like to periodically fix smaller problems with your directory catalog. It's a great idea, in fact.*

7.2 DiskWarrior is our favorite tool for attempting file recovery operations on the road, because sometimes its approach has amazing results.

One of the many benefits of using a Mac running Mac OS X is that you don't need to spend much energy worrying about viruses, at least not most of the time. If, however, you traffic in Word and Excel files that employ Microsoft's macro language, you could be susceptible to one or more of the myriad macro viruses inhabiting that pocket universe. They won't do any damage to your Mac, except for possibly spreading to your various Word and Excel template files, but you could easily become the software equivalent of a carrier, spreading the virus to other computers.

Additionally, if you spend a lot of time running old applications in Classic, there are viruses that will attack your Classic System Folder and applications. In these instances, a virus-fighting utility is useful. Currently, McAfee's Virex is available as a free download for .Mac subscribers, or you can purchase a subscription. Other virus applications include Norton Antivirus (www.symantec.com) and VirusBarrier by Intego (www.intego.com).

Finally, for diagnosing hardware problems, it's a good idea keep on hand the Hardware Test CD that Apple ships with your laptop.

Wires and cables

Previously, in discussing the portable first aid kit, I touched on the basic set of cables you should consider taking with you on the road. When operating from your office or home, you don't have nearly the space or weight constraints, and the diversity of cables you can keep on hand grows significantly.

✦ **Phone cable.** If you ever use your Mac's fax capability, either sending or receiving, or you have a dial-up Internet connection, this cable is absolutely necessary.

✦ **USB cables.** Consider keeping a varied collection of USB cables on hand. For example, we always have a couple of spare 6-pin to 6-pin cables, at least one USB extender cable, a 6-pin to 4-pin USB cable, and a pair of 6-pin to mini-USB cables (for digital camera use), as well as a powered USB hub.

✦ **Power cables and batteries.** One major downside to laptop use is that there are so many different AC cables available, and only one of them will be right for your hardware, and they're all very expensive when compared to the very standardized male-to-female grounded power cords that are used with desktop computers, printers, hard drives, scanners, and so many other pieces of computer hardware. Similarly, every different model seems to use a proprietary battery and, regardless of the advertised battery life, you'll likely run out of juice at a critical time with no place to plug in and recharge. Because the spare battery is considered a vital component in the laptop traveler's kit, you want it recharged for when you leave your home base. You should consider an extra battery and power adapter as necessary supplementary equipment (just like additional RAM).

Note *Anecdotally, in a quarter century of personal computer usage, only Dennis has had one standard AC cable/plug go bad (his teething puppy was at fault) out of literally dozens. Conversely, between the two of us we've had six portable power adapters or cords fail, due to kinking as the cord gets rolled up and unrolled or rolled over by a chair or serving cart and the adapter getting inserted or removed from the outlet. The more you manipulate cabling and connectors, the more opportunity for mishap.*

✦ **FireWire cables.** Like USB cables, keep a variety on hand. If your Mac supports both FireWire 800 and FireWire, you should have at least one cable of each type. We also recommend at least one 6-pin to 4-pin FireWire cable—the one usually required to connect a mini-DV camcorder to your Mac. Even if you don't own a camcorder, that doesn't mean one of your friends or coworkers won't have one and some footage that you really need or want.

✦ **Ethernet cables.** Sometimes called Cat 5 cables, keep at least one crossover cable and one straight patch cable around for when you need to create a network or add a new piece of

hardware to your existing network. If your laptop typically offers only basic AirPort (802.11b) support, you'll experience a speed increase by switching to a wired Ethernet connection when you're at your desk. If your network hub supports the 100BaseT or 1000BaseT (sometimes called "gigabit Ethernet") standards, you even get a speedup by using Ethernet when compared to AirPort Extreme (802.11g).

✦ **AV cables and adapters.** Invaluable when you want to connect to an external display, a projector, or a TV set, there are a variety of video cables you might need, each dependent upon which Mac laptop you have and what your external video device(s) might be. Check your Mac's User Guide to see what video-out capabilities it supports. You likely have one or more of the cables and adapters in the box that came with your PowerBook or iBook.

What to keep on disk

If we can recommend one item that can save you a lot of time if disaster strikes, it would be the downloaded updaters for your OS X software and applications. Of course, we don't recommend that you save this (only) on your hard drive—keep a backup of these installers and updaters. If you ever have to reinstall your system software or an application, running an updater that you already have saves you a great deal of time over having to acquire it through a download (or snail mail) and then running the update. For the items acquired through Apple's Software Update, the process of saving the update is very simple, as illustrated in figure 7.3.

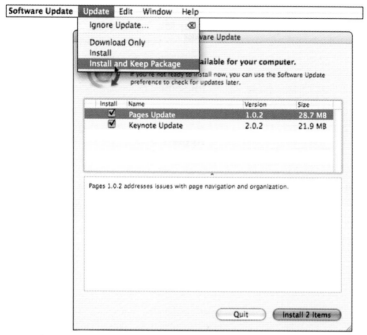

7.3 Software Update lets you save the package you're about to install.

Software Update's Update menu offers a few options not seen in the main window. In our opinion, the most useful of these is Install and Keep Package. When you make this choice, the update takes place as usual, but when the installation process is completed, you'll find a PKG (or MPKG) file in the /Library/Packages folder. From this point forward, if you need to reinstall the software to which the update applies, you already have the updater at hand.

Tip *Choosing Update ⇨ Install and Keep Package also provides you the option of downloading the updater only once if you need to perform the update on more than one computer. This can be particularly advantageous if you aren't blessed with a high-speed Internet connection.*

Another item you should at least consider keeping on disk is a third-party disk utility. We like DiskWarrior, as you might have gathered from earlier discussion.

Addressing Common Problems

There are three main areas where you can encounter problems when using any computer: electrical, hardware, and software. Each of these three areas can manifest itself in a number of ways. The following discussions address problem symptoms and walk you through determining into which problem category the symptoms indicate the actual difficulty lies.

Startup problems

When you press your laptop's Power button and nothing happens or you hear the startup sound but your Mac doesn't make it to the login screen or your Desktop (if you have autologin enabled), you probably experience a sinking feeling in the pit of your stomach.

The first problem, nothing happening, is almost always a hardware or electrical problem. Some remedies to try include:

✦ **If your laptop is not plugged into an AC outlet, plug it in and try again.** If that works, then you probably were just suffering from a dead battery. Leave it plugged in to recharge or swap in a fully charged battery.

✦ **If supplying AC power didn't work or you were already plugged in, try connecting a different AC adapter.** This will help determine whether there is a problem with the cord, connector, or adapter. (Of course, you should make sure that the outlet is supplying power by plugging something that you know works into the outlet and checking — sometimes, a circuit breaker has been tripped or a wall switch has been turned off.) Leave it plugged in for a minute or two before pressing the power button to make sure that all circuitry is ready to go.

> **Note**
>
> *Dennis has a PowerBook G3 that doesn't get a lot of use now that he also has a PowerBook G4. When he hasn't used the G3 for a month or two and plugs it in, nothing happens, but if he leaves it plugged in for at least 24 hours and tries the power button again, it starts up. If you have an older model PowerBook, you might want to keep this in mind.*

✦ **You may have an issue with your Mac's power manager and/or battery and AC power adapter.** Check out the section "Battery life and power manager" for some additional options.

✦ **If none of these other options work, take your laptop in to an Apple Store or other authorized service center.** You likely have a problem that necessitates a repair bill unless your laptop is still under warranty or you purchased AppleCare.

Assuming that your Mac is getting power, but just doesn't make it through the startup process, the following list of diagnostic checks should be attempted, in the order given, until you either have isolated the problem or run out of checks to try.

1. **Disconnect all external devices (printers, external keyboards and mice, external drives, cameras, and so on) and attempt to restart.** If that clears things up, you know that one of your devices or its connection (cable, port, or connector) is causing the problem. Plug in one at a time and try startup again until you isolate the problem device.

On occasion, everything will be fine after you reconnect all your external devices. If that is the case, you either have a device whose connector was not solidly attached or you have an intermittent cable/connector/port problem. If the problem recurs at a later date, assume the intermittent connection problem and work to isolate the bad cable, connector, or port.

2. **Restart your laptop while pressing Option.** This should bring your Mac up in the Pick a device to boot from screen. If your target disk is present on this screen, select it and then click the arrow on the right of the screen. If your target disk isn't present, it means that your Mac doesn't recognize a valid startup (System) folder on that volume. If another bootable volume is present, start from it and see whether your target volume is there, albeit with a damaged System. If the volume is there with a damaged System, you can attempt to restore from your backups (you do back up your Mac, don't you?), repair the disk using Disk Utility or some other recovery program like DiskWarrior, or, failing all else, reinstall your System after backing up any files you want preserved to another volume (CD, DVD, external hard disk, key drive, and so on).

3. **Try booting from another source, such as your OS X installation DVD or CD or a recovery tool's startup CD.** To restart from a CD or DVD, insert the disc in your optical drive and restart while pressing C. If pressing and holding C doesn't work, try Option and proceed as in Step 2. If neither works, you're starting to run out of things to try.

4. **The last thing to try before giving up and contacting an Apple service technician, is to see whether you can see your computer's hard drive when using FireWire Target mode.**

With your Mac powered off, connect the FireWire 400 ports of your laptop and another Mac. Restart your laptop while pressing T. If your screen and hard drive are functioning, a blue screen appears with a bouncing FireWire logo on your laptop's monitor and your hard drive should appear as a volume on the other Mac's Desktop (or in the Finder sidebar).

Tip

If your hard drive does mount, this would be an opportune time to back up all the data present on your laptop's drive before attempting any software-based recovery tools or the more drastic step of reformatting and reinstalling your OS.

Assuming that you were able to see and back up your data at some point in the previous steps, it is time to attempt repair or reinstallation. Use your recovery software of choice to attempt to recover or restart with your OS or laptop's Install disc. Or, assuming that you have cloned your drive (as described shortly), reformat the hard drive and restore from the cloned backup, adding whatever files you were able to back up that had changed since you cloned the drive.

If all of the previous suggestions fail, you need to see an Apple service technician, or if your data is important enough to you and your wallet/credit card can stand the hit, you could contact DriveSavers (www.drivesavers.com) to recover your data (if your data is that critical and you haven't been backing up regularly, shame on you!).

Back It Up or Clone It

Both Dennis and I are big fans of backing up our systems. Not only is our data important, but the hassle of resurrecting our finely tuned working environments is extremely distasteful. I use my office network scheme to keep files backed up in the office and my iDisk for backup on the road.

Dennis, in addition to backing up his data regularly, likes to *clone* (make an exact copy of) his entire hard drive to an external drive whenever he makes a major change (just before upgrading to a new OS release, for example). Two popular utilities for performing this cloning operation are SuperDuper! (www.shirt-pocket.com, $20) and Carbon Copy Cloner (www.bombich.com, donationware). SuperDuper! has more options, including setting checkpoints that allow you to time-travel to a specific point in your system's life; however, if all you seek is the basic drive-cloning functionality, Carbon Copy Cloner is free.

Application problems

Almost all Mac OS X application-related problems stem from improperly set permissions, corrupt preference (PLIST) files, or problems with third-party applications. (Even worse are third-party hacks. Yes, those little Unsanity hacks (www.unsanity.com), as useful and as attractive as they are, often come at a price paid in lessened stability for your Mac.)

The most basic application problem occurs when you attempt to launch an application and it immediately quits or fails to respond. Follow these steps, as they apply to your situation, to try to fix the problem:

1. **The most straightforward fix to attempt is to log off and then log back on and try it again, or to restart, log on, and reattempt launching the application.**

2. **Launch the Console application from your Utilities folder and display the Logs pane (click Logs in the toolbar, shown in figure 7.4, or choose View ⇨ Show Log List).** Expand the ~/Library/Logs list and then expand the CrashReporter entry. Select the crash in which you're interested, and an assortment of low-level details meant for techies appears on the right, describing what was going on when the crash took place. If you're not nerdy enough to make sense of this, skip on to the next suggestion. (Of course, they might be of interest to a technical support person or to the author of the application that crashed, if you get a hold of them via the Internet, for example.)

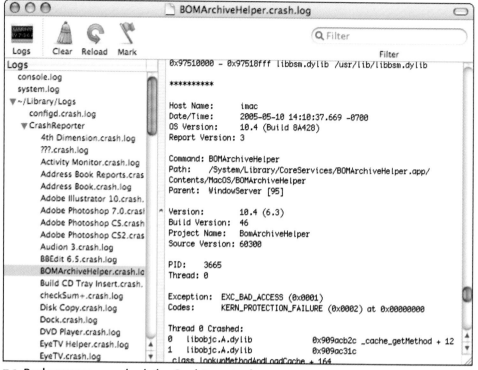

7.4 Real programmers check the CrashReporter logs.

3. **Launch Disk Utility, and in the First Aid tab, tell Disk Utility to Repair Permissions, as described earlier in this chapter.** I reiterate here that repairing disk permissions should be a prophylactic exercise performed after installing or updating software.

4. **Locate and remove the application's preferences file.** This file is almost always located in the Preferences folder inside your personal Library folder, which is inside your Home folder's and has a name like com.company.programname.plist — for example, iTunes's preference file is com.apple.itunes.plist.

Keeping an Account for Testing

I suggest keeping an unused-except-for-testing user account on your Mac. (You create it using the Accounts pane, which is discussed in Chapters 3 and 4.) When you encounter a problem with one of your applications, log on to this clean account and see whether the problematic application's misbehavior occurs there. If it doesn't, then the preference file is almost assuredly at least part of the problem; if the problem occurs in the clean account tool, then the preference file is less likely to be at fault (though it still might be a contributing factor).

5. **Check your application enhancers (sometimes called *haxies*) and background applications.** For example, some document scanners include a background logon application to implement one-touch scanning that can interfere with more generic scanning software's access to the scanner. You can determine what background applications are running by checking in Activity Monitor (in your Utilities folder). Startup (actually logon) items can be located in your Accounts System Preferences pane, on the Login Items tab.

   Most enhancers appear in the Other row of System Preferences main window. The actual files will be located in /Library/PreferencePanes or ~/Library/PreferencePanes. Remove suspect items and restart. You might have to run an uninstaller for some — if you're using haxies, you really need to have read the documentation that came with them to know how individual haxies are disabled.

6. **Run a third-party utility like DiskWarrior to check and, if necessary, repair disk directory problems.** You'll need to restart from another volume or the DiskWarrior CD to fix problems on your normal startup volume.

7. **If everything up to now has failed, it is time to consider reinstalling the application software.**

File problems

What can you do when a file won't open or attempting to open it crashes the application? There are so many answers to this question that whole books can be, and have been, devoted to the subject. Consequently, this section just hits the high points — the most commonly encountered causes and remedies.

Problem: One of the most common examples is actually application-specific, so I'm covering it first. You double-click a Photoshop document, Photoshop launches, but the document doesn't open in a window.

Solution: The reason for this is most often that you have just upgraded your operating system version and Photoshop's Scripting Additions didn't get moved into the new Library folder. Either copy the Scripting Additions folder from your backup or the Previous Systems directory, if you did an archive and install upgrade, or reinstall Photoshop.

Problem: You attempt to open a graphics file and Preview, iPhoto, QuickTime Player, or some other graphics program complains that it is corrupt.

Solution: Try opening the file with GraphicConverter (www.lemkesoft.de). It is likely that you have a corrupt or incomplete JPEG file here, but GraphicConverter recovers as much of it as can be read and warns you of the problem. You can then save the result and, hopefully, have enough content to work with so that you can work around the missing or corrupt data.

Problem: You attempt to open a file and Mac OS X tells you that you don't have sufficient privileges to open the file.

Solution: This is one of the simplest file problems to correct. Choose File⇨Get Info and expand the Ownership & Permissions panel. Click the Details disclosure triangle to show who can do what with the file. Unlock the padlock, provide an Administrator account and password, and then change the ownership or permissions, as shown in figure 7.5.

Problem: You attempt to open a file and the application unexpectedly quits (that's Apple's polite euphemism for crashing).

7.5 Change ownership or permissions on a file.

Solution: You might not be able to work around this problem. There is a strong likelihood that the document is corrupt and the authors of the program didn't make it robust enough to deal with that eventuality. If, however, it is a document type that can be opened by another application, try using another application and see whether you can now open the file and recover some, or all, of the contents. For example, TextEdit can open most Word files as can Pages, although some formatting will be lost, as will revision tracking information, and some other higher-end features. Your best hope is to have a noncorrupt copy of the document on one of your recent backups.

> **Tip**
> The first thing to do when an application crashes is to take Apple up on its offer and send it a crash report. (You'll need to be online to do this.) Panther and Tiger make the process very easy—all you have to do is respond to the prompts your particular OS version presents.

Problem: You have trouble with crashing in Safari or another Web browser.

Solution: Assuming the problem isn't occurring because of an incompatibility between Safari and the Web site you're trying to visit, frequent crashing may suggestion corruption in one of the files that Safari accesses frequently such as the history or bookmarks files, or perhaps with Safari's cache files. If you suspect that's the case, clear Safari's cache files by choosing Safari ⇨ Empty Cache or History ⇨ Clear History. If the problems seem more severe than that, choose Safari ⇨ Reset Safari to clear out data from any of the tracking files, which might help eliminate the problem. If you're not working in Safari, you'll find that other Web browsers such as Internet Explorer and Firefox offer similar cache- and history-clearing commands.

Problem: You can't launch Mail or have trouble when working in Mail.

Solution: If you're having issues working with a current Mailbox within Mail, particularly if it simply seems too slow, you can select it and use the Mailbox, Rebuild Mailbox command to give it a fresh start. This will sometimes fix problems with corruption, although a corrupt e-mail message is often its own issue — if you can track down the offending e-mail and delete it, that's usually the best tactic. Sometimes the solution to a file that won't completely download or that otherwise times out and causes problems when you're trying to receive e-mail is to log into the Webmail interface for your e-mail account and download the offending message (or delete it) from your browser, then continue the download operating in Mail.

Battery life and the power manager

After a number of years the battery in a PowerBook or iBook starts to fade, and eventually it may need to be replaced. If you notice that your Mac's performance time slowly fades more and more when it's on battery power, the battery may be part of the reason. Even with today's technology, batteries eventually wear out.

One thing that doesn't happen with modern lithium-ion batteries is that they don't have the same memory issues that you may have heard of in the past in reference to laptop batteries. In previous generations and technologies, working with a portable computer's battery meant that it was important for you to drain the battery completely before recharging (or, at least, to do so frequently) and then to recharge fully before use. With lithium-ion battery technology, that's not the same issue it once was.

That said, a modern PowerBook or iBook does occasionally need to be recalibrated so that the battery monitor built in to the Mac agrees with the battery itself; after a while, your Mac may start to inaccurately report the amount of time remaining. The solution is to:

1. **Charge your Mac fully by connecting it to AC power.**

2. **Disconnect the Mac and run it until it runs down completely.** It should go beyond the battery level warnings until it puts itself into Sleep mode.

3. **Connect the AC adapter again and charge your Mac continuously until it's once again completely charged.** This should calibrate the Mac's sensing system so that it reports remaining battery power as accurately as possible.

Tip

Most Apple batteries have a small button on the outside of the battery (the side that faces out when the battery is installed or mounted) that you can press to quickly see what level of charge that battery thinks it has; if that rough percentage (two dots is 50 percent, three dots is 75 percent) doesn't agree with what your Mac thinks is remaining, that could be a sign of a problem with the power manager, the seating of the battery, or other issues.

Having said all that, if your Mac portable's battery suddenly starts giving only a fraction of its original charge, it can be a sign of another problem. Under certain circumstances it can be important to reset the power manager, which is circuitry that's unique to iBooks and PowerBooks. Many of today's portable Macs, for example, rely on the power manager to control when the screen dims, when the Mac puts itself to sleep, and when the hard drive spins down. Over time, the data in the power manager can become corrupt, requiring a hard restart of the power manager. This is especially true if your Mac is erratic in behavior, such as failing to charge batteries, failing to wake up, or not responding appropriately when plugged into an AC adapter.

Caution

Although resetting the power manager shouldn't damage your Mac in any way, know that it's more of a last-resort solution than it is First Aid. Problems such as crashing or file corruption don't have anything to do with the power manager — instead, we focus specifically on Mac portable issues that have to do with batteries, AC adapters, and turning on or waking from sleep.

Different models have different instructions for resetting the power manager. Here's a look at the sequence that's involved for modern PowerBook and iBook models, according to Apple:

✦ **PowerBook G3.** The original PowerBook G3 (similar in design to the PowerBook 3400) is reset by shutting it down, then pressing and holding the reset button next to the serial port on the back of the Mac for 10 to 20 seconds. It should restart on its own.

✦ **PowerBook G3 Series.** The clamshell-style PowerBook G3 models are reset by turning the computer off, pressing Shift+Fn+Ctrl+Power simultaneously for at least five seconds, and then pressing the Power button again.

✦ **PowerBook G3 (Bronze Keyboard).** This oddball model is reset by turning off the PowerBook, pressing and releasing the reset button for at least five seconds (it's located on the back of the PowerBook near the modem port), and then turning the PowerBook back on by pressing the Power key.

✦ **PowerBook G4 (early Titanium models).** If your 15-inch Titanium PowerBook has a reset button on the back near the external video port, then you reset by shutting down your Mac, pressing that button, waiting five seconds, and then pressing the Power button again.

✦ **PowerBook G4 (later Titanium models).** Shut down the Mac, and then raise the keyboard by releasing the keyboard latches between the Esc and F1 keys, and the F8 and F9 keys. There, next to the

Power button, you see a small reset button. Press the button, and then wait five seconds. Replace the keyboard and press the Power button.

✦ **PowerBook G4 (early Aluminum models).** Shut down the Mac, simultaneously press and hold Shift+Ctrl+Option+Power, then release them. Wait five seconds, and then press the Power button to restart.

✦ **PowerBook G4 (later 15-inch 1.5GHz., 1.67Ghz, and 17-inch 1.67Ghz, Aluminum models).** Shut down the Mac, then disconnect AC power and remove the battery. Press and hold the Power button for five seconds, reconnect AC and battery, and then press the Power button.

✦ **iBook G3.** This one has a number of steps. First, shut down the Mac. Next, unplug the Mac from AC and remove the battery. Now, press and release the reset button (with a straightened paperclip), which is in a recessed location above the Power button. Wait five seconds, reconnect the AC adapter, reinstall the battery, and then press the Power button.

✦ **iBook G4 (early models).** The instructions for this model depend on whether or not it has a reset button located near the audio out jack. If so, then shut down your Mac, unplug it, remove the battery, press the reset switch with a straightened paperclip, then wait five seconds. Now, connect the AC, install the battery, and press the Start button. If you don't have a reset button, then you have a later model.

✦ **iBook G4 (later models).** If your iBook doesn't have a reset button, you should be able to reset by shutting down your Mac, pressing Shift+Ctrl+Option+Power on the keyboard simultaneously, and then releasing those keys. Wait five seconds, and then press the Power key to start up again.

 Note

Resetting the power manager on some models may reset your Mac's clock and calendar, which you can reset using the Date & Time pane of System Preferences.

Clumsiness, carelessness, and acts of nature

Portables are expected to receive rougher handling than desktop units and are built accordingly. For example, the cases are much harder to open, more closed to user modification, and drives are shock-mounted. There is a limit, however, to how much physical protection can be built in to the computer without increasing the size and weight to unacceptable levels. Barring extraordinary impact, the insides of your Mac laptop are probably safe; however, the same cannot be said for the hinges and other parts of the case.

A laptop's compact, all-in-one nature places the monitor, keyboard, and pointing device (also known as a trackpad) all in one case with the logic board—a unique situation as even iMacs have external keyboards and mice.

If you spill coffee into a desktop computer's keyboard, you are likely to damage the keyboard, but plugging in a new keyboard would get you back to operation. However, if your Venti Non-fat Latté spills into your PowerBook's keyboard, some of that liquid could find its way to the logic board below the keyboard, with disastrous results. The best course of action here is to minimize the possibility of such accidents. While Dennis admits to keeping a large diet soda at hand while working at his desktop computers, we both make an effort to disallow any liquids on the same table as our laptops, nor do we take a sip while typing or scrolling lest an accident occur.

If your precautions come to naught and you spill some liquid onto your keyboard, proceed as follows:

1. **Quit your running applications and shut down your Mac.**

2. **With the lid open, turn your laptop upside down to promote draining the liquid as quickly and thoroughly as possible.** In fact, if you can perform the Quit and Shutdown steps with the portable inverted, do so.

3. **Using a dry, absorbent cloth or towel, pat the affected surface until it is dry.**

4. **Open your laptop's case and separate the keyboard from the logic board.** This only works for iBooks and certain PowerBook models that have a keyboard that separates easily. With others, you'll have to stick with simply turning it over. The instructions for this operation vary from one model to another, but usually it involves removing some screws from the bottom of your computer, popping some tabs that hold the keyboard in place, and letting it dangle.

5. **Give the components time to dry.** If it was a sticky substance, such as soda pop, you're probably going to have a residue and you should take your computer in for service.

6. **Reassemble after everything is completely dry — wait hours, if possible — and try to start up.** If you were quick (and lucky) your Mac laptop will still be functional.

Alternatively, take your Mac in for service — sometimes the repair will actually be covered under your warranty or Apple's extended warranty AppleCare service.

Operating Temperatures

Your laptop comes with a very thin Owner's Guide. One of the few items in the Owner's Guide to which you should pay careful attention, though, is the section that relates to permissible operating temperatures. If you attempt to operate your laptop in a too-cold environment, the heat produced as components operate can result in electrical short circuits or components cracking. Conversely, if you operate your computer in a too-warm environment, overheating can cause delicate circuits to melt. As you might imagine, it's always good to keep your portable Mac in a temperature-controlled environment—the trunk of your car for long periods is probably a mistake.

Upgrading Your Portable Mac

If your Mac didn't come with everything you need out of the box, you'll want to upgrade it. There are a few internal upgrades you can perform and modern portable Macs feature a number of ports that you can use for adding peripherals, which are covered in this appendix as well.

Caution *This Appendix discusses opening your portable Mac for upgrading purposes; while most of these are Apple-approved for user upgrades, you should only open up your Mac if you're comfortable with the idea. Also, you should know that static electricity can harm computer components – you should particularly take care if you live in a dry area where you conduct a lot of static. If you live in an area where static electricity is an issue, stop into a computer or electronics store and buy a static electricity wrist band, which is connected to metal or a ground and keeps you from zapping your Mac's components.*

Note *The System Profiler, found in the Utilities folder inside your main Applications folder, can be used to see what you already have installed on your Mac, including the number of RAM modules and whether or not a slot is free. This is an important step to take before buying RAM, because if you find out that your portable Mac has all of the memory modules it can handle, then you'll need to decide whether it's worthwhile to replace an existing module with a newer, larger RAM module.*

The Original iBook

The original iBook was designed to be a portable iMac of sorts, with its colorful exterior and curved design. The iBook was the first of Apple's computers to sport an AirPort card slot, which is designed for easy access under the keyboard. It had fewer ports than later iBook models, but offered internal upgrading options for adding wireless networking and additional RAM.

Ports

The original iBook sports an Ethernet port, which was a relatively new addition for any consumer-oriented computer at the time, much less a portable. The Ethernet port made it easier to connect the iBook to a local network or to the broadband modems that were just becoming popular when the iBook was released. The original iBook also has a modem port, a USB port, and an audio-out port that is ideal for headphones. Later, the iBook DV added a FireWire port, which could be used for connecting a digital video camcorder for editing.

Expansion options

The original iBook could accept two internal upgrades: an AirPort card and a RAM module. The AirPort card needs to be Apple's original AirPort card, which is compatible with the 802.11b standard. This model of AirPort card can be shipped with a green circuit board that it connects to; you need to remove it from this circuit board (it slides out) so that you install only the small card in your iBook.

Both RAM and the AirPort card are installed beneath the keyboard. Here's how to get into the Mac:

1. **Shut down your Mac and unplug it from the wall.**

2. **Turn the iBook over and remove the battery.**

3. **Between the Esc and F1 keys and the F8 and F9 keys, use your fingernails on the small tabs to pull them away from the display.**

Note *The iBook's keyboard has a small screw that's used to lock the keyboard into place; if it can be lifted easily, you may need to turn that screw a half-turn counterclockwise or so to release the keyboard. This screw is located between the F4 and F5 keys.*

4. **Flip the keyboard over on top of the wrist pad (see figure AA.1).**

AA.1 On all iBook models, you add RAM or an AirPort card by lifting the keyboard.

5. **Touch one of the metal surfaces inside the iBook in order to discharge any static electricity.**

> **Note** *When your replace the keyboard after upgrading, place the bottom edge of the keyboard under the lip of the bottom of the keyboard area, so that the metal is below the plastic. You can then lower the keyboard toward the display and hold down the plastic clips until the keyboard is flush; then release the tabs to lock it down.*

Adding an AirPort card at this point is relatively simple. (Note that you wouldn't want to install the AirPort card before installing RAM, which is discussed next.) Here's how:

1. **There's a small wire bracket that holds the AirPort card; it must be lifted so that the card can slip beneath it.** The area that accepts the AirPort card should be obvious — it's a depressed area that has the card's slot hidden up under the trackpad side of the keyboard opening. The bracket will actually pivot upwards, so you'll want to apply a little pressure to the bracket where it latches under the edge of the keyboard area, and then let it swing upward to make way for the AirPort card.

2. **Plug the antenna's cable into the port on the AirPort card.** It's the cable found right next to where the wire bracket was latched.

3. **You can now slide the card into its place in the iBook; note that it goes in with the AirPort label facing down.** The card slides into some pins that receive it snugly; make sure you're seeing the codes that are on the "back" of the card with the AirPort logo facing toward the innards of the iBook.

4. **That's it — if you only install the AirPort card, you can close up your iBook by replacing and latching the keyboard, fire it up, and test.**

While the iBook is open, you may want to install additional RAM modules. The original iBook requires an SO-DIMM (small outline Dual In-line Memory Module), which can be up to 512MB in size; it needs to be 1.25 inches or smaller. Here's how to install the module:

1. **With the keyboard open, remove the AirPort card from its slot if you have one installed.** You can leave the antenna plugged in and put the card off to the side if desired.

2. **Remove the two screws that secure the metal tray that holds the card; it's also a shield for the RAM.** With the tray removed, you should see an open RAM socket, which you can use to install the RAM module.

3. **Line up the notches on the module with the notches on the RAM slot, then insert the module at about a 30-degree angle into the slot.**

4. **Use light pressure to spread the two locking tabs on either side of the module while pressing the module down into place.** It should lock into the tabs and fit securely, with no pins on the memory module showing.

5. **With the module clicked in, you can replace the shield, return the AirPort card to its place, and replace the keyboard.**

Tip *Apple offers more and more do-it-yourself help on its support site at* www.apple.com/support/ *including instructions and kits for changing the feet on the bottom of an iBook or even, when necessary, changing out a damaged keyboard. Consult the site for details.*

The "iceBook" and iBook G4

Apple's all-new iBook model in 2001 gave up the toilet-seat shape and the handy carrying handle in order to move to a small, sleek, and lighter-weight iBook. In this iteration, the iBook includes two USB ports, a FireWire port, and a PowerPC G3 500Mhz or faster processor; the 600Mhz model and higher could be had with a 14-inch display as well. Again, these models are easy to upgrade either by adding external devices or by opening them up and adding RAM or an AirPort card.

Ports

The iBook G3 features two USB ports on the side and a FireWire 400 port. It also offers an Ethernet port, modem port, and audio out. The iBook doesn't offer audio in. The iceBook (often called the dual USB model in Apple's literature) was the first iBook model to include a video-out port, which is a special RGB output port that requires a VGA or video-out adapter in order to connect to a computer display or to a television monitor or other recording device, respectively.

The iBook G4 offers remarkably similar ports, with the addition of support for USB 2.0 devices, which doesn't actually change the USB ports themselves. In terms of the case itself, the major difference is the less transparent white color and it offers a slot-loading optical drive instead of a tray-loading design.

Expansion options

As with the original iBook, the expansion options are essentially limited to an internal AirPort card and RAM modules. How you get into the iceBook is also very similar to the original iBook — you raise the keyboard and get in that way.

Here's how to remove the keyboard:

1. **Shut down your Mac and unplug it from the wall.**

2. **Turn the iBook over and remove the battery.**

3. **Between the Esc and F1 keys and the F11 and F12 keys, use your fingernails on the small tabs to pull them away from the display.**

Note *The iBook's keyboard has a small screw that's used to lock the keyboard into place; if it can be lifted easily, you may need to turn that screw a half-turn counterclockwise or so to release the keyboard. This screw is located between the F5 and F6 keys.*

4. **Flip the keyboard over on top of the wrist pad.**

5. **Touch one of the metal surfaces inside the iBook in order to discharge any static electricity.**

Note *The iBook G3 models support the same SO-DIMM RAM modules used for earlier iBook models; the iBook G4 switches to DDR (Double Data Rate) modules that need to have the correct specifications (PC2100 SDRAM).*

For the iBook G4, Apple switched to the AirPort Extreme card to support 802.11g speeds. Most iBook G4 models have the AirPort Extreme card built in, but it must be removed in order to access RAM slots. Once the keyboard is removed, you can follow these steps to add RAM:

1. **There is a small wire bracket that holds the AirPort card; it must be lifted so that the card can be slipped out from beneath it.**

2. **Remove the card and unplug the antenna cable from it.**

3. **Remove the four screws that secure the metal tray that holds the card; it's also a shield for the RAM.** With the tray removed, you should see an open RAM socket, which you can use to install the RAM module.

4. **Line up the notches on the module with the notches on the RAM slot, and then insert the module at about a 30-degree angle into the slot.**

5. **Use light pressure to spread the two locking tabs on either side of the module while pressing the module down into place.** It should lock into the tabs and fit securely, with no pins on the memory module showing.

6. **With the module clicked in, you can replace the shield, return the AirPort card to its place, and replace the keyboard.**

PowerBook G3 Series

Apple has slowly dropped support for PowerBook G3 models, with the FireWire-equipped Pismo models being the only remaining PowerBook G3 that is supported by Mac OS X 10.4. (Earlier models, of course, can continue to use Mac OS 10.3.x and earlier.) The PowerBook G3 Pismo was the first PowerBook to support FireWire and AirPort, and to drop external SCSI support for SCSI hard drives and scanners.

Ports

The PowerBook G3 bronze keyboard model includes an Ethernet port, a SCSI port, two USB ports, and a VGA-style video-out port, which can be used to both mirror the display or expand your Mac's Desktop from the PowerBook's internal display to an external display. (This enables you to mouse from the PowerBook's display to another display that sits next to it, effectively increasing the amount of Desktop real estate you have to work with.)

 Tip *Most PowerBook models, including the PowerBook G3 bronze keyboard can be used in clamshell mode, meaning you can plug in an external display, keyboard, and mouse and then wake the PowerBook up and use it without opening its top. This enables you to use only external peripherals with the closed Mac, giving you a desktop-like computing experience.*

The PowerBook G3 Pismo models dropped the SCSI port in favor of a FireWire port and added support for an internal AirPort card.

The PowerBook G3 bronze keyboard and Pismo models offer 16-bit stereo miniplug ports for sound in and sound out, which can be used with a microphone and headphones, respectively. Finally, these models have an S-video-out port that can be used for connecting the Mac directly to video playback or recording devices, or in many case to overhead projection equipment for presentations.

Expansion cards and bays

The PowerBook G3 Pismo offers an internal AirPort card slot as well as a slot for adding RAM modules. Both the bronze keyboard and Pismo models offer a PC Card slot that supports credit-card-sized expansion cards for a variety of purposes, such as to add networking or wireless access capabilities or for plugging in external storage, additional expansion ports (USB and FireWire), and so on. The PC Card slots support one Type I and Type II card, or a CardBus card.

 Note *The term PC Card doesn't refer specifically to Windows-compatible PCs in any way — it's a cross-platform standard that used to be called PCMCIA. CardBus is the technology that allows a PC Card expansion card to offer bus capabilities, which usually translates into ports such as FireWire expansion ports. If you shop PC Cards, you'll find that some say they require CardBus support — all PowerBook models that are compatible with Mac OS X 10.4 support the CardBus standard.*

To add a PC Card upgrade you simply orient it correctly and slide it into the PC card slot until it locks into place; the card should be recognized by your Mac and made available as a peripheral. (You may need to install a software driver to make it work correctly or configure the card in, for instance, the Network pane of System Preferences if it's a network card.)

To remove the PC Card, eject it from within the Mac OS (if necessary) or shut down your Mac if required by the card. (This may be important for some cards with low-level functionality such as adding FireWire ports.) Then press the release button next to the PC Card slot to eject the card; it should pop out part of the way so that you can pull it out completely.

The PowerBook G3 bronze keyboard and Pismo models also offer a special expansion bay on the right side of the machine, which can be used to swap internal peripherals such as optical drives (CD and DVD drives) and to add third-party peripherals such as an external Iomega Zip drive. The expansion bays are also used for the PowerBook G3's batteries, such that both bays can support a battery to extend battery life.

To remove an expansion bay item, first eject it in the Finder (if appropriate) or shut down the Mac. Now, pull the lever at the front of the bay toward you to eject the module slightly; you can then pull it out once it's unlocked from its connector. If you have another module you want to place there, simply orient it correctly and slide it in until it connects, then press the lever back in to lock the expansion device into place. If you don't have a module you want to put in the expansion bay, you should insert the dummy expansion bay device that came with the PowerBook in order to save weight but keep the expansion bay from accumulating dust or debris.

Upgrading AirPort

The AirPort card slot in the PowerBook G3 Pismo sits beneath a heat shield, which, in turn, is beneath the keyboard. You need to remove both to add the card. Here's how:

1. **Shut down your Mac and unplug it from the wall.**

2. **Eject the battery from its expansion bay by pulling forward on its lever at the front of the PowerBook.** That should eject the battery part of the way so that you can pull it out of its bay. (You don't need to pull it all the way out for this upgrade.)

3. **Between the Esc and F1 keys and the F11 and F12 keys, use your fingernails on the small tabs to pull them away from the display.**

   Note *The PowerBook G3's keyboard has a small screw that's used to lock the keyboard into place; if it can be lifted easily, you may need to turn that screw a half-turn counterclockwise or so to release the keyboard.*

4. **Lift the keyboard slightly toward the screen to clear the small tabs at the bottom of the keyboard from the case, and then flip the keyboard over on top of the wrist pad.**

5. **Touch one of the metal surfaces inside the PowerBook in order to discharge any static electricity.**

6. **Using a small Phillips-head screwdriver, remove the two screws at the bottom of the heat shield (a flat metal piece that's right in the middle of the keyboard area), and then lift it out of the PowerBook.**

7. **Plug the antenna cable into the AirPort card and orient the card so that the bar code and numbers are facing upward.**

8. **Slide the card into its slot until it plugs securely into the connector.**

9. **Replace the heat shield and return the keyboard to its latched position.** If you plan to install more RAM, you can do that at this phase in the instructions as well.

Upgrading RAM

The PowerBook G3 accepts SO-DIMM modules, which are the same modules supported by all iBook G3 models as well as the iMac G3.

If you plan to upgrade the RAM, you need to complete the steps in the previous section to expose the RAM module slot. Once you complete those steps, follow these steps to upgrade the RAM:

1. **With the heat sink removed, you should see an open RAM module slot.** If there's a module in it, then you need to remove that module to add the new one, assuming the new module offers higher capacity than the existing one.

2. **Line up the notches on the module with the notches on the RAM slot, and then insert the module at about a 30-degree angle into the slot.**

3. **Use light pressure to spread the two locking tabs on either side of the module while pressing the module down into place.** It should lock into the tabs and fit securely, with no pins on the memory module showing.

4. **With the RAM module clicked in, you can replace the shield, return the AirPort card to its place, and replace the keyboard.**

PowerBook G4 Titanium

The PowerBook G4 looked dramatically different from most notebook computers when it was introduced, sporting a wide-screen 15-inch display and a thin case. It did away with the PowerBook G3's flexible expansion bays, while also doing away with quite a bit of the weight that came along with the PowerBook G3's design. The early PowerBook G4 Titanium models support many of the same ports, except sound-out, and include PC card expansion.

Ports

The PowerBook G4 Titanium models include a 100BaseT Ethernet port (upgraded to Gigabit Ethernet for the PowerBook DVI models at 667MHz and higher), two USB ports, a FireWire port, and a VGA-style video-out port, which can be used to both mirror the display or expand your Mac's Desktop from the PowerBook's internal display to an external display. With the advent of the PowerBook G4 DVI models, Apple switched to a DVI port for video out, making the PowerBooks more compatible with digital LCD displays.

The PowerBook G4 Titanium models offer 16-bit stereo mini-plug ports for sound out or headphones, as well as an S-video-out port that can be used for connecting the Mac directly to video playback or recording devices, or in many cases to overhead projection equipment for presentations.

Expansion options

The PowerBook G4 Titanium has an internal AirPort card slot and an accessible slot for adding RAM modules. It also offers a PC Card slot that can accept one Type I and Type II card, or a CardBus card.

To add a PC Card upgrade you simply orient it correctly and slide it into the PC card slot on the left side of the PowerBook's case until it locks into place; the card should be recognized by your Mac and made available as a peripheral. (You may need to install a software driver to make it work correctly or configure the card in, for example, the Network pane of System Preferences if it's a network card.)

To remove the PC Card, eject it from within the Mac OS (if necessary) or shut down your Mac if required by the card. (This may be important for some cards with low-level functionality such as adding FireWire ports.) Then press the release button next to the PC Card slot to eject the card; it should pop out part of the way so that you can pull it out completely.

In the PowerBook G4 Titanium the RAM slot is easy to reach, but the AirPort card slot is a bit more of a challenge. Regardless, you need to remove the keyboard first. Here's how:

1. **Shut down your Mac and unplug it from the wall.**

2. **Close the Mac, turn it over, and remove the battery.**

3. **Turn the Mac back over and open the clamshell.**

4. **Between the Esc and F1 keys and the F8 and F9 keys, use your fingernails on the small tabs to pull them away from the display.**

> **Note** *The PowerBook G4's keyboard has a small screw that's used to lock the keyboard into place; if it can be lifted easily, you may need to turn that screw a half-turn counterclockwise or so to release the keyboard.*

5. **Lift the top of the keyboard up, and then flip the keyboard over on top of the wrist pad (see figure AA.2).**

AA.2 For the PowerBook G4 Titanium series you lift the keyboard in order to upgrade the RAM.

6. **Touch one of the metal surfaces inside the PowerBook in order to discharge any static electricity.**

Now that the keyboard is out of the way, you can work on upgrading the RAM by following these steps:

1. **With the keyboard removed, you should immediately see the RAM slot that is available (it's toward the bottom of the keyboard cavity).**

2. **Line up the notches on the module with the notches on the RAM slot, and insert the module at about a 30-degree angle into the slot.**

3. **Use light pressure to spread the two locking tabs on either side of the module while pressing the module down into place.** It should lock into the tabs and fit securely, with no pins on the memory module showing.

4. **Now you can replace the keyboard to its latched position.**

The AirPort card installation is a bit trickier. You do not need to remove the keyboard to install an AirPort card. Follow these steps:

1. **Shut down your PowerBook and disconnect from AC power.**

2. **Open the clamshell and turn the Mac back over so that its bottom is facing up.** Apple recommends placing the Mac on a table with the display hanging off toward your lap and the keyboard supported by a soft cloth or towel.

3. **Remove the battery and touch metal inside the battery's area to discharge any static electricity.**

4. **With a Phillips-head screwdriver, remove all of the screws holding the bottom in place.**

5. **With the screws removed you find that the bottom of the PowerBook has catches at all four corners; lift up on the corners to release the bottom.**

6. **Slide the bottom away from you; then rotate the button up from the side closest to the display; then remove the bottom from the case.** This reveals the slot for the AirPort card.

7. **Connect the card to the antenna cable and slide it into its slot.**

Zap PRAM

If your Mac doesn't seem to recognize your AirPort card or if it has trouble starting up, you may find it helps to "zap PRAM" as you start up your Mac, which resets a small portion of RAM that's set aside for storing some very basic options. To zap PRAM, hold down the ⌘+Option+P+R keys immediately after hearing the startup tone on your Mac. You may have to restart your Mac first if it's managed to start up but can't find the AirPort card. Keep holding the keys until you hear the startup tone two more times; then release them and let your Mac finish the startup process.

8. **When the card is flush in its slot, make sure the cable and small plastic tab are inside the edges of the case.**

9. **Replace the bottom of the Mac and tighten all eight screws.** Insert and attach all screws loosely; then use an alternating pattern to tighten them down. (That is, start on the left side and tighten one, then move to the right side to the tighten the next, and so on.) That helps to ensure that you don't mis-align the case bottom as you reattach it.

10. **Return the battery to its compartment; then turn the Mac over; if necessary plug it in.**

You can now start up the Mac and see if the AirPort card is recognized by launching System Preferences and opening the Network pane.

PowerBook G4 Aluminum

Apple's most recent PowerBook G4 Aluminum models are really three different computer designs — the 12-inch, 15-inch, and 17-inch PowerBooks, designated as such for the size of their displays. In terms of

upgrading, all share at least one common design trait — a panel for upgrading RAM that's found on the bottom of the PowerBook. None of these models sports the lift-up keyboard found on previous gen-erations (or on the current iBook G4 models at the time of this writing), which makes for a slightly more stable keyboard with less opportunity for damage. Some of these models also have AirPort Extreme support built onto the logic board in such a way that they don't offer a card for upgrading, because AirPort isn't an option on those models, including all iterations of the 17-inch PowerBook and many of the latest 15-inch PowerBooks.

Ports

The different PowerBook G4 Aluminum models offer different ports if only because the 12-inch PowerBook is so much smaller than the 17-inch PowerBook that it has an abbreviated feature or two. All of these models sport two USB 2.0 ports, as well as FireWire 400, Ethernet, and a modem con-nection. The later 15-inch and 17-inch mod-els have a FireWire 800 port as well as a FireWire 400 port, and a full-sized DVI port as opposed to the mini-DVI port found on the 12-inch model. The 15-inch and 17-inch models also offer an S-video-out port for connecting to a television or video recorder; the 12-inch model can offer an S-video port using a special Apple video adapter. All three models offer 16-bit audio in and out via a mini-plug connection.

Expansion options

All three of these PowerBook models offer a quick-access RAM module door on the bottom of the Mac, making them easy to get into and expand for memory. All three also support the same type of memory module (either PC2100 DDR SDRAM or, on 1.25GHz models and faster, PC2700 DDR SDRAM) in the form of a SO-DIMM designed to fit a PowerBook.

Here's how to replace the RAM:

1. **Shut down your Mac, and turn it over.** Apple recommends waiting five minutes for it to cool down.

2. **On the 12-inch and 15-inch models, use a coin to release the battery lock, and then remove the battery.** The 17-inch PowerBook has two sliding latches on either side of the battery for easy removal.

3. **Touch a metal surface in the battery area to discharge any static electricity.**

4. **Locate the RAM panel (see figure AA.3) and remove the four small Phillips screws.** This reveals the memory slots.

Note *Your Mac's lid latch has a magnet that's built into it and if you don't hold onto small screws tightly, the lid's magnet may grab the screws. If so, look first on the edge of your Mac to see if it's being held there magnetically. (The latch can also be an amusing place to store a space paperclip — magnetically.)*

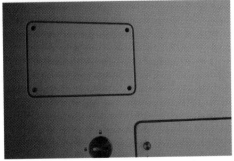

AA.3 The PowerBook Aluminum series offers a special panel just for upgrading RAM.

5. **If the top slot is open, you can add a memory module by lining up the tabs in the slot with the indentations in the module, then inserting the module at about a 30-degree angle.** If the top slot isn't open, you need to replace that existing memory module with your new one, assuming that the new one is a higher capacity.

6. **Use light pressure to spread the two locking tabs on either side of the module while pressing the module down into place.** It should lock into the tabs and fit securely, with no pins on the memory module showing.

7. **Replace the battery compartment's panel using the four screws.**

8. **Replace the battery and turn its lock.**

9. **Start up your Mac and check the About this Mac command (Choose About this Mac from the Apple menu) or the System Profiler to see if the RAM is recognized.**

As for an AirPort card, only early 15-inch models and most 12-inch models enable you to insert an AirPort Extreme card, as the circuitry is built in to other PowerBook G4 Aluminum models such as all the 17-inch models. Here's how to get at the AirPort card (or slot, if you're installing a new card).

1. **Shut down the Mac and turn it over.** Apple recommends waiting five minutes for it to cool down.

2. **On the 12-inch and 15-inch models, use a coin to release the battery lock, and then remove the battery.** The 17-inch PowerBook has two sliding latches on either side of the battery for easy removal.

3. **Touch a metal surface in the battery area to discharge any static electricity.**

4. **Locate the AirPort Extreme card slot, which is found in a wall of the battery compartment.** The diagram on the bottom of the battery compartment should help you locate it.

5. **If you're installing a new card, then first move the antenna cable out of the way, and then, with the bar code and numbers on the card facing upward, slide the card almost all the way into the slot.**

6. **Attach the antenna cable to the card; then press the card all the way into its slot.** It should fit flush with the walls of the slot.

7. **Bend the plastic tab up and over the card and into the slot so that it secures the antenna cable and is out of the way of the battery.** You should now be able to replace the battery, lock it down, and turn your Mac over to start it up. Once started, open System Preferences and the Network pane to test and make sure the card is recognized.

To remove the AirPort card, all you need to do is get access to that plastic tab on the card (according to Apple, a "black stick" is handy for this, which is just a plastic stick that doesn't conduct electricity — you can get one from a good electronics store). Pull the card out slightly, remove the antenna cable, and then pull the card the rest of the way out.

Index